Five Hundy by ....

PRESENTS

The Outsiders' Guide *to* Las Vegas

TIM DRESSEN

OTINGTON
PRESS

OTINGTON PRESS
Roseville, Minnesota
www.OtingtonPress.com

The Outsiders' Guide to Las Vegas

Paperback edition ISBN 978-0-9962906-0-9.

Cover design and interior layout by Tim Dressen and Cathy Zielske.

All photos by Tim and Michele Dressen except the author photo
by Cathy Zielske and outside back cover photo
by blvdone/Shutterstock.com.

Printed in the United States of America.

Dedicated to:

Michele
For supporting my Las Vegas obsession,
encouraging my creative endeavors,
and making every day entertaining

Also, Bob Stupak

Contents

PREFACE

Long Live the Las Vegas Outsider

Las Vegas is a city of legends—most of which are complete bullshit. You probably know them well. Bugsy Siegel stood in the middle of the desert and had a vision of what would become the Las Vegas Strip. Bullshit. Casino operators pump oxygen through their ventilation systems to keep gamblers alert and playing longer. Bullshit. Tourists are at risk of being drugged and waking up in a bathtub full of ice sans one kidney. Bullshit. For $4.95, you can get a steak and eggs breakfast and a blowjob at Sam's Town. OK, that one may be true, but I don't recommend it.

Tales like these, the town's mob history, and the What Happens Here Stays Here slogan contribute to a mystique unique to Las Vegas. Whether they've visited the city or not, many people perceive Las Vegas to be a place filled with secrets. And they believe that knowing the right person—a Las Vegas insider—is the key to unlocking all the magic Vegas has to offer. Unfortunately, most so-called insiders either have a vested interest in providing slanted information or simply don't know what the hell they're talking about.

THE MEDIA

The Las Vegas public relations, tourism, and media industries coexist with an unspoken "I'll scratch your back if you scratch mine" agreement. On behalf of their hotel, casino, restaurant, nightclub, and retail clients, PR departments churn out mountains of freshly spun news releases and media pitches daily. They proclaim the opening of every new nightclub as a "game-changer." They describe every new shopping mall as a "groundbreaking retail and dining experience." And they throw around terms like "vibe dining" and "curious class" as though they actually mean something.

Traditional and new media outlets alike eat this stuff up. Far too often, they simply regurgitate what the PR reps feed them without raising doubts, offering criticism, or saying anything that could jeopardize either precious advertising dollars or—even worse—access. When a Las Vegas blogger gets paid only $25 to write a show review, attending press junkets where food, booze, tickets, and performer access flow freely is a big deal. Being too harsh in the review—even if the show blows goats—risks the blogger's removal from future guest lists.

Conflicts of interest spew from the city's PR and media machine. An editor freelances for a casino company she appears to be covering objectively. A blogger posts glowing reviews about the resort where his spouse works. A gossip columnist writes about a hotel while on the payroll for voiceover work. Such scenarios are common in Las Vegas. Writers shun conflict-of-interest disclosures, and their readers are none the wiser.

SERVICE INDUSTRY EMPLOYEES

People working in the Las Vegas service industry deserve loads of respect. Dealing with the general public in any customer service setting is tough. Free-flowing booze consumed by many Las Vegas visitors pours fuel on the asshole fire. However, most servers, bartenders, hotel employees, and casino workers offer good service day in and day out.

It makes sense that tourists would look to these folks for insider advice. After all, they live in Las Vegas and spend countless hours in the middle of the action. So they must have insight into everything happening on the Strip and Downtown. Right? Not so much.

Most Las Vegas locals are busy living their lives. They may check out a show once in a while or try a restaurant on the Strip on occasion, but few of them are hanging out there regularly when they aren't working. The exception, of course, is the crew at The Montecito. Danny McCoy and the gang spend most of their free time chilling over drinks at the same place where they work.

If you live in a major metropolitan area, how tuned in to your city's tourism scene are you? Probably not so much. Hell, I live 15 minutes from the Mall of America and haven't set foot inside the place more than four times in the past decade—despite my well-documented love of shopping malls.

Surely employees have inside information about what's happening in the hotels where they work. Right? Again, not so much. Once in a while, a hot rumor from a bartender will actually play out as stated. But more often, he's passing along the same type of workplace gossip you hear at your job. Either it's not true or it's of no interest to anyone who doesn't work there. I'm sorry the new head of Food and Beverage is a dick, but that doesn't help me figure out whether to eat at the Mex-Italian fusion place that famed multi-racial chef José-Luis Stefanini just opened across from the casino cage.

Chatting with personable bartenders in Vegas can be entertaining and fun, but their inside information is often nonsensical. Listeners of *Five Hundy by Midnight*, the Las Vegas podcast I cohost with my wife, often share these rumors. About a year after The Cosmopolitan opened, a bartender at the hotel's Vesper bar claimed the hotel was planning to tear out an exterior wall and bring in food trucks that gamblers could access directly from the casino floor. Sure, that sounds like the type of hipster nonsense Cosmo would try, but it never happened. I made the mistake of giving far too much credence to a Backstage Bar and Billiards bartender shortly before its sister venue, Fremont Country Club, opened. He told me they had booked a couple major bands to perform intimate club shows and attract publicity for the new bar. Based on his info, I posted the rumor that Coldplay would play a concert at the club. Never happened and never will. Lesson learned. They did book Hanson, however. Mmm... bop!

CABBIES

Like service industry employees, cabbies are locals. They're more worried about picking up a frozen pizza at the end of a shift than whether Aria is a fun place to gamble. That, however, won't prevent them from telling you the casino has the best blackjack in town, along with a multitude of other "facts" about Aria that have little basis in reality.

In the late 1990s, an old airplane was located on an otherwise empty lot not far from Las Vegas Boulevard. I think there were plans to turn it into a restaurant. Upon driving by the plane on our ride from the airport, a cabbie told my brother and me that it was the legendary Spruce Goose. The plane wasn't even wooden. Other than that, the story was solid.

Before you fire off an e-mail telling me about a super knowledgeable cabbie who gave you nothing but great advice and knew more about Las Vegas than anyone you've encountered, don't bother. I believe you. I've had some great cabbies too. They're out there, but the number is far lower than those who are full of shit.

My point? Simply living and working in Las Vegas doesn't make someone a reliable source of information on the hotels, casinos, restaurants, bars, shows, and other fun stuff that keeps us outsiders returning again and again. Often it is we, the obsessive tourists, who offer the most valuable perspective on Las Vegas. We share our experiences directly with each other on message boards, podcasts, and blogs without hidden agendas. We aren't afraid to say when something sucks or scream at the top of our lungs when something is great. We don't care about losing special access because we never had special access anyway. We simply want to share our passion for the best vacation spot in the world with other people who feel the same. I'm proud to be a Las Vegas outsider. I'd like to share with you the myriad of information I've picked up from fellow outsiders throughout my many years visiting Las Vegas and cohosting *Five Hundy by Midnight, the Original Las Vegas Podcast*.

About This Book

Having access to information about everything with a quick Google search can make planning trips to Las Vegas both super convenient and super overwhelming. Third-party travel agency websites, message boards, official resort pages, blogs, podcasts, and content farms can fill your brain with every detail about Las Vegas you could ever want to know. Weeding through the virtual mountain of details and figuring out which sources are trustworthy, however, is daunting. PR fluff gets repackaged over and over—sometimes under the guise of independent reviews—and some sources provide questionable advice. *The Outsiders' Guide to Las Vegas* is intended to help you cut through the fluff, narrow your choices, and improve your Las Vegas trips. Used in tandem with online trip research, the book is designed to help readers figure out the best use of their limited time in the city.

Part travel guide, part unfiltered commentary, this book offers honest insight, pointing out what's great and what's not so great about the best vacation destination on the planet. The three sections cover planning, experiencing, and recovering from a Las Vegas vacation. Because so much of the Las Vegas experience centers around its hotels and casinos, much of the book focuses on the noteworthy aspects of each major hotel and casino on and near the Strip and Fremont Street. Rather than dump every detail about every property into this book, each hotel and casino review includes a Jackpot section and a Tilt section. Jackpot covers exceptional, interesting, or unique features about the property. Tilt covers underwhelming, disappointing, or completely horrible aspects.

The book focuses mainly on the tourist areas of the city—the Strip (Las Vegas Boulevard between Mandalay Bay and Stratosphere) and Downtown (on and near Fremont Street). In many cities, popular areas are filled with nothing but chain restaurants and lame tourist traps. This is not the case in Las Vegas. The Strip and Fremont Street are far more compelling for visitors than the city's outlying neighborhoods. While there are certainly some nice hotels, casinos, restaurants, and other attractions off-Strip, this book focuses on the areas where most visitors are likely to concentrate the majority of their time.

Whenever possible, the book includes recommendations for reliable websites that offer additional information. This book will not teach readers how to play all of the different casino games, for example, but it provides an overview and suggests resources for learning strategies. Similarly, because pricing and business hours change often, check official websites for those details.

Listeners of *Five Hundy by Midnight, the Original Las Vegas Podcast*, will recognize the book's tone—a little snarky, a little cranky, and a little off-color. (If you're not listening to *Five Hundy*, consider giving it a listen. The hosts are brilliant.) Anyone who truly loves something sees not only its best features, but also its worst. Those of us with nerdy obsessions are often the biggest critics of flaws we find with our chosen passions. So some parts of the book skew negative or even a tad harsh. If you're seeking all sunshine and lollipops, stick to the official PR-generated pablum, but don't be surprised when the "game-changing" restaurant turns out to be an overpriced variation on Olive Garden.

If you consider certain words, like "assclown" and "fuckstick" to be "bad words," you probably won't love this book. I, however, find the words "moist" and "ointment" to be far more disturbing, so I pledge to you that those words will not appear anywhere else in this book.

Finally, because the ever-evolving nature of Las Vegas, the Updates page at *www.lasvegasoutsidersbook.com* will list openings, closings, and other changes that alter the content of this book.

The Road to Happy Town

The magic of a Las Vegas vacation doesn't begin upon first seeing the row of hotels from Stratosphere to Mandalay Bay in the distance as Las Vegas Boulevard inches closer. It doesn't begin at the hotel check-in desk. It doesn't begin with the first cocktail at the casino bar or the first winning hand at the blackjack table. The joy of a Las Vegas vacation begins immediately upon deciding to go.

Having "Las Vegas" noted on the calendar provides days, weeks, or even months of happy thoughts and dreams of what awaits. However, these Vegas-inspired dreams have little chance of becoming a reality without proper planning. Hastily booking the cheapest flight and hotel room may save you time and money, but will likely result in an uncomfortable trip on Unanticipated Fees Airline and an unpleasant stay at Skank-by-the-Hour Motor Lodge. Embrace the planning process. Taking the time to research options will build anticipation for the many ~~drunken errors in judgment you'll make~~ good times you'll have and ultimately result in a great vacation.

CHAPTER 1

The Miracle of Flight

If you've begun planning a Las Vegas trip, don't live within short driving distance, and are excited to begin wagering, there's no need to wait until you've arrived. Figuring out the optimal time to book your flight presents the perfect chance to test your luck. If you book too early, you may miss out on a fare sale. If you hold out for a better rate, you may ultimately pay more. Airlines frequently manipulate pricing, each with a different, ever-evolving secret formula.

Because airlines usually introduce fare sales on Tuesdays, that day has long been considered the optimal time to get the best deals. However, the September 2014 Air Ticket Advanced Purchase Analysis from Airlines Reporting Corporation found that travelers booking domestic flights on weekends get the best rates. The average ticket prices on Saturdays and Sundays are $439 and $432, respectively, compared to between $498 and $503 on weekdays. The study also suggests booking between 100 and 50 days before departure is likely to yield the best fares. Of course, these are simply averages, and individual experiences vary widely. United Airlines may introduce a winter travel sale on a Tuesday in October for flights taking place December through February, resulting in substantially lower fares than you'd get booking on a Sunday between 100 and 50 days before your trip.

So, what's the best strategy?

- **Be obsessive.** Check rates early and often. Using a travel site like Kayak, Expedia, or Hipmunk, compare prices for your target trip dates to get a sense of typical rates. If Southwest Airlines flies out of your market, you'll need to check those rates separately, as they don't appear on most third-party online travel agency sites. If Spirit or Allegiant Airlines appears in the search results, change your search criteria to eliminate them from the mix unless you're willing to endure cramped seats, delayed flights, and fees for everything except using the restroom. (However, I hear they're considering a staggered fee structure based on the combination of time in the bathroom and total offload weight.) Their pricing models frequently make them appear as substantially cheaper options, but additional fees for everything from reserving a specific seat to traveling with carry-on bags will ultimately chip away at the savings. Unless you fully understand what you're getting into with Spirit and Allegiant, resist the urge to book solely on the airline's seemingly irresistible base fares. The no-frills experience may put you in a sour mood to start your vacation.

- **Use online tools to help determine rate drops.** Kayak (*www.kayak.com*) includes a Price Trend feature, which predicts whether rates are likely to increase or decrease over the next seven days. Yapta (*www.yapta.com*) uses Kayak's search engine but adds a feature allowing users to set e-mail alerts, notifying them if rates for specific flights drop.

- **Be prepared to book without hesitation.** If you're traveling with others, agree in advance on a booking strategy—acceptable flight days, times, and rates, and who has the authority to book if a decent fare pops up. If rates are hovering around $350, but you think there's a good chance they'll drop below $300, get everyone's buy-in to proceed as soon as that rate appears. Having to contact others to get approval after the rate drops may lead to missed opportunities. If you find a rate you like, don't hesitate. Many fare fluctuations don't last long.

- **Book directly through the airline.** Unless you have a specific reason for booking through a third-party site—participation in a loyalty program, use of a gift certificate or discount code, or unbeatable flight/hotel package deal—book directly. If there's a problem, you may have an easier time dealing with the airline when there's not a middleman involved.

- **Once you've booked, quit looking.** The wheels are in motion, and there's no turning back. Don't punish yourself with the knowledge that if you had only waited another week, you could have saved another $20. You're better off not knowing. Focus on planning other aspects of your trip and leave well enough alone. If your frequent flier status or airline policies offer the rare ability to get a refund for a price drop, set up Yapta alerts to notify you.

BRING YOUR NICKELS AND DIMES

Increasingly, airlines charge additional fees for checked luggage, priority boarding, and preferred seating. Most carriers follow a similar model, but a few discount airlines buck the trends. Southwest has endeared itself to travelers by allowing up to two checked bags at no charge. With competitors making millions from checked bag fees, it may be just a matter of time before Southwest caves and joins the dark side. Spirit, Allegiant, and Frontier charge for checked and carry-on luggage. I anticipate one of them instituting a fee for pocketed items to prevent creative travelers from loading up a pair of cargo shorts for the weekend. Kayak maintains a list of the most common fees assessed by each airline at _www.kayak.com/airline-fees_.

Requiring travelers to pay for both carry-on and checked bags seems a tad greedy. However, from an efficiency standpoint, I wouldn't mind seeing airlines charge for carry-ons _instead_ of checked bags. Since the onset of luggage fees, enduring the boarding process has become more tedious than sitting through a _Murder She Wrote_ marathon on the Hallmark Channel. I often find myself mentally pleading for sudden injury to temporarily incapacitate the jagoff in 16F trying to cram the overhead bin with a backpack containing enough supplies to survive a trek up Kilimanjaro. I'd like to see the airlines implement a fee system for the amount of time it takes to get from the airplane door to your seat with all items stowed and your seatbelt fastened. Upon having their boarding passes scanned, each passenger receives a bracelet containing a sensor. One passenger boards at a time. Upon entering the plane, the sensor triggers a timer, which automatically stops when their seatbelt snaps closed. The first 10 seconds are free. Each additional five-second block of time results in a $25 credit card charge. How rewarding would it be to know the asshole trying to pass off the Prius with a duct-taped handle as a carry-on bag just racked up a $1,400 Discover Card charge? Hell, if they install a large LED timer at the front of the plane, some of us would gladly pay a $25 priority boarding fee to wager on our fellow passengers' times. Let's make this happen, Delta.

THE PARTY BEFORE THE PARTY

Just because your vacation is happening in Las Vegas doesn't mean you have to wait until touchdown for the fun to begin. If you have extra time after the TSA's routine stripping, scanning, and—if you're especially lucky—backroom fingering, swing by the airport bar for a quick pre-flight drink. A little alcohol will take the edge off and ease you into the Vegas mindset. Don't overdo it, though. Getting drunk before you set foot on the plane is an amateur move. It's all about pacing. Get a nice buzz going and try to maintain it throughout the flight.

Unlike flights elsewhere, planes headed for Las Vegas hum with excitement. You'll hear passengers discussing their hotel choices, comparing plans, and offering each other dining and entertainment tips. Other than a dozen poor bastards in matching polo shirts headed for three 12-hour days at the convention center trying to sell their "viable turnkey solutions" to other corporate schmucks, everyone has a hopeful, happy aura.

If you're one of those genetic freaks capable of sleeping on an airplane, nodding off for a couple hours will help give you additional energy to make the most of your first day in Las Vegas. For the rest of us, the flight offers a chance to cram in some last-minute Las Vegas mental prep. Watch *The Hangover*, listen to *Sinatra at the Sands*, or practice your blackjack and video poker strategies. If you're drinking, maintain your buzz, but don't get too sloshed. You'll never live down the shame if you arrive, check in at your hotel, and promptly pass out because you shot your vodka wad on Flight 423.

For an extra comfortable Vegas pre-party, there's no beating first class. Unfortunately, advance rates are usually way too expensive for most of us to justify the cost. However, some airlines offer discounted upgrades if first-class seats remain available at check-in. I've become spoiled by the frequent availability of $145 same-day upgrades from Minneapolis. The benefits of flying first-class include:

- **Priority boarding:** No more worrying about overhead space for your carry-on. The plane is empty, so shove your bag anywhere you see fit.
- **Comfortable leather seats with substantial legroom:** When you're over six feet tall and haven't skipped a meal since the Carter administration, avoiding the ever-shrinking coach seats alone is almost worth the cost.
- **Food:** Long the punch line in every hacky comic's bit on airlines, the meals served in first class have gotten pretty good considering they're served in a glorified bus with wings. It's nice to arrive in Las Vegas with a calzone in my gut, ready to absorb whatever poisons I pour down my gullet.
- **Booze:** Drink service begins upon boarding and lasts until about 15 minutes before landing. Resist the urge to try and drink enough alcohol to cover the cost of your first-class upgrade. You'll never do it, and your attempt will make your first hours in Las Vegas a sloppy mess.
- **Instant snobbery:** Each pre-flight beverage served in first class contains a droplet of elitism lasting the exact duration of the flight. A feeling of superiority washes over you as everyone seated in coach parades by, and you look at them with smug pity—all for the price of your upgrade.
- **Low-traffic restroom:** When the sky waitresses properly enforce access, the first-class restroom is a delight compared to the high-traffic shitter in coach. The restroom is still the size of half a broom closet and not an ideal place to relax and catch up on Tom Clancy novels. However, with only about a dozen or so people using it, the chances are fairly slim that some inconsiderate dolt who neglected to dump before leaving home will shit it up just before I need to make room for more booze. Unfortunately, some flight attendants don't send the peasants from coach back to the appropriate restroom when they wander up to first class. The airlines should equip the people seated in the last row of first class with stun guns. If anyone crosses over from coach for any reason during the flight, they are free

to zap at will. If passengers in the exit row have the authority to open the emergency doors, surely first-class passengers can be trusted to keep the riff-raff back in their section.

Be warned that treating yourself to a first-class upgrade will ruin you for life. Every future coach flight will feel like you're being smuggled into a drive-in theater in the trunk of a 1977 Chevy Vega. That said, Las Vegas trips are all about immediate gratification, so if it's a reasonable option, embrace the unnecessary luxury of first class and enjoy the flight.

CHAPTER 2

Selecting a Hotel

Few cities offer the variety of hotels found in Las Vegas. With more than 40 options on the Strip and Fremont Street, plus dozens more off-Strip, every visitor can find the perfect hotel soul mate. While figuring out where to stay can be a fun part of the lead-up to a Vegas trip, narrowing down the choices at times seems daunting.

Everybody has slightly different wants and needs when it comes to their ideal accommodations. Some Las Vegas visitors view their hotel room as nothing more than a place to crash for a few hours between binges. If the room has a bed and a bathroom, they're happy. Some people love to spend a ton of time relaxing in the sun, so access to a great pool area is essential. Still others place a high value on personalized service and feeling pampered. A nongaming hotel with a great spa may be their best choice. Typically, the hotel decision comes down to some combination of personal taste, location, price, and amenities.

Following are several considerations to help you choose your next Las Vegas hotel. Because most Las Vegas visitors want to stay where the action is, we're going to confine our tips and suggestions to the Strip and Fremont Street. If you're wondering whether to give the rent-by-the-hour Stickit Inn on Maryland Parkway a shot, you're on your own.

LOCATION

Although getting around Las Vegas is fairly easy, staying close to the casinos and attractions where you plan to spend the most time can simplify your trip. Consider how you prefer to use your hotel room to determine the importance of your hotel's location. If you typically leave your room before breakfast and don't return until you're ready to crash for the night, location may not be your top consideration. However, if you prefer to swing back to your room to change clothes, recharge your phone, or grab a mid-day wank, staying in a central location may be the most important aspect when choosing a hotel.

Chapters 9-13 offer additional insights into some of the most notable (and sometimes cringe-worthy) aspects of each property to help you consider the place where you may want to stay. Following is a breakdown of the general locations for each hotel. The maps in Appendix C may also be helpful.

- **South Strip:** This area includes Mandalay Bay, Delano, Luxor, Excalibur, Tropicana, New York-New York, MGM Grand, and Monte Carlo.
- **Center Strip:** The largest and most concentrated area of the Strip includes Mandarin Oriental, Aria, Vdara, The Cosmopolitan, Planet Hollywood, Bellagio, Paris, Bally's, The Cromwell, Flamingo, Caesars Palace, The Linq, Harrah's, Casino Royale, The Mirage, Treasure Island, The Venetian, and The Palazzo.
- **North Strip:** Currently underdeveloped, the North Strip is on the verge of a significant facelift. Several announced and under-construction projects will likely make this area a much more popular part of the Strip in a few years. Hotels include Wynn, Encore, Circus Circus, SLS, and Stratosphere.
- **Downtown:** Hotels on and near Fremont Street in Downtown Las Vegas include Main Street Station, California, The Plaza, Golden Gate, Golden Nugget, Fremont, Four Queens, The D, Downtown Grand, and El Cortez.

BUDGET

For most Las Vegas visitors, hotel rates matter when choosing accommodations. Those who are simply seeking the cheapest available room in a specific area of the Strip or Downtown have the easiest time selecting a hotel. All they have to do is compare rates using a third-party booking service like Orbitz or Kayak and sort by price. Find the cheapest option and book it—problem solved. Most of us, however, seek a balance between rate and perceived quality. Circus Circus frequently offers rooms below $30 a night (sans taxes and fees), but the location sucks and the casino has a certain sticky quality many people don't enjoy. As a general rule, Downtown hotels skew cheaper than those on the Strip, but many people find Downtown's old-school grit to be too gritty for their tastes. Mid-tier hotels won't break the bank but offer a step up from the lowest price options. Mid-tier value options worth considering include Tropicana (South), Bally's (Center), Treasure Island (North), and The D (Downtown).

When comparing rates, take advantage of past casino visits. Some hotels—particularly those that are part of large multi-property players club networks like Total Rewards, Mlife, and BConnected—allow customers to review customized rates and room offers online. Even if your gambling history at a property is minimal, logging in to check rates or calling the phone number listed on the back of the players club card (rather than the hotel reservation number) and speaking with the casino marketing department may yield a discounted "casino rate." Simply provide your name and players club number. Tell them you're thinking about staying there and would like to check on the lowest available rate for your travel dates.

AMENITIES

If you could happily subsist in a Ted-Kaczynski-style Montana shack, go with the cheapest room option. A quick-and-easy booking experience and a frill-free room await if you want nothing more than a place to sleep and shower. Quite honestly, I'm a bit jealous of tourists with the "hotel room is nothing more than a place to sleep" mindset. They spend little time considering options and next to no money on their rooms. Those of us who desire a hotel with specific amenities, however, need to expend a bit more energy.

Seeking a fun pool area? Consider Mandalay Bay, Monte Carlo, MGM Grand, Flamingo, or Golden Nugget. Want on-site access to a great spa? Take a look at Caesars Palace, Encore, Bellagio, or The Venetian. Do you hate walking long distances? Stay Downtown, or choose a small hotel like The Cromwell or Casino Royale. Want a relaxing experience without a casino? Try Mandarin Oriental, Vdara, or Four Seasons.

LAS VEGAS ROOM TYPES

After narrowing your hotel options, evaluating room types is the next challenge. Unfortunately, hotels often make this task cumbersome. If you've ever spent five minutes in a hotel room monkeying with an unfamiliar style of shower knob, you're already aware that hotels don't always make things easy. I'd like to wash the secondhand smoke out of my hair without having to solve a fucking Rubik's Cube before getting hot water. For whatever reason, hotels like to keep guests on their toes by making common items like shower knobs and lamp switches as confusing and inconsistent as possible. It wouldn't surprise me if the rooms at The Cosmopolitan offer 12-prong electrical outlets common to Belarus, Slovakia, and certain regions of the Czech Republic.

This unnecessary complexity is also a problem when comparing room types. The number of options within a single hotel can drive a person mad. Caesars Palace offers more than three dozen room types with names like Forum Deluxe King and Augustus Luxury Two Queen. The king and queen part are pretty easy to figure out. However, the difference between "deluxe" and "luxury" may not be as obvious. To help cut through the confusion, following is an attempt to translate common Las Vegas hotel room terms you may encounter.

- **Deluxe:** Las Vegas hotels never want you think something about their property is simply average or normal, so they avoid the term "standard" when describing the basic room tier. Instead, they go with "deluxe." Depending on the hotel, your deluxe room may be a complete shithole, but at least the name sounds good. If you encounter a problem with your accommodations, using the full room name when reporting the issue may make you feel better. Calling the front desk and saying, "My fourth-floor deluxe king room headboard has a large blood stain" still makes the place seem slightly classy, despite the recent homicide.

- **Classic/Vintage:** "Classic" and "vintage" are the hotel code words for outdated. Your classic room is likely to be pleasantly affordable. It also hasn't been renovated since Dean Martin was headlining at Bally's. Expect the décor to include burnt orange bathroom tile, shag carpeting, and a lovely macramé owl. Don't be surprised if the television is a 400-pound Magnavox console topped with rabbit ears. Classic rooms are a step below deluxe.

- **Superior/Luxury:** Superior or luxury rooms are usually one step up from deluxe. For an additional $10 to $40, these rooms offer one feature slightly better than deluxe rooms. Depending on the hotel, these rooms may be recently renovated, include an additional 100 square feet or, in the case of The Cromwell, provide a partial view of Las Vegas Boulevard rather than facing the wall that helps support the weight of the rooftop pool. Yes, technically the rooms are superior but not by all that much. Some hotels skip the "deluxe" label for standard rooms and use "luxury" instead. Consistency be damned in Las Vegas.

- **Premium/Premier:** Premium rooms are likely to be both larger and more modern than their lower tier counterparts. If superior or luxury rooms include one significant feature nicer than deluxe rooms, premium rooms frequently include a couple additions. These rooms have a little extra square footage and a newer or more elegant design.

- **Resort:** The Mirage, Wynn, and Bellagio skip the deluxe and luxury labels completely, using "resort" for their standard rooms. At Planet Hollywood, resort rooms are an upgrade from the standard Hollywood Hip rooms. They include better views and more square footage. Regardless of whether you have a resort room, you'll pay a resort fee, but we'll get to that now-standard (or should I say "deluxe") hotel scam shortly.

- **Panoramic/Strip-View/Fountain-View:** If falling asleep and waking up with a righteous view is important to you, seeking out a room with "panoramic" or "fountain-view" in the name may be worthwhile. These have sprawling views of a large section of the Strip or overlook the Fountains of Bellagio. Depending on the hotel, rooms labeled as Strip-view, however, may offer only a partial view of Las Vegas Boulevard if you look out the window at a less-than-ideal angle.

- **Junior/Mini Suite:** Junior suites and mini suites generally offer just enough bonus square footage for some additional seating and perhaps room for a little late-afternoon interpretive dance practice, but don't expect multiple rooms.

- **Suite:** In most cities, staying in a suite means having a bedroom and separate living room. This is not necessarily so in Las Vegas. Rio may have set the tone for redefining "suite" by referring to larger-than-average standard rooms as such. The Venetian and The Palazzo followed suit with large rooms that separate the bedroom and living room spaces with a couple stairs and a decorative railing. Although most hotels do offer larger multi-room suites, don't get your hopes up too high when you think you've stumbled upon the deal of the century—a suite for $149. It very well may be a lovely, oversized room, but it's unlikely to come with 10,000 square feet and a butler.

- **Penthouse/Villa/Bungalow:** If you're staying in a Las Vegas room labeled as a penthouse, villa, or bungalow, you're living large. These rooms are typically multi-room suites, possibly occupying multiple floors and including private swimming pools. Having one of these rooms without hosting a party, complete with illicit drugs, hookers, and a tiger or two is just a waste.

- **Hotel-Specific Quirks:** Although these terms give you a bit of insight into what type of room you may actually be booking, each hotel throws in plenty of additional terms to maximize confusion. Many refer to specific hotel tower names. Booking at SLS for example, you'll encounter Lux, World, and Story rooms, referring to the hotel's three towers. Caesars does the same with Roman, Forum, Palace, Augustus, Octavius, and Nobu towers.

  Likewise, hotel-specific branding throws another confusing twist into the mix. In addition to Planet Hollywood's Hollywood Hip rooms, you may encounter Flamingo's Fab and Go rooms, for example. This is just some marketing wanker's attempt at making standard and slightly better than standard rooms sound impressive. El Cortez is perhaps the biggest offender for mislabeling rooms. At most hotels, use of the word "cabana" indicates the presence of a swimming pool. And although Las Vegas is notorious for a bastardized definition of "suite," the word still implies a larger-than-standard room. El Cortez has no pool, and the size of its Cabana Suites makes a standard Holiday Inn room look like the Taj Mafuckinghal. The rooms are nice and among the best hotel values Downtown, but "Cabana Suites" couldn't be a less accurate description.

Ultimately, comparing Las Vegas rooms is always at least a minor pain in the ass, even when you have a reasonable understanding of the terms they use to simultaneously dazzle and confuse you. Within a specific hotel, room price provides a pretty good indicator of how each tower and individual room style ranks. Even when booking through a third-party site, comparing descriptions and pricing on the official hotel site is worthwhile.

WHY ARE HOTEL RATES SO HIGH?

Las Vegas hotel rates fluctuate constantly based on supply and demand. Because of its enormous room supply, attendee appeal, and a vast variety of meeting, exhibition, and entertainment space, Las Vegas draws numerous conferences and special events annually. These events are a double-edged sword. Those who are either required or compelled to attend have an excuse to plan a Las Vegas trip under the guise of official business. Unfortunately, degenerate fun-seekers with no interest in these events face high room rates resulting from the influx of attendees. When planning a trip, scanning the Las Vegas Convention and Visitors Authority convention calendar at _www. vegasmeansbusiness.com_ may clarify why rates are high during a specific week. Although a single event with 10,000 or 20,000 attendees will spike room rates in the immediate area where it's being held, hotels in other parts of the city are unlikely to be significantly affected. Multiple concurrent events of this size or single events attracting as many as 350,000 visitors, however, drive up rates everywhere. Expect long cab lines, busy restaurants, and crowded hotel bars. Several recurring events spike room rates annually.

- **Consumer Electronics Show:** Held in early January, CES attracts more than 150,000 attendees. Tech companies announce and demonstrate new televisions, phones, computers, and other personal electronics. Tech nerds run amok.

- **Super Bowl:** Marketed as the "Big Game," because the National Football League defends its trademarks almost as well as it protects the wife-beaters, rapists, and other criminals who play in the league, the Super Bowl brings football fans and sports bettors to Las Vegas in early February. Have a theory on which side of the game coin is more likely to land face up on natural grass when the temperature is below 40 degrees with wind blowing from the northeast? Then this is the event for you. Ridiculous proposition bets are all the rage. Many casinos host parties for VIP customers or anyone willing to buy a ticket.

- **MAGIC International:** More than 80,000 well-dressed, fully coiffed fashionistas overtake Las Vegas in mid-February and late August for the fashion industry's largest tradeshow. Many celebrities endorse or unveil their clothing lines during this event.

- **March Madness:** Although the games occur elsewhere, Las Vegas is a mecca for sports bettors during the NCAA men's basketball tournament. With more than 50 games played in the first six days, sports books and bars are packed during the initial rounds in mid-March. The excitement of watching these games in person pales in comparison to viewing them with a room full of people who have money riding on the outcome.

- **National Association of Broadcasters:** Each April, 100,000 broadcast professionals learn about new technologies and content options at the NAB show. If you've ever wondered how a show like *Paternity Court* ends up on TV, it's probably a safe guess that a drunken night in Las Vegas during NAB led to a regrettable multiyear syndication deal.

- **Electric Daisy Carnival:** Held at Las Vegas Motor Speedway, the EDC electronic music festival draws as many as 150,000 fans of dance music, wacky costumes, and casual drug use each June.

- **Automotive Aftermarket Industry Week:** During the first week in November, more than 140,000 gearheads descend on Las Vegas to learn about the latest in automotive rust protection and spinning rims. Casinos replace their usual scents with WD40, and slot machine buttons often become caked with axle grease.

- **National Finals Rodeo:** Shit-kickers unite! The nation's largest annual rodeo event descends on Las Vegas for ten days each December. More than 170,000 adults who love Coors Light, Kenny Chesney, and giant hats overtake the Strip. Expect cranky waitresses and bartenders because rodeo fans are notoriously rowdy drunks and bad tippers.

- **New Year's Eve:** The most popular holiday in Las Vegas, New Year's Eve typically includes a massive fireworks display from several Strip hotels. Las Vegas Boulevard converts into an auto-free, pedestrian party zone. Plan for high room rates, wall-to-wall drunken revelers, and a night of delicious regrets.

RESORT FEES: A SHITTY FACT OF LIFE

Several years ago, Las Vegas hotels began implementing resort fees. They bundled several amenities, perks, and services—some which were previously free—into a mandatory per-night fee paid directly to the hotel. Fees range anywhere from $5 to $30 per night—and they continue to increase. Listed amenities include such items as:

- Parking
- WiFi or wired Internet access
- Newspaper
- Coffee
- Fitness room admission
- Local and toll-free phone calls
- Fax service
- Bottled water
- Show, bar, or restaurant discounts

- Boarding pass printing
- Notary service

Depending on the hotel and the services a guest is likely to use each day, these fees may feel like a great value or a tedious, nickel-and-dime ripoff. Many of us would prefer to pay individual fees for only the services we need. However, someone who needs daily WiFi, runs on a treadmill every morning, and faxes a lot of notarized documents may find the mandatory fee to be worthwhile.

MGM Resorts properties were among the early adopters of resort fees in an attempt to improve online search result placement and decrease commissions to third-party travel agencies. Caesars Entertainment countered the MGM strategy in 2010 with a "No Resort Fees" publicity campaign, featuring company spokesboob Holly Madison proclaiming that customers should pay for only the services they use. Unfortunately, three years later, Caesars changed course and began implementing fees at all of its Las Vegas properties. The company claimed that guests were increasingly demanding a package price rather than separate fees. Unfortunately, as soon as Caesars caved, nearly all Strip and Fremont Street hotels followed suit.

Resort fees irritate hotel customers *almost* as much as bed bugs, demagnetized key cards, and maids who knock on the door despite the do-not-disturb sign. So why would hotels take this strategy rather than simply increasing their rates and making the supposed benefits complimentary for all guests?

A significant number of tourists research and book their rooms through online travel agencies, including Priceline, Expedia, and TripAdvisor. When searching these sites, most users sort the results by price from lowest to highest within whatever star rating they are willing to accept. A hotel's failure to appear on the first page or two of search results can result in thousands of lost dollars daily. Add-on fees—even those that are mandatory—are disclosed before booking, but they rarely appear in the initial search results. If Flamingo charges a $25 resort fee, this gives the hotel the flexibility to lower its standard rate by $6, $8, or $10—even the full $25—to ensure it places on the first page of search results without losing money. In addition, customers pay these fees directly to the hotel, so the travel sites don't receive a commission, as they do with the standard rates for rooms booked through their sites.

Resort fees may irritate customers, but about 95 percent of hotels in the major tourist areas of Las Vegas have adopted them. Unfortunately, they will continue to be an unpleasant fact of life unless the U.S. Federal Trade Commission decides to crack down on the practice or third-party booking sites stand up to the hotels.

Major Strip and Downtown hotels not yet charging resort fees include:
- Casino Royale
- Elara (timeshare property attached to Planet Hollywood's Miracle Mile Shops)
- Hilton Grand Vacations (timeshare properties)
- California
- Four Queens
- Fremont
- Main Street Station

HOTEL LOYALTY PROGRAMS

You've probably noticed that consumer loyalty programs are a big deal these days. For decades, casinos have used players clubs to reward customers for their gambling and, ultimately, drive repeat business. In addition to their casino loyalty programs, many Las Vegas hotels belong to nationwide or global hotel loyalty programs. Frequent travelers can earn free room nights and other perks by choosing hotels that belong to their preferred program. Following is a list of Las Vegas hotels affiliated with national hotel loyalty programs.
- **Best Western Rewards:** Casino Royale
- **Choice Privileges:** Downtown Grand
- **Hilton HHonors:** Elara, Hilton Grand Vacations (all locations), SLS, Tropicana
- **Hyatt Gold Passport:** Aria, Bellagio, Delano, Excalibur, Luxor, Mandalay Bay, MGM Grand, MGM Grand Signature, The Mirage, Monte Carlo, New York-New York, Vdara
- **IHG Rewards:** The Palazzo, The Venetian
- **Lexington Rewards:** The D

- **Marriott Rewards:** The Cosmopolitan
- **Starwood Preferred Guest:** Bally's, Caesars Palace, The Cromwell, Flamingo, Harrah's, The Linq, Paris, Planet Hollywood, Rio, The Westin

CHAPTER 3

Renting a Car

When planning your trip and considering transportation options, don't immediately assume you need to rent a car. Because most Las Vegas tourist attractions are concentrated on the Strip and Fremont Street, visitors can easily see the sights without driving. If, however, you have a burning desire to see Hoover Dam, Red Rock Canyon, or Sam's Town, having a car will give you the freedom to hit the road whenever you desire. Fortunately, car rental rates in Las Vegas tend to skew lower than many U.S. cities. Following are a few tips for renting a car.

- Online travel agencies offer convenient price comparison searches to begin narrowing down options.
- Car rental discount codes are readily available with a quick Google search or by checking *www.rentalcodes.com*, *www.rentalcarmomma.com*, and *www.carrentalsavers.com*.
- If you find a good deal directly through a car rental company's website, book it. As with hotel room bookings, you can typically cancel and rebook if you find a better rate later. Make sure to read the terms of service to ensure this is the case. Cheaper pre-paid deals may be exempt. Periodically search for cheaper deals after booking, as rates fluctuate often.
- Even if you need a car for only one day, the price of renting for your full trip may justify doing so. Rental rates for pickup and drop-off at hotels are sometimes higher than at the airport. Factor in transportation to and from the airport if you would otherwise use a cab. Run the numbers before assuming a one-day rental is the best option.
- AAA, AARP, Costco, and some credit cards offer members-only discounts, so check their benefits information if you belong.

- Bidding on a rental car through Priceline (_www.priceline.com_) can yield some substantial discounts, but renters pay in advance and fees are nonrefundable.

- Rentals booked through AutoSlash (_www.autoslash.com_) are automatically rebooked whenever a lower rate becomes available. The site also offers tracking of rates for reservations booked through other sites.

Major car rental services in Las Vegas include Advantage (_www.advantage.com_), Alamo (_www.alamo.com_), Avis (_www.avis.com_), Budget (_www.budget.com_), Dollar (_www.dollar.com_), Enterprise (_www.enterprise.com_), Hertz (_www.hertz.com_), National (_www.nationalcar.com_), and Thrifty (_www.thrifty.com_).

Ultimately, the decision to rent a car may hinge on your perception of freedom when vacationing. Frequent Las Vegas visitors who rent a car every trip love the ability to drive anywhere in the city at a moment's notice with no dependence on anyone else. They hate dealing with dishonest cabbies and don't want to hassle with public transportation. Those of us who rarely rent a car enjoy leaving the driving to others (due in part to our tendency to overindulge in alcohol in Las Vegas). We don't want the responsibility of a vehicle on vacation, don't particularly enjoy navigating unfamiliar streets, and view dealing with the car rental process, valets, and parking garages as unnecessary inconveniences. There are certainly pros and cons to both, so consider your personality and your desire to wander off the beaten path when planning your trip. Chapter 7 offers additional insight into Las Vegas transportation options.

CHAPTER 4

Finding the Sweet Spot

Many factors come into play when determining the optimal trip length. Available vacation time, commitments at home, frequency of visits, and budget are among the most obvious considerations. However, more than anything else, each of us has a Las Vegas Tolerance Threshold, the point at which we've simply had enough of the city for a while. Figuring out how much damage you can take will help you plan the ideal length for your trip. The only way to determine your personal threshold is through trial and error.

For most first-time visitors, three nights is the optimal trip length. New visitors hit the town with gusto and fail to properly pace themselves. They want to see everything, do everything, and consume everything possible—sleep be damned. After a long weekend, they're exhausted, broke, and ready to go home. If, however, at the end of a three-nighter you feel like you haven't had enough, tack on a fourth night the next time around. Follow this process for subsequent trips until you go home feeling like you wish you had left a day earlier. I've done a few six-night trips, but they're rarely as satisfying as those that last five nights. That's my sweet spot. Within a few days of a five-nighter ending, I'm ready to begin planning my return visit. After a six-nighter, I usually don't want to think about returning for at least a few weeks. That extra day burns me out almost every time.

The longer you stay, the more important it is to not shoot your Vegas wad on the first night, getting way too drunk and/or losing way too much of your bankroll. Trying to cram in all the fun at once is a quick road to disaster. Inevitably, you'll end up either so hungover you can't get out of bed or so pressed for cash you'll spend your last days selling $20 handjobs in the Slots-A-Fun men's room to avoid going home broke. Spread out the fun. Pacing is everything.

Some Las Vegas visitors make annual pilgrimages lasting a month or more, bouncing between hotels to take advantage of multiple cheap or comped room offers. Even though they may not have a home in Las Vegas, these people function much more like temporary residents rather than tourists. Maintaining a tourist pace over several weeks would tax even the most diehard Vegas visitor's vital organs and budget. I respect their ability to demonstrate self-control in the face of the many temptations Vegas offers. I don't think I could do it though. At this stage in my life, I still prefer to keep Las Vegas as a refuge from reality for five nights several times during the year rather than one or two longer stretches.

CHAPTER 5

Companions, Work, Kids, and Other Annoying Considerations

If you're traveling to Las Vegas with only a spouse, partner, or friend, it's fairly easy to plan a trip that will meet both of your expectations. Group trips, work trips, family trips, and—in some cases—solo trips carry additional complications worth addressing before finalizing plans.

"HEY, WE SHOULD ALL GO TO VEGAS TOGETHER!"

That suggestion, thrown out at countless dinners, parties, and family gatherings, signals the beginning of fun Vegasy adventures. Family, friend, bachelor/bachelorette party, and multi-couple trips can be a blast, creating memories that last a lifetime. The night your buddy Todd got thrown out of Marquee and wet his pants after passing out on the sidewalk will live in infamy and fuel mockery for years to come. However, if not executed properly, Las Vegas group trips can be the stuff of nightmares. The more people who are involved, the greater the chance for disagreements, hurt feelings, and unnecessary drama. Such problems can be avoided by discussing expectations before the trip begins. Most likely, everyone will be so excited about the prospects of a Las Vegas trip that they will focus on all the fun times ahead. "We should all spend the morning lounging by the pool." "I've heard Drai's is amazing!" "It would be fun to have a blowout dinner on the last night at Gordon Ramsay Steak." This all sounds great two months before the trip, and may be fine if everyone in the group wants to do the same things. However, all-for-one all-the-time trips rarely work. What if Janelle finds pool lounging to be a boring waste of Vegas time? What if Ben hates nightclubs? What if Brian refuses to dine in any restaurant that serves meat because he's a staunch animal rights activist? Someone needs to step up, suggest setting a few ground rules, and disinvite Brian because he's a guaranteed buzzkill.

Every two years, my three brothers (David, Mike, and Dan), my oldest nephew (Phillip), my dad (Bill), and I head to the Promised Land for a guys' trip. This tradition began in 1999 to celebrate Dad's 60th birthday. We all had such an amazing time that it became a recurring tradition. Never once in our nine trips have we had any disagreements or hurt feelings about how things would play out. This success is the result of a rule Dad set out at the beginning of the first trip: "Everyone is responsible for their own fun. If you're not having a good time, go do something else." We all agreed. As a result, we sometimes split off into groups and head in different directions. If we're all gambling at Tropicana and Phillip gets bored, he may wander off to do a little shopping at the Miracle Mile Shops. While we're all getting drunk on cheap beer at Casino Royale, I may suggest we all go to Circus Circus as a goof. Everyone declines except Mike, who inexplicably indulges my idiocy, and the two of us head for Clownville. Dad inevitably wants to take the shuttle to Gold Coast—probably because most gamblers there are in their 90s, and it makes him feel young. David and Dan join him, but the rest of us stick to the Strip. Each afternoon, we gather in a designated hotel room for happy hour. We drink beer for a couple hours and tell stories about our day. Although it would be perfectly acceptable if someone missed happy hour because he was having a good run in the casino, none of us has ever skipped one. We bust balls and laugh a lot. It's the best part of the day. Before heading out for the evening, we agree on a time and location for breakfast. Again, our group breakfast is optional, but inevitably everyone shows up. At the end of breakfast, we agree on a late lunch location, and we're on our way. We may all hang out together for a while, or we may splinter. For us, having a few planned daily gatherings and the rest of the time less regimented works out perfectly. I'm not suggesting this as a perfect recipe for every group, but rather pointing out the importance of figuring out a workable level of togetherness early instead of leaving it to chance.

Depending on the mix of personalities, some groups may find it more beneficial to plan out specific activities a bit more. If a golf outing, show, or upscale dinner is in the mix, reservations may be needed. If everyone knows each other well and typically enjoys the same activities, perhaps spending the entire trip as a group will work. Regardless, sorting out these details and setting expectations early is essential to a harmonious trip. To broach the topic, simply say something like, "I've heard stories about group trips turning ugly because not everyone wanted to do the same things. We should figure out plans for a few full group activities and time for people to do whatever they want." It may not be perfect, and your super codependent friend Jill will likely end up throwing a hissy fit at some point anyway. But at least you've done your best to preemptively keep the peace.

WORK TRIPS

Congratulations. Your boss just e-mailed you an approval to attend the upcoming Edutunities Conference. As luck would have it, Aria is hosting this year's event, so you're getting a free trip to Las Vegas, courtesy of your beloved employer. A working trip to Las Vegas can be both a blessing and a curse. On one hand, you'll be in Las Vegas. On the other hand, work responsibilities will consume much of your time. What's a lady to do?

Your ability to maximize your Vegasness during a work trip depends on several variables.

- **Are you simply attending the event or are you working at it, either as an exhibitor or on behalf of the company holding the event?** If you are merely an attendee, you'll likely have some free time to hit the casino, see a show, or enjoy the sights. Exhibitors frequently get stuck spending all day in an expo booth and all night wining and dining clients. Sucks for them.

- **Will your boss or coworkers also attend?** Your ability to live life to the fullest may suffer if you're traveling with a boss or a coworker who doesn't share your enthusiastic attitude about taking advantage of your location. The fewer people you know there, the easier it is to slip out early, skipping nonessential or unappealing sessions and networking functions.

- **Do you have to share a room with a coworker?** If your company is cheap, requiring you to share accommodations with a colleague, you're fucked. Your roomie will be privy to the hours you keep, which will inevitably be shared with others back at the office. So forget about dominating the craps table until 4 a.m. Also, you'll probably hear your coworker snore, smell his sleep farts, and possibly see him naked. Proceed with caution.

- **Can you travel with a spouse or guest?** If company policy doesn't prohibit bringing a travel companion, you can give a loved one a decent excuse to sneak in a Las Vegas trip they otherwise wouldn't have taken. You'll forever endear yourself to that person, plus you'll have someone fun to hang out with if your coworkers are boring.

- **Can you extend your trip beyond the conference dates?** If work obligations prevent you from enjoying your time in Las Vegas during the event, tack on a couple days at the end. Your company won't be picking up the tab for your room and meals, but at least you'll get to take full advantage of your free flight. Also, knowing you have a couple vacation days at the end decreases the frustration of being in Las Vegas but not truly experiencing the city during the conference.

NO KIDDING AROUND

This is the point in *The Outsiders' Guide to Las Vegas* when approximately 11 percent of readers get upset, curse my existence, and swear they'll never again pay attention to anything I say. I know this because it happens whenever we discuss traveling to Las Vegas with kids on the podcast. The subject elicits strong feelings, and for good reason. Nobody likes having their parental choices judged—especially by someone who doesn't have kids (that's me!).

Many *Five Hundy* podcast listeners have bemoaned the challenge of balancing the responsibilities of parenthood with the desire to occasionally return to the most fun place in the universe. I understand and empathize with the dilemma. That said, knowing some of you are already crossing your arms and muttering that I'm a know-nothing asshole, I'll do my best to lay out a case for leaving the kids at home, preferably with adult supervision.

When considering family vacation destinations, you have a whole range of options. At one end of the family-friendly spectrum, you'll find the obvious choices for child-centric fun—anywhere with a theme park. The more theme parks in a concentrated area, the more suitable it is for family fun. I'm fairly certain traveling within a 50-mile radius of Orlando, Fla., legally requires the accompaniment of at least one child. Fortunately, Orlando International Airport includes several lease-a-kid services, located conveniently next to the Thrifty Car Rental counter. At the other end of the scale are locations barely suitable for adults, let alone children. Boasting the most murders per capita for two years running, San Pedro Sula, Honduras, takes this honor. Every other location falls somewhere on the family vacation continuum between Happy Fun Land in Florida and Murder City in Honduras. The closer to Happy Fun Land, the better the choice for a trip with your beloved little darlings, Briston and D'Jennica.

So where does Las Vegas land on the family vacation continuum? Obviously it's not one of the worst places on the planet. That, however, does not make a good defense when arguing in favor of taking your kids to Las Vegas. "There are worse places we could take them" doesn't make Las Vegas a good choice. That's like saying, "I haven't acknowledged my son's birthday in seven years, but I'm a better dad than Darth Vader." Just because you haven't cut off your kid's hand in a lightsaber battle doesn't make you Ward Cleaver. When looking at what makes Las Vegas a popular tourist destination, the city skews far more adult-oriented than child-oriented. Yes, Las Vegas offers a handful of entertainment options for kids. However, the majority of Las Vegas fun is aimed at adults. For every Adventuredome theme park, Fun Dungeon arcade, and Mandalay Beach wave pool, there are a dozen pornslappers, 100 casinos, and 10,000 drunken gamblers.

Walk down Las Vegas Boulevard in the evening and really pay attention to the environment. (If doing so requires you to walk slowly, please move to the right. The world doesn't need more inconsiderate moseyers.) Notice the mobile billboards rolling by, featuring nearly nude models, promoting strip clubs and "dancers direct to your room." How many people are sucking down football-sized beers? Look, there's a guy in a g-string posing for photos. Step inside the nearest casino for a healthy view of several of the world's favorite vices—gambling, smoking, and drinking. Which part of this is for kids? This observation sometimes leads to another defense: "I don't want to shelter my kids. It's good to show them to the darker side of life too." There's a difference between not sheltering them and intentionally exposing them to something. When they inevitably get caught watching bukkake videos online, you'll have a chat about it. That doesn't mean you should preemptively sit down as a family in front of YouPorn to watch coeds get sprayed in the face like they've been eating vanilla ice cream cones in a wind tunnel.

Next on the weak defense list is the argument that plenty of kids grow up in Las Vegas, and they turn out perfectly fine. Absolutely true, but that has nothing to do with this debate. Those of us opposed to treating Las Vegas as a family destination don't claim that exposing your kids to the adult aspects of the Strip will result in a life of crime. Parents in Las Vegas deal with raising kids within the unique realities of their environment just like parents in any other location. Whether the city provides a good location for raising a family is an entirely different subject outside the scope of a book about Las Vegas vacations.

Las Vegas isn't chosen as a family vacation destination because it's a great place to bring the kids. It's chosen because mom and dad love it, and there happens to be enough stuff for kids to give them a good time. If you're going to choose a vacation destination more for your enjoyment than for your kids', why bring them at all? Leave them with grandma and grandpa or, if that's not an option, go somewhere closer to Happy Fun Land on the family vacation destination continuum.

Some of you will ignore this advice, writing it off as preachy and ignorant. So be it. Your love of Las Vegas cannot be stopped, family be damned. So, I offer the following suggestions for taking kids to Las Vegas without drowning them in the adult nature of their surroundings, courtesy of longtime *Five Hundy* listener Chris from Santa Cruz. He provided these tips in response to a kids-in-Vegas discussion on the podcast.

- *Stay somewhere that doesn't have a casino. Yes, this is a pain in the ass if you're an adult and you like to gamble. Deal. Stay at The Signature at MGM Grand, Four Seasons, or somewhere like that. If you have to stay somewhere with a casino, make sure that you don't have to walk through the casino to get to the kid activities such as the pool. The pool complex at Mandalay Bay is a great example of this. You can get to the pool from the Mandalay Bay hotel elevators without going through the casino.*
- *Plan your day so your kids can have something to do. See Hoover Dam, Red Rock Canyon, or the Pinball Hall of Fame.*
- *At night, hire a babysitter to stay with your kid in the hotel. Most of the more upscale hotels will be more than happy to arrange babysitting with bonded, safe, reputable sitters. This will not be cheap. Again, deal. It was your decision to bring them. Be a responsible parent. DO NOT leave them in the Circus Circus or Excalibur arcades. This does not count as babysitting.*

  All of this only works from ages 8 to 13. Any younger and you should just stay home. Any older and the kids are going to be difficult to contain in the room unless they can bring a friend.

Unfortunately, seeing kids waiting for mom and dad near the casino while they gamble is all too common. Nevada law prohibits minors not only from gambling but also from loitering in casinos. They're allowed to walk through with an adult, but they cannot hang out with you while you gamble or even watch from the edge of the casino floor. Because casinos can lose their gaming licenses if caught allowing kids to linger in the gaming area, security rarely ignores the issue. After being told the kids need to leave, security won't hesitate to eject parents who continue to violate the law. So either skip the casino or figure out a reasonable way to ditch the kiddies while you gamble.

If you insist on choosing Las Vegas for a family trip, visit _www. vivatotvegas.com_, a blog from Dr. David Schwartz offering advice, reviews, and other information for Las Vegas visitors traveling with small children.

SOLO TRIPS

Nobody enjoys spending time with me more than I do. So, occasionally, I'll find myself alone in Las Vegas. Fortunately, the city caters nicely to independent travelers. Hotels, restaurants, bars, and attractions throughout the city are accustomed to solo convention attendees, travelers who are going it alone because companions overindulged the previous day, and people who simply choose to visit the city on their own. People who don't normally travel alone may feel self-conscious and worry about what others think of them. If you're one of those people, I gladly offer you some free tough-love-style therapy:

GET OVER YOURSELF.

If you think anyone in Las Vegas gives half a shit about why you're spending time alone there, you have major narcissism issues. Few people book trips to Las Vegas with the goal of mocking solo travelers. Other tourists are too focused on their own fun to worry about what you're doing. They probably won't notice you, and even if they do, they likely won't dedicate five seconds of thought to you. Las Vegas employees see solo travelers every day. Their desire is getting you in and out of their establishments efficiently and with a smile on your face so you'll tip them generously and leave positive Yelp reviews. It's highly unlikely they're going to stand on a table in the employee cafeteria during lunch, clap their hands to get everyone's attention and announce, "You're not going to believe this. I had a customer today who was dining by herself!" On the unlikely chance someone gives you a strange look, it's probably because you have a piece of toilet paper stuck to your shoe or a giant booger precariously dangling from your right nostril.

If someone questions your solo status—again, highly unlikely—be prepared with a bogus story that makes him feel like the douchenozzle he is. "I promised my husband that immediately following the funeral I would come to our favorite city and visit all of the places where we laughed together." With a comment like that, you've put him in his place and entertained yourself simultaneously. Bonus.

A few tips to make your solo experience enjoyable:

- **Be safe.** Don't stray from the well-populated, relatively safe Strip and Fremont Street areas, especially at night.

- **Reel in the booze consumption.** If you're alone and noticeably liquored up, you may become a target for nefarious figures looking for a victim.
- **At restaurants, ask to be seated at the counter or bar.** These common options are perfect for solo travelers. Vegas bartenders tend to be very welcoming and social, so you may find yourself having a nice conversation. If not, there's probably a TV behind the bar to hold your attention.
- **Get social.** Find a blackjack table with players who appear to be having a good time. Choose a slot machine next to someone with a friendly demeanor. Make a comment about something simple like the weather or your cocktail to the person sitting next to you. If you're not used to putting yourself out there in that manner, it may feel awkward at first. However, you may end up having a great conversation and some laughs.

When planning your solo adventure, visit _www.vegassolo.com_ and _www.solofriendly.com_, two blogs by Gray Cargill. They are packed with useful articles, tips, and reviews to help make your solo travels—not only to Las Vegas, but anywhere—more enjoyable.

CHAPTER 6

Vegas Lent

U nable to completely shed my Catholic upbringing, I long ago misappropriated the term "Lent" for my Vegas-related amusement. Vegas Lent describes the 40 days leading up to a Las Vegas vacation. Unlike actual Lent, during which many Christians choose to give up chocolate, swearing, or some other relatively harmless vice, Vegas Lent requires no sacrifice. Rather, this time is spent in solemn preparation for an upcoming desert journey. Vegas Lent includes no formal rules or requirements. Instead, use the time for any activities that prepare you for your trip or put you in a Las Vegas state of mind.

GAMBLING PREPARATION

Lasting just over a month, Vegas Lent provides a reasonable amount of time to sharpen your gambling skills before hitting the casino floor. Figure out which games you're most likely to play and begin practicing. It may seem a little strange to practice for vacation. However, ensuring you know the proper strategy for your favorite games can help stretch your bankroll and give you confidence when you plant your ass at a table or machine. Consider using training apps for your phone, tablet, or computer to become a master at blackjack and video poker. Even if you're confident in your abilities, you'll likely be surprised at the number of false choices you're unwittingly making. Chapter 16 provides a helpful overview of the many games you're likely to encounter in Las Vegas.

Recommended training apps and websites include:

- **Blackjack:** A quick Web search finds many free blackjack training websites. Unfortunately, they tend to be slow, clunky, and cluttered with online casino sales pitches. Pony up a few bucks for a proper training app instead. For iOS devices, the

Blackjack Strategy Practice app ($3) offers strategy cards, customizable rules, and even an option to practice strategy for dreaded 6:5 tables. Blackjack Trainer Lite (free) and the more comprehensive Blackjack Trainer Pro ($5) offer similarly solid options for Android users. Players who wish to move beyond basic strategy and try card counting can hone their skills using the Blackjack Card Counting Trainer Pro app ($3) for iOS.

- **Video Poker:** The WinPoker iOS app is the gold standard of mobile video poker training programs. Don't sweat the $9.99 price. It will quickly pay for itself via reduced errors during your next video poker session. Unfortunately, neither WinPoker nor a comparable app is available for Android devices. Video Poker Expert offers the largest variety of game options on an Android app, and it's free. Video Poker for Winners (Windows only) and Optimum Video Poker (Mac, Windows, Linux) are useful computer software applications with a robust set of features, but the $50 and $55 price tags are a tad steep. Sticking with mobile options or more basic (and free) Web-based trainers may be better options. Try *FreeVideoPoker.com*, *WizardofOdds.com*, and *VideoPokerTrainer.org*.

- **Other Games:** For pretty much any game you'll encounter in a casino, *WizardofOdds.com* offers comprehensive information about odds and strategies. Even if you don't have the option to practice using training software, you can pick up useful tips and learn which bets to avoid if you hope to stretch your gambling bankroll.

SCOPE OUT DEALS

Upon finding out you're heading to Las Vegas, some people may tell you there are no good deals there anymore. They'll wax poetic about the days of yore, when no meal cost more than $2, casinos showered even low-rolling guests with gifts beyond their wildest dreams, and blumpkins were free for the asking. Today, they'll tell you that you can't cross the street without having to pay for the privilege. They're full of shit. Ignore them. It's true that casino owners have increasingly sought to maximize profits in areas that once were loss leaders. However, Las Vegas still offers plenty of value if you're willing to seek out some deals during Vegas Lent. Here's how:

- **Follow hotels, bars, casinos, and attractions on Facebook and Twitter.** You'll have to endure a fair amount of noise generated by the PR and marketing departments. However, between photos of jackpot winners and inane questions—"If you could eat in any of our restaurants today, which one would you choose?"—you'll likely find some useful information. Keep an eye open for happy hour food and drink specials and limited-time discounts.

- **Join a community.** Tons of online Las Vegas forums connect Las Vegas travelers. You'll pick up useful information by simply scanning recent discussions every day or two. I'm partial to the *Five Hundy by Midnight* Facebook group (*www.facebook. com/groups/fivehundy*), which spun off from my podcast. There, you'll find discussions about all things Las Vegas from a knowledgeable and entertaining collection of fellow outsiders. Simply as a result of the sheer volume of users, the TripAdvisor Las Vegas Travel Forum (*http://www.tripadvisor.com/ShowForum-g45963-i10-Las_Vegas_Nevada.html*) provides a wealth of information as well.

- **Visit SmarterVegas (*www.smartervegas.com*) and Travel-Zoo (*www.travelzoo.com/entertainment/las-vegas*) to find deals on show tickets compiled from multiple sources.** If you're interested in same-day ticket discounts, visiting *www. tix4tonight.com* will give you a pretty good idea of the types of show discounts often available upon arriving in Vegas.

FINALIZE PLANS

In the days and weeks before your trip, firm up your travel plans. Double-check room and car rental rates, and rebook if prices have dropped. If your plans include dinner at an upscale restaurant, make reservations early. While it's often easy to get reservations within a day or two, some new and extremely popular restaurants book early. It's better to reserve and cancel if necessary than to wait and risk getting shut out. Many restaurants offer online booking via OpenTable (*www.opentable.com*), so you won't even need to deal with the annoying hold music and voice prompts that come with phone reservations.

If you're an iPhone user, download the VegasMate app (*www.vegasmate. com*) and make an informal itinerary for your trip. Even though plans are likely to change once you arrive in Las Vegas, plotting out restaurants, attractions, and sites you plan to visit will save time when you arrive. This type of planning also helps build anticipation for the awaiting Vegasy fun.

MAKE VEGAS YOUR SOUNDTRACK

What better way to get into a Vegasy mood than by making and listening to a customized soundtrack of songs about gambling and Las Vegas? If you're a past visitor, you probably have a few songs that bring back fond memories and put you in a Vegas state of mind. Put together a playlist of all your favorites—perhaps that unforgettable Bellagio fountains song or that shitty Smashmouth tune that was playing during the most incredible dice session you've ever had. To help you complete your soundtrack, I've compiled a list of songs with a Las Vegas or gambling theme. See Appendix A.

HAVE A LAS VEGAS FILM FESTIVAL

Holding a multi-day Las Vegas film festival will undoubtedly get you in the Vegasy frame of mind for an upcoming trip. Seeing Las Vegas scenery with the knowledge you'll be there in just a few days will make your heart beat faster and your mind race with visions of yourself in those same locations. Countless movies have been filmed there, but many include only short Las Vegas scenes or aren't quite the right tone for trip preparation. Some are heavy on eye candy but light on plot. I'm looking at you, *Night of the Running Man*. Others, like *Top of the World*, are set in the city but have few if any actual Las Vegas locations beyond stock establishing shots. And, then you've got films that have good storylines and plenty of scenery but just don't make good pre-trip viewing. *Leaving Las Vegas* may be a fine piece of work, but watching someone slowly kill himself in a shitty motel won't exactly get you amped up to conquer the Strip. To help you weed through the many Las Vegas movie options, following is a curated film selection for your consideration.

- *Casino* **(1995):** Ace Rothstein (Robert DeNiro) runs Tangiers Hotel and Casino on behalf of the mob. His hot mess of a wife (Sharon Stone) and his hot-tempered mobster friend (Joe Pesci) make life difficult for Ace. Nearly all of *Casino* takes place in Las Vegas, and dozens of scenes highlight Strip and Downtown locations. In addition to numerous interior shots filmed at Riviera, eye candy includes Peppermill's Fireside Lounge, The Plaza's glass-domed restaurant (currently occupied by Oscar's), and the long-gone Glass Pool Inn. Based on the true story of Frank "Lefty" Rosenthal, *Casino* is the definitive Las Vegas mobster movie. It includes gambling cheats getting the backroom treatment, government officials on the take, and Midwest mob bosses skimming profits. Bonus points for a cameo by legendary mob lawyer and former Las Vegas mayor Oscar Goodman.

- *Fear and Loathing in Las Vegas* **(1998):** Based on the Hunter S. Thompson novel, *Fear and Loathing in Las Vegas* stars Johnny Depp and Benicio del Toro. Visiting Las Vegas to write about the off-road Mint 400 race for a magazine, they get fucked up on mescaline and other assorted substances. If nothing else, this film teaches us that visiting Circus Circus (called Bazooko Circus in the movie) while on LSD could actually make that casino tolerable.

- *The Hangover* **(2009):** Bradley Cooper, Zach Galifianakis, Ed Helms, and the guy who plays Doug head to Las Vegas for a bachelor party. Things quickly get out of hand because some people just can't handle Vegas. Many of us have had drunken Las Vegas evenings with brief memory gaps. *The Hangover* takes that experience to the extreme. It's not *Citizen Kane*, but *The Hangover* won't soon be topped as the definitive Las Vegas party movie. Establishing helicopter shots of the Strip, nighttime shots from the roof of Caesars Palace, the Caesars Palace pool and porte cochere, Atomic Liquors, and the casino at Riviera highlight the Las Vegas scenes.

- *National Lampoon's Vegas Vacation* **(1997):** Chevy Chase, Beverly D'Angelo, and their kids head to Las Vegas for yet another zany Griswold family adventure. Like all of the National Lampoon Vacation movies, *Vegas Vacation* includes incredibly silly scenarios and unrealistic plot twists. Who cares? It's a mindless comedy. More importantly, it's packed with Las Vegasy goodness, including underage gambling that results in multiple car jackpots, a trip to a less-than-flashy off-Strip casino, and Wayne Newton. The movie has plenty of great Strip and Downtown eye candy, including scenes at The Mirage, MGM Grand, and the Neon Boneyard.

- *Ocean's 11* **(1960):** Frank Sinatra, Dean Martin, Sammy Davis Jr., and their military buddies hatch a plan to rip off Desert Inn, Flamingo, Riviera, Sahara, and Sands on New Year's Eve. The definitive Las Vegas heist movie, *Ocean's 11* moves a little slowly by today's standards. However, it's packed with old-timey Strip casino shots, a fun plot, and the Rat Pack. What more could you want from a classic Las Vegas movie?

- *Ocean's Eleven* **(2001):** Inspired by the 1960 original by the same name, the modern reboot of *Ocean's Eleven* stars George Clooney, Brad Pitt, Matt Damon, and a bunch of other big-time stars. Clooney and his criminal pals plan to knock off Bellagio, MGM Grand, and The Mirage simultaneously. The Las Vegas eye candy in *Ocean's Eleven* is delicious, with several casino scenes and an unforgettable ending at the Bellagio fountains. Las Vegas plays an essential role in the film, evident from the clunker of a sequel that was *Ocean's Twelve*—not set in Las Vegas.

- *Ocean's Thirteen* **(2007):** A successful return to form for the Ocean's franchise, Clooney, Pitt, Damon and crew return to Las Vegas. They plan to knock off The Bank, a new casino owned by Al Pacino, after Pacino squeezes their friend, Elliott Gould, out of his share of the property. Although not as solid as *Ocean's Eleven* and not as packed with on-location scenes, *Ocean's Thirteen* has enough Vegasy action to make it worth viewing.

- *Showgirls* **(1995):** Nomi Malone (Elizabeth Berkley) travels to Las Vegas because she has a dream—a dream to dance. After losing everything she owns, she becomes a stripper but soon finds herself working at Stardust in a big-time Las Vegas show. When a movie centers around showgirls, there's really no-where else it could be set. Fortunately, most of the movie was filmed on location. Internal shots include the Forum Shops, Riviera, and Stardust. External scenes include Peppermill, Luxor, Riviera, Stardust, Fremont Street, and Barbary Coast. Notoriously bad acting makes *Showgirls* one of the greatest Hollywood train wrecks of all time and mandatory viewing for any Vegas fanatic.

- *Swingers* **(1996):** Vince Vaughn and Jon Favreau drive from Los Angeles to Las Vegas for a night on the town. Their plans to get comped by acting like high rollers doesn't work so well, but they still end up with the company of two lovely Las Vegas locals. Much more of an L.A. movie than a Vegas movie, *Swingers* gets a spot on the *Outsiders' Guide* film festival list for a couple reasons. The Vegas scenes, filmed at Stardust (external shots) and Fremont (casino scenes), are a memorable and funny part of an overall great movie. Plus, a line from the L.A.-to-Vegas driving scene includes the dialogue that inspired the name of my podcast, *Five Hundy by Midnight*. So how could I not include it on the list?

This list of Vegas film festival essentials can be bulked up, if needed, with the multitude of other movies filmed in the area. Honorable mentions include: *Austin Powers: International Man of Mystery* (1997), *Bugsy* (1991), *Diamonds Are Forever* (1971), *Get Him to the Greek* (2010), *Go* (1999), *The Hangover 3* (2013), *Honeymoon in Vegas* (1993), *Indecent Proposal* (1993), *Last Vegas* (2013), *Mars Attacks* (1997), *Paradise* (2013), *Rain Man* (1988), *Rush Hour 2* (2001), *21* (2008), *Very Bad Things* (1998), and *Viva Las Vegas* (1964).

The Experience

As fun as it can be planning a Las Vegas trip, that entire process pales in comparison to the trip itself. The Las Vegas Strip and Fremont Street areas offer limitless opportunities for seeing cool sights, sampling delicious tastes, and experiencing a place unlike any other.

When arriving in Las Vegas, visitors are faced with a myriad of choices. Which show should I see? Where should I eat? Which casinos should I visit? Knowing what to expect and understanding the different options available can help narrow down the choices.

If you're preparing for your first Las Vegas visit, the following chapters will help you prioritize how and where to best spend your time. If you're a Las Vegas veteran, this information may open your eyes to aspects of the Strip and Downtown you haven't yet explored—or confirm that you made the right decision ignoring them during past trips. Either way, these chapters include many liberally scattered tips, ideas, and anecdotes to help improve your time in Las Vegas.

CHAPTER 7

Transportation

GETTING TO YOUR HOTEL

Unless you're driving from Southern California or Arizona, your Las Vegas experience likely begins at the airport. Arriving at McCarran International, you exit the airplane, walk up the jetway with purpose, and step into the terminal. Your heart begins beating faster as the moment you've been thinking about nonstop for the past several weeks morphs into reality: "Holy shit! I'm in Las Vegas." Scanning the gate area, you make eye contact with one of the poor suckers waiting to head home. You ignore the brief thought that you'll have the same shell-shocked look on your face in a few days when you're in their position. You'll deal with that reality when it comes. For now, you have a mission—get to your hotel as quickly as possible, check in, dump your bag in the room, and hit the casino floor. Tunnel vision kicks in as you scurry past more departing tourists giving the Wheel of Fortune slots one more shot. A quick tram or escalator ride to baggage claim gets you a little closer to the bonanza of fun you've been awaiting. Luggage from your flight hasn't arrived yet, so you anxiously wait, struggling to stand still because you're inching ever closer to as much fun as you can pack into the next several days. You second-guess whether you could have squeezed everything into a carry-on bag and skipped this annoying speed bump. The next five minutes feel like an hour. Blaring video screens flash ads that encourage you to see Celine Dion, "voted the best show in Las Vegas." When the next commercial promotes Terry Fator, "voted the best show in Las Vegas," you mentally question the prestige, exclusivity, and legitimacy of being voted the best show in Las Vegas. Finally, a red light flashes, a buzzer sounds, and baggage carousel 8 begins to spin. "Please let my bags drop first," you think. Three dozen suitcases later, just as you begin to worry about whether your stuff got misrouted, your bags arrive. Just a few miles of pavement stands between you and your room.

As with just about every aspect of your Las Vegas trip, it's decision time. What's the best way to get to your hotel?

BUS

The cheapest—not necessarily the best, but simply the cheapest—way to get to Las Vegas Boulevard or Fremont Street is by bus. At only $2, the Westcliff Airport Express (WAX) and Centennial Express (CX) lines more than compensate for their lack of luxury and style with unbeatably low pricing. And while their extremely limited number of stops makes for a fairly efficient ride, you'll likely have a significant stroll in store unless one happens to be in front of your hotel. On the Strip, the WAX bus stops only at Las Vegas Boulevard and Tropicana. The CX bus stops only at Las Vegas Boulevard and Sands. If traveling with anything larger than a carry-on bag and staying anywhere on the Strip other than the hotels immediately adjacent to the bus stop, the hassle outweighs the benefits of saving a couple bucks. You'll end up lugging baggage in potentially pedestrian-dense areas, walking as much as a mile to the hotel entrance or paying a couple bucks more to take the monorail from MGM Grand to another part of the Strip. Totally not worth it. Downtown, WAX stops at 4th and Carson, while CX stops at Fremont Street and Casino Center Drive. Because Downtown isn't as congested, and because the hotels are all relatively close together, walking with luggage to any of the area hotels isn't as cumbersome as on the Strip. At the airport, the CX line stops only at Terminal 3, so you may need to take an inter-terminal shuttle to get to and from the bus. Because routes and fares change, consult _www.rtcsnv.com_ for the latest bus information.

SHUTTLE

There's no easier way to kill your Vegas buzz than by taking a shuttle from the airport to your hotel. Your excitement to begin your trip will slowly drain from your body as you wait for the shuttle to load and then spend nearly an hour riding from hotel to hotel because you're the lucky sucker who's getting dropped off last.

The shuttle option is best suited for solo travelers on a tight budget. If you value saving a few bucks more than saving some of your limited Vegas time, several shuttle services offering van or minibus transportation to and from McCarran International Airport can meet your needs. Per-person rates begin at $7.50 for one-way Strip trips and $9 to Downtown, or $14/$18 round-trip. Reservations and walk-up service are available. The more people traveling together, the less economical shuttles become compared to simply taking a cab. Shuttle service contact information is available on the McCarran transportation web page at *www.mccarran.com*.

CAB

The line to get a cab at the airport may look intimidating, but it's efficient and moves quickly. Most waits are less than 15 minutes at Terminal 1, but during peak convention weeks and holiday weekends, it may take up to an hour. Because Terminal 3 is not yet operating at full capacity, cab lines rarely exist. Walk right up and get in a car. Travelers arriving at the D gates with only carry-on bags can take a short tram ride to Terminal 3 (instead of a slightly longer tram ride to Terminal 1 baggage claim) to take advantage of more expedient cab access.

Many Las Vegas cabbies will rip you off if given the chance. Taking an indirect route from the airport to the hotel—usually via the highway, which may be quicker but is rarely cheaper than taking city streets—happens frequently. The practice, called long-hauling, is illegal, but weak enforcement efforts have done little to curb the problem. Upon giving the driver your destination, he will likely begin making small talk. "Where are you from?" and "Is this your first time in Las Vegas?" may seem like friendly banter, but he's sizing up your familiarity with the proper route to the hotel. If he thinks you're an infrequent visitor, his odds of getting away with an extended trip are good. Because it's illegal to take passengers for a longer-than-necessary route without their approval, he may try to get you to consent to go the long way by suggesting the roads are congested, or there's an accident messing up traffic. He'll probably suggest that the highway will be quicker or simply ask, "City streets or highway?" knowing most people assume the highway is a faster and, thus, cheaper option. If asked, choose city streets. If you don't specify a route and, upon exiting the airport, you find yourself heading through a tunnel and onto the highway, congratulations, you're getting ripped off. To avoid getting long-hauled, tell the driver you don't want to take the highway, or—better yet—specify your preferred route. In 2014, the Nevada Taxicab Authority posted signs at the airport recommending the following routes.

- **Las Vegas Boulevard:** Aria, Circus Circus, The Cosmopolitan, Excalibur, Luxor, Mandalay Bay, Mandarin Oriental, Monte Carlo, New York-New York, The Palazzo, Paris, Rio, Treasure Island, Vdara, and The Venetian
- **Paradise Road:** All Downtown hotels, Bally's, Bellagio, Caesars Palace, The Cromwell, Encore, Flamingo, Harrah's, The Linq, MGM Grand, The Mirage, Stratosphere, Treasure Island, Tropicana, and Wynn

Average cab fares to Strip hotels run from $16-$24 (plus tip), with Downtown hotels averaging $25-$30 (plus tip). Trips from Terminal 3 cost an additional $2-$3. If you neglect to specify your route and the cabbie takes the highway, you're not out of luck. Upon arriving at your destination, tell him you know he took a longer route than necessary and that he needs to discount your trip or you'll call the taxicab authority. If you want to know how much the fee should be, ask a bellhop what the typical cab fare from the airport is. Smelling a possible tip, he'll gladly help. If the cabbie protests, note his name and cab number, and call the Nevada Taxicab Authority. The number is posted prominently in every cab.

LIMO

There's no better way to relive the fond memory of not getting laid on prom night than by hiring a limo. At the airport, walk-up service can yield a car for between $40 and $70, depending on destination and demand. Don't be afraid to negotiate. Offer $40 and see what happens. If a driver has been waiting for business for an hour, he may accept.

For the full big-shot treatment, book a limo in advance. The driver will monitor your flight's arrival, meet you at baggage claim, and transport your luggage while escorting you to the car. For several years, Presidential Limo (_www.presidentiallimolv.com_) has offered dependable round-trip service between $100 and $250, depending on the type of vehicle (sedan, stretch limo, SUV limo, party bus).

Another company, Bell Limousine (*www.belllimousine.com*) offers an economical car service with slightly fewer frills. Unlike most limo services, the fee for this deal is per person ($28 each round-trip to the Strip or $38 to Downtown). Upon arrival, check in at the Bell Limousine desk. The clerk will confirm the reservation and direct you to a waiting area. The first available sedan, limo, or SUV takes you to your destination. Technically, this is a shared shuttle service, so you may end up in the car with strangers and stop at another hotel or two to drop them off. However, historically, this rarely occurs. Your chances of getting your own car are very good. For the solo traveler, the Limo Share-a-Ride Special is cheaper than cabbing it. Find Limo Share-a-Ride Special details on the company's Web Specials page.

RENTAL CAR

Travelers who reserved a rental car for pickup at McCarran should follow signs to baggage claim and then doors 10 and 11 at Terminal 1 or doors 51-54 or 55-58 at Terminal 3. The McCarran Rent-A-Car Center shuttle departs approximately every five minutes for the three-mile ride to the rental hub. At the Rent-A-Car Center, proceed to the counter for the appropriate company.

If you rent a car or skipped the airport commute entirely by driving to Las Vegas, you'll be faced with the decision whether to self-park or valet when you arrive at your hotel. Unfortunately, there's no one-size-fits-all rule for choosing self-park or valet. As with many Vegas decisions, the choice is one of preference, comfort, and convenience. Some Vegas drivers swear by valet, while others—fearing the Ferris Bueller treatment—never trust a valet. Self-parking is free at resorts on the Strip and for hotel guests Downtown. Valet parking is free, but tipping a few bucks when dropping off and retrieving a vehicle is customary. If you anticipate dropping off or retrieving your car at an especially busy time, self-park will likely be quicker than waiting for the valet. However, some hotels' self-park lots are far less convenient than using the valet—especially when transporting luggage. Planet Hollywood, for example, has a notoriously inconvenient parking ramp requiring a long walk to the hotel. And, of course, horror stories abound about valets returning cars with scratches, dents, and mystery miles. If you prefer the peace of mind that comes with knowing the location of your car and accessing it without assistance, go with self-parking. If you enjoy the convenience of pulling up to the hotel door, and you trust that valets are professionals who park hundreds of cars daily with few incidents, use the valet.

GETTING AROUND TOWN

Although some Vegas visitors get the shakes if they don't have access to a car (see Chapter 3), many relinquish driving responsibilities once they've arrived at the hotel. For those who plan to stick close to the Strip and Fremont Street, walking supplemented by the occasional cab, bus, shuttle, or monorail adventure works perfectly well.

WALKING

Las Vegas and Clark County attempt to make tourist areas pedestrian-friendly, and in most cases do a decent job. Pedestrian overpasses along Las Vegas Boulevard reduce the likelihood of a vacation-ruining encounter with the grill of a Cadillac Escalade. And the 1995 repurposing of Fremont Street as a pedestrian mall makes Downtown casinos readily accessible by foot even by those who have consumed multiple yard-long margaritas. Despite these efforts to ensure the smooth flow of foot traffic, several barriers remain.

Moseyers

The biggest impediment to pedestrians is other pedestrians. Taking a leisurely stroll can be pleasant. After all, this is a vacation, so what's the rush? I'll tell you what the rush is. My vacation is only five days long. I have limited time to pack in as much fun as possible. I don't need your slow ass blocking my otherwise quick jaunt from Bally's to The Cosmopolitan for happy hour at Estiatorio Milos. It lasts only 90 minutes, and I don't want to miss a second of it. So let's pick up the pace, Tortuga Jones.

In all fairness, the massive, ridiculous, and unique architecture of Las Vegas Boulevard's hotels and the classic neon of Downtown invite gawking. Even repeat visitors who have seen it all numerous times will occasionally slow down and marvel at the impressiveness and silliness of their surroundings. The problem with Las Vegas moseyers isn't so much their pace, but their tendency to completely disregard the two dozen people behind them who are trying to get on with life. These are the same people who take their young kids to Subway at peak lunch hours and find it adorable to have little Braxman and Jolyssa order for themselves. Come on, mom. Johnny Dockers doesn't have a two-hour lunch break. He needs to cram a six-inch Italian B.M.T. down his gullet and get back to work. Teach your ankle-biters life's lessons on your own time.

By all means, enjoy all the ambiance Las Vegas has to offer. Take it in. Stop and smell the roses. Actually, you may want to skip smelling the roses—a homeless guy just pissed on them. But please treat the sidewalks and casino walkways as though they were freeways. Keep the slow traffic to the far right, giving others the ability to pass on the left. Don't walk four people across, blocking the entire sidewalk. Bunch up. And, for the love of all that is good, when you get to the end of an escalator or moving sidewalk, don't step off and stop to consider where you're heading next.

When you encounter Las Vegas moseyers (and you will), avoid the temptation to drop a snarky, "excuse you." You'll just be lowering yourself to their inconsiderate level. Either wait patiently for a passing opportunity to present itself or politely say, "excuse me," and hope they get the hint. Everybody is trying to have a good time. Throwing out a sarcastic comment will likely just lead to unnecessary verbal sparring, prolonged interaction, and increased aggravation.

Timeshare Sales Reps

Because I'm a raging hypocrite, my suggestion to avoid sarcastic comments doesn't apply when approached by people peddling timeshare properties. Unlike oblivious moseyers, these bottom feeders are intentionally trying to prevent you from successfully reaching your destination quickly. Their chosen profession requires getting you to stop and speak with them, taking valuable time from your vacation. They deserve whatever abuse they receive. The obvious responses—ignoring them or telling them to go fuck themselves—are effective, but ultimately unrewarding. Rather, a more measured response provides an opportunity to amuse yourself, your companions, and nearby strangers.

Timeshare sales scumbags try to engage couples they assume are married by posing a question. The most common questions and sample responses are provided here for your convenience.

> **Question:** Where are you from?
> **Response:** I don't speak English. (Say it as clearly as possible. Momentary confusion will cause the sales rep to pause, just long enough for you to walk out of her immediate pestering zone.)

> **Question:** Are you going to be in town tonight?
> **Response:** No. We left this morning.

> **Question:** Are you two married?
> **Response:** To each other? No.

> **Question:** How about taking your lady to a free show tonight?
> **Response:** She gets a free show from me every night.

Costumed Characters

Costumed characters offering to pose for photos in exchange for tips litter Fremont Street and the Strip. Some of their costumes are sad, like the obviously unauthorized Elsa from *Frozen*, who looks more like Rocky Dennis from *Mask*. Others are just lazy, like the multitude of off-the-shelf *Despicable Me* minion costumes. A few are admittedly impressive. The guy who dresses like Captain Jack Sparrow looks like he spends more time in the makeup chair than Johnny Depp did while filming the actual *Pirates of the Caribbean* movies.

Regardless of the quality of the costume, avoid the temptation to tip these people. Sure, they add to the nutty atmosphere of the Strip and Fremont Street, but consider whether you really want to support a meth head's habit so you can have a wacky new Facebook profile photo. And by all means, please don't have your kid pose next to these creeps. A

Stormtrooper costume is the perfect choice for that sex offender to hide the raging hard-on he just got from putting his arm around your 11-year-old son.

Pornslappers

Walking the Strip, Las Vegas visitors are sure to encounter tiny immigrants distributing business cards promoting adult entertainers. The "dancers" shown on these cards (or a slightly more saggy, leathery, game-used version thereof) are willing to appear in any Las Vegas hotel room for a flat fee of somewhere between $30 and $90. What a city! Their official marketing representatives are known as pornslappers, so named for the slapping noise they make with the cards—considered porn by some despite most naughty parts being discreetly shielded by starburst clipart.

Some visitors find the content of the cards offensive. How dare someone compromise the otherwise family-friendly Las Vegas Strip with photos of nearly naked women! If people tolerate this sort of thing, pretty soon the whole place will be overrun with smoking, gambling, and public drunkenness. Others simply don't like having ads of any nature shoved in their face. Fair enough. There are only four viable options for dealing with pornslappers.

- **Ignore them.** Unlike many of the other pests you'll encounter, pornslappers aren't persistent. If you stroll past them, they won't follow you or yell at you.
- **Tell them to fuck off.** This is pointless, as few of them speak English.
- **Take the cards and immediately throw them on the ground.** Pornslappers are required to keep the area around them free of their literature. If they see someone drop the cards, they face fines for not picking them up. Yes, this makes a point, but it's not going to lead to the disappearance of pornslappers, and it's a dick move.
- **Accept the cards for future use.** No, not ordering a hooker… uh… "adult entertainer." These cards have other uses. A stack discreetly tucked in the suitcase of your travel buddy with the uptight wife is sure to provide a relationship-strengthen-

ing bonding experience when he returns home. Likewise, what better way to show a fun-loving coworker what he missed than by leaving a few in his top desk drawer when you return to the office? Consider it either a valuable team-building exercise or a chance to spend some quality time getting to know your company's Human Resources Director. Be creative and have fun. Pornslapper cards provide countless opportunities to bring a little Vegas joy home with you.

Budding Hip-Hop Stars

Have you ever dreamed of being the next Clive Davis? Well, you don't own a record label so give up the dream. It's stupid. And if by chance your name *is* David Geffen, you're unlikely to discover the next Snoop Dogg selling his latest hip-hop CD in front of Bellagio. So ponying up $10 to MC All-You-Can-Eat is a waste. If he had any talent, he'd be a contestant on BET's *So You Think You Can Rap?* And if he had any brains, he'd be building an audience on YouTube rather than hassling tourists. There's a pretty good chance the guy selling the CD isn't an actual musician anyway. When you get home and discover you've purchased a blank CD-R or a pirated dub of the *Twelve Inches of Snow* album, don't be surprised.

Water Water One Dollar

On Las Vegas Boulevard and its pedestrian overpasses, burgeoning entrepreneurs offer ice-cold bottles of water for just a buck each. Technically, they're offering the water for free with the expectation of tips because they aren't licensed to sell such merchandise. Regardless, I'm sure it's all on the up-and-up, and that Uncle Sam is getting his cut. Unlike many Las Vegas peddlers, pushers, and scammers, these folks provide a useful product. The desert air is dry, and staying hydrated is essential to avoiding sickness and warding off the bottle flu. Buying from these folks may be quicker than wandering into one of the CVS or Walgreens stores dotting the Strip, but it includes some risk. You're buying from an unauthorized, unlicensed vendor—perhaps more than a little less trustworthy than a recognizable chain store.

Some people believe these peddlers refill used bottles from the tap and sell them for fun and profit. It's certainly possible, but breaking down this theory, I find it difficult to believe. In order for Stanley the Water Guy to run this scam, he would need to spend significant time rummaging through garbage cans and recycling bins to find empty water bottles and their caps, cart them back to his house, fill them, and cap them. If this guy wanted to work that hard, he'd be able to hold down a real job. It's much easier to swing by the local Albertson's, buy a case of 24 bottles for $4, throw them in a cooler and make an easy $20 profit. If I'm parched, I'll occasionally throw one of these guys a buck for a bottle. If all the bottles in the cooler have the same packaging, I'm willing to take the chance that they're factory sealed. I haven't come down with dysentery yet, and just about anything could have caused these persistent mouth sores.

CAB

On the Strip and Fremont Street, finding a cab is a cinch. This isn't New York City, so standing on a Las Vegas Boulevard curb and raising your hand while dozens of available cabs zip by will make you look like a dope. Regulations prohibit cabbies from picking up passengers on Las Vegas Boulevard, so head to the cabstand at the main entrance of any hotel. There's usually a lineup of cars, so you shouldn't have to wait for more than a few minutes except after major events, on weekend nights, or when conventioneers overrun the city.

A doorman will signal the next cab to pull forward, open the door, and ask you for your destination, which he will convey to the driver. Tip him a buck or two. It's part of the Vegas culture, even though the service he's providing is largely unnecessary. In fact, during busy times, the cab line process rivals casino players club desks as the most inefficient operations in Las Vegas. There's a line of people, a line of cabs, and plenty of room for multiple cars to load simultaneously. Instead, they insist on handling one cab at a time. I'm sure there's some logic about traffic flow, but it probably comes down to minimizing the number of employees and maximizing the amount of cash changing hands. It's bullshit, but it's the way things are. If a doorman opens the cab door when you arrive at your destination, don't bother tipping unless he assists with bags. I have no idea why opening the door to leave garners a tip while opening the door to arrive doesn't, but that's how it works. For more information on America's other nonsensical tipping customs, see Chapter 8.

Cab rides get expensive, so plan on using them only when necessary or when the convenience outweighs the cost. Sometimes at the end of a long day, you want nothing more than to get back to your hotel as quickly as possible so you can crash for the night. Spending $12 for a ride from Mandalay Bay to Planet Hollywood may be worth it if you just don't feel like walking anymore.

As previously noted, some cabbies will attempt to long-haul riders if given the chance. For simple Strip-hotel-to-Strip-hotel trips, you're less likely to be taken on an unnecessary tour of Clark County than Strip-to-Downtown trips. Unless traffic is crawling on the Strip and Paradise, city streets offer a cheaper route to and from Downtown than the freeway. Feel free to tell the driver you prefer to take city streets. If he balks, tell him you're a superstitious gambler and that you always have bad luck after taking the freeway. This pretty much always halts any protest because Las Vegas is teeming with superstitious gamblers. Of course, when traffic is bad, all bets are off, and you're best just surrendering to the will of the cabbie and hoping his chosen route isn't excessive.

My biggest irritation with taking cabs is the effect it has on my self-esteem. Whenever I'm in a Las Vegas cab, I realize that my social life pales in comparison to every former third-world resident with a cab license. These guys get more phone calls than Crazy Johnny and the Morning Zoo Crew offering free Taylor Swift tickets. What could they possibly be discussing? Because I'm not fluent in whatever system of tongue clicks makes up the native language of remote tribes in Zimbabwe, I'm oblivious to the content of their discussions. I have two theories. The first is that they're planning an elaborate surprise party. Tracking down a caterer who can prepare goat meat stew and fried ox kidney with peppers for 75 people takes a lot of work. My second theory is that these calls are between drivers passing the time by mocking their passengers. "I just picked up a fat guy too lazy to walk from Mandalay Bay to Planet Hollywood." "I'm taking two drunk girls from The Cosmopolitan to SLS. We just passed Green Valley Ranch." As soon as I finish writing this book, I plan to buy Rosetta Stone and become fluent in Zimbabwanese so I can get to the bottom of this.

RIDE-SHARING SERVICES

In 2015, ride-sharing services, including Uber and Lyft, received approval to operate in the state of Nevada. Although controversial for functioning much likes cabs but without the same level of regulation, these services are poised to provide a more consumer-friendly alternative. For more information about these services and to download their mobile apps, visit *www.uber.com* and *www.lyft.com*.

BUS

There's nothing quite like public transportation in a major city. Where else can you experience the colorful sites, sounds, and smells of tourists and locals alike for only two bucks? When choosing a seat, make sure to examine it closely for urine and vomit stains. Few things can ruin a day as quickly as the ominous squish of your butt landing in still-warm barf.

One of the cheapest, easiest ways to travel the Strip and Downtown is via bus. The Regional Transportation Commission of Southern Nevada offers two popular options—The Deuce and the Strip/Downtown Express (SDX). The Deuce transports riders on double-decker buses 24 hours a day, arriving at designated stops every 15-20 minutes. The single-level SDX buses run from 9 a.m. to midnight, also arriving approximately every 15 minutes, but with fewer stops. If you're looking for a leisurely cruise down the Strip, hop on The Deuce. It stops about every 15 feet, so you'll have plenty of time to take in the sights. If you value your time and don't want to piss away your day on the bus, give the SDX a shot. Single rides cost just $2. Two-hour, 24-hour, and three-day passes are available for $6, $8, and $20, respectively. For a list of stops for each route and additional information, visit *www.ridethestrip.com*.

Although both The Deuce and SDX take riders from the Strip to Fremont Street, the previously mentioned Westcliff Airport Express offers the quickest bus option for travelers on the South Strip. With only one Strip stop at Tropicana and Las Vegas Boulevard, the WAX bus picks up riders approximately every hour, dropping them Downtown at 4th and Carson about 15 minutes later (compared to 30+ minutes on the SDX and up to an hour on The Deuce). The return trip leaves Casino Center and Fremont Street, again stopping at Tropicana and Las Vegas Boulevard.

The Centennial Express bus offers a similar option for riders from the North Strip, picking up at Sands/Spring Mountain and Las Vegas Boulevard, dropping at 4th and Carson, and departing from Casino Center and Fremont Street, returning to Sands/Spring Mountain. Rides for the WAX and CX routes are $2 each way.

FREE TRAMS AND SHUTTLES

Las Vegas visitors can save a few bucks on transportation by taking advantage of free trams and shuttles between hotels. The major downside to free transportation is wasting valuable vacation time waiting for them to arrive. If a shuttle bus gets stuck in traffic, its schedule may get thrown off track for the rest of the day. Schedules change, so shuttle riders should double-check arrival and departure times with the appropriate hotel. When schedule details are available online, a link to the current schedule is provided.

- **Mandalay Bay, Luxor, Excalibur Tram:** The Mandalay Bay to Excalibur tram runs every three to seven minutes. The northbound tram leaves the Mandalay Bay station, stopping at Luxor and Excalibur. The southbound train leaves the Excalibur station, located near the Las Vegas Boulevard pedestrian overpasses to Tropicana and New York-New York. The southbound train does not stop at Luxor. Trams run from 9 a.m. to 10:30 p.m. daily.

- **Monte Carlo/Aria, Crystals, Bellagio/Vdara Tram:** Arriving approximately every seven minutes, this four-car tram runs north from Monte Carlo station, located near the Street of Dreams shops. This station is accessible from Aria via a short walkway. The Crystals station is accessible via escalator from the mall's second level. The Bellagio stop is located near the spa tower and Sensi restaurant. A short walkway connects the station to Vdara. The tram runs from 8 a.m. to 4 a.m. daily and stops at all three stations in both directions.

- **The Mirage, Treasure Island Tram:** Arriving approximately every 10-15 minutes, this tram runs north from The Mirage station, located outside, near the hotel's main entrance. It arrives at the Treasure Island station, located near the parking garage. The tram runs in both directions from 9 a.m. to 1 a.m. (2 a.m. on Friday and Saturday).

- **Harrah's, Rio Shuttle:** Running approximately every 30 minutes from 10 a.m. to 1 a.m., the Rio shuttle bus leaves Harrah's, near the hotel lobby. The return trip leaves the Rio entrance near the Carnival World Buffet. Total Rewards diamond and seven stars members board first.

- **Bally's, Rio Shuttle:** Running approximately every 30 minutes from 10 a.m. to 1 a.m., the Rio shuttle bus leaves the Bally's bus drop-off entrance on the north side, near Flamingo Road. The return trip leaves the Rio entrance near Carnival World Buffet. Total Rewards diamond and seven stars members board first.

- **Bally's, Gold Coast, The Orleans Shuttle:** Leaving from the Bally's food court entrance approximately every 30 minutes, shuttle buses stop at Gold Coast and The Orleans. Shuttles run from 9 a.m. to 12:30 a.m. Gold Coast and Orleans hotel guests board first.

- **Harrah's, Sam's Town Shuttle:** Shuttle buses to Sam's Town from the Strip leave Harrah's, near the hotel lobby, from 9:30 a.m. until 9:10 p.m., approximately every 80-90 minutes. Sam's Town hotel guests and BConnected players club members board first. Schedule: _www.samstownlv.com/stay/shuttle-service_. Legend has it that once you get to Sam's Town, you can take another shuttle to pretty much any location in the city for free.

- **Fremont, California, Sam's Town Shuttle:** Shuttle buses to Sam's Town from Downtown leave Fremont, near the hotel lobby, from 8:15 a.m. until 8:45 p.m., and California, near valet parking, from 8:30 a.m. to 9 p.m., approximately every 75 minutes. Sam's Town hotel guests and BConnected players club members board first. Schedule: _www.samstownlv.com/stay/shuttle-service_.

- **Fashion Show Mall, M Resort Shuttle:** Shuttle buses to M Resort leave Fashion Show Mall, near valet parking, from noon until 11 p.m., approximately every two hours. M Resort hotel guests board first. Schedule: _www.themresort.com/visito-rinfo/visitor_info.html._

- **Fashion Show Mall, Planet Hollywood, Tropicana, Town Square Mall Shuttle:** Shuttle buses to Town Square leave Fashion Show Mall, near valet parking; Planet Hollywood, near the Miracle Mile entrance; and Tropicana, near the valet area; from 10:30 a.m. until 8:30 p.m. approximately every 90 minutes. Schedule: _www.mytownsquarelasvegas.com/shuttle.html._

LAS VEGAS MONORAIL

Running a monorail along the entire length of the Las Vegas Strip sounds like a great idea. In theory, this type of transportation should provide fast, efficient travel for tens of thousands of tourists daily. Unfortunately, the Las Vegas Monorail suffers from three major flaws, making the train useful only in limited cases.

- **Monorail Fail #1:** Located behind the Strip hotels, the monorail is barely visible from Las Vegas Boulevard. Out of sight, out of mind. Visitors can easily spend a week in Las Vegas and never see the monorail.
- **Monorail Fail #2:** Getting to many of the monorail stations requires a significantly long walk through a large casino. In some cases, walking from the Strip to the station, waiting for the monorail to arrive, taking it to the next location, and walking from the station into the destination casino takes longer than just walking along the Strip. If you're at one of the casinos on the west side of the Strip, don't even bother. You'll need to pack supplies, rent a donkey, and hire a Sherpa just to get to the closest station.
- **Monorail Fail #3:** The monorail doesn't connect visitors to the airport or Downtown. Since even before opening in 2004, several plans have been floated for monorail extensions. However, because of opposition from the city's taxicab industry and the original phase's lackluster performance, lining up support and funding make such an extension unlikely.

Despite these problems, some visitors will find the monorail to be extremely useful.

- Visitors staying at hotels located Center Strip or South Strip near a monorail station while attending an event at the Las Vegas Convention Center.
- Guests at Westgate who plan to spend time on the Strip and vice versa.
- Guests at SLS who want to visit Center Strip or South Strip, and vice versa.
- Guests staying at or near MGM Grand who want to travel directly to Harrah's or The Linq relatively quickly.

The monorail runs from 7 a.m. to 2 a.m. (3 a.m. on Friday through Sunday). Station locations include MGM Grand, Bally's, Flamingo, Harrah's/The Linq, Las Vegas Convention Center, Westgate, and SLS. Do not be misled by the official names of the stations. The supposed Flamingo/Caesars Palace Station is at least a 10-minute walk from the Caesars Palace entrance.

Passes are available beginning at $5 for a single ride. Unlimited one-day passes are $12, and multi-day passes run from $22 to $56 depending on length. Discounts may be available for advance purchases at _www.lvmonorail.com_.

CHAPTER 8

Maximizing Your Las Vegas Experience

UPGRADING YOUR ROOM

At many Las Vegas hotels, registration clerks have significant freedom to upgrade guests to a better room than the one initially booked. Guests can attempt to obtain an upgrade using several different tactics.

Ask

From the moment you approach the check-in desk, be upbeat and friendly. When the clerk is looking up your room information, ask for exactly what you want. If you are seeking a pseudo-upgrade—a standard room but with a Strip view or located close to the elevator—you have a decent chance of getting it simply by being cordial and asking. Sometimes you may even get a more significant upgrade. If you're celebrating a special occasion, it can't hurt to drop this into the conversation. "We're very excited to be celebrating our 10th wedding anniversary here. If there are any complimentary suite upgrades available or anything you can do to make our stay even more special, we'd appreciate it." The worst-case scenario is that you'll be wished a happy anniversary and told no free upgrades are available. You're not out anything, and it was worth a shot.

Negotiate

If you have a specific type of room in mind, ask how much it would cost to upgrade. If the clerk tells you the additional cost is $100 per night, respond by telling her that rate is a little out of your price range. However, if she could give it to you for $50 per night, you'd take it. The clerk may accept your offer, decline it, or counteroffer with a different rate.

Depending on hotel policy and the clerk's level of authority, she may check with a supervisor first. If you don't mind paying for a larger room but are ultimately content with whatever you initially booked if it doesn't work out, this is a reasonable option.

Tip

The so-called "$20 trick" is simply a tip to the hotel registration clerk in an effort to procure a better room. When the clerk asks for your identification and credit card, include a folded $20 bill between the cards. Make sure the bill is visible. As you hand the Andrew Jackson sandwich to the clerk, ask, "Are any complimentary corner suite upgrades available today?" Be specific but realistic with your request. If you booked a standard room, you are not going to get the 16,000 square foot penthouse suite for a $20 tip. However, you may get a junior suite or even a standard suite. Before your trip, scope out the hotel's website so you know the specific room types—shoot for something a couple levels above what you booked.

The clerk may respond in one of several ways.

- **Immediately decline, sliding your $20 back to you.** He may say hotel policy prevents them from accepting tips or the hotel is at capacity, and no upgrades are available. Oh well. It didn't hurt to try.
- **Spend a few minutes checking the room inventory but find no available upgrades.** He will typically return your $20. If it seems like he gave it a decent effort, you may opt to tip anyway.
- **Decline the specific type of upgrade you requested but offer something different.** The counteroffer may be something basic like a view of the Strip. You may have received that view just by asking, but at least it's something.
- **Accept and give you what you requested or something better.**

Because the $20 trick is carried out in a semi-covert manner, it may feel like you're doing something untoward. It's common to get a little nervous before slipping the clerk the money simply because you're not used to this sort of transaction. However, it's highly unlikely that members of the SWAT team will suddenly shoulder-roll out of the back office, aim their AK-47s at your skull, and demand that you drop to the ground. I've heard of that happening only once or twice, but Planet Hollywood was under different ownership back then.

Frequently, when Las Vegas online forum participants discuss the $20 trick, someone will object, saying it's a bribe and, thus, unethical. If your strict moral code prohibits you from participating in this activity, it's probably best that you use the $20 for something more virtuous during your Vegas visit, like gambling or consuming grotesque amounts of alcohol.

For me, slipping a hotel clerk $20 in hopes of gaining some additional square footage for the week is the most I'll ever feel like James Bond. When it turns out well, it's a cool way to begin a trip. Plus, there's the added bonus of looking like a big shot back at the office the next week when casually mentioning that "pulling a few strings at the front desk" resulted in a 1,200 square foot Jacuzzi suite.

So, if $20 works, will $50 work better? The crew at the Five Hundy Center for the Study of Las Vegas Hijinks has not yet issued its formal report on the effectiveness of higher denomination tips. However, few people are ever motivated to make less of an effort when faced with the prospect of more money. If you have the cash to blow and don't mind making that first wager of the trip a little larger, give it a shot. Whether it pays off or not, you're in Las Vegas and your trip is just beginning. So you're still a winner.

STRATEGIC RESTROOM PLANNING

Unless you have unrealistic plans to venture back to your hotel room every time nature calls, you'll inevitably need to use public restrooms during your Las Vegas visit. This experience can range from an uneventful afterthought to a life-altering tragedy, requiring years of psychotherapy. You just never know what sensory assaults await when it's time to drain your rum tank or restock Lake Mead with brown trout. Proper planning and some basic strategy can decrease your chances of a day-ruining restroom visit. Consider these tips:

- **When it comes to waste management, nothing beats the home field advantage.** While you're in Las Vegas, your hotel room provides the closest you'll come to the private, low-pressure, distraction-free toilet time you get at home. The best time to offload yesterday afternoon's buffet lunch is just before leaving your room. In the unfortunate event you plug the toilet, you can call down for a plumber, exit the room for the day, and avoid facing the poor bastard whose morning you just ruined. Don't forget to leave a $10 or $20 guilt tip for the assistance.

- **As you go about your day, consider the likely quality of the restrooms at your next destination before arriving.** As a general rule, the nicer the casino, the better maintained the restrooms. Wynn doesn't want to risk losing the business of a Japanese high roller offended by the sight of a stray pube resting on the edge of a urinal, so restrooms are kept as tidy as the rest of the resort. At Casino Royale, on the other hand, your chances are about one in four of encountering a churning cauldron of buttstew in one of the stalls. So if you plan to spend some time at one of the slummier casinos, make a pit stop at a nicer joint along the way.

- **Avoid restrooms close to the Strip and Fremont Street entrances.** Tourists who fail to strategize inevitably find themselves strolling along Las Vegas Boulevard or Fremont Street, suddenly realizing it's go time. In a high-pressure situation, they have little choice but to head for the nearest restroom. As a result, the most accessible restrooms from the street are also the messiest. Two years after glimpsing the aftermath of an assplosion that occurred in the Planet Hollywood men's room across from BurGR, I still have traumatic flashbacks that would make most Vietnam War vets feel sorry for me.

- **Lock the stall door.** Kids should learn this lesson on the first day of kindergarten, but apparently some people still haven't received the memo. It's unlikely you want someone busting in while you're copping a squat, and nobody wants to see what you're doing in there. So please save us both the embarrassment of an extremely awkward restroom encounter by latching the door.

- **Avoid the temptation to seek more information.** At some point during your Las Vegas visit, you're likely to hear a bizarre conversation or, worse yet, questionable noises coming from a restroom stall. Don't linger to discover the source. Your memories will be better if you let your mind create an image of whoever is responsible for the things you're hearing.

  At the original O'Sheas (RIP), I heard the unmistakable rhythmic grunts emanating from a stall of someone engaged in sexual activity. Rather than just accept my initial assessment that someone was banging a hooker at 10:30 a.m., I glanced beneath the door to see how many feet were visible, discovering there were only two. OK... someone was whacking it. Rather than leave it at that, upon exiting I sat at a nearby slot machine, waiting to see who had been enjoying his own company. Soon a small, wrinkled man in his 70s shuffled out and joined his wife in the food court. Good for him, I guess, but I would prefer to have the memory of hearing someone drilling a streetwalker over an old dude tenderizing his meat.

- **Guys, don't discount the benefit of pissing in a stall instead of at the urinal.** Receiving this advice, you probably assume I'm recommending the increased privacy that prevents neighboring pissers from glancing at your junk. Well, I'm sorry to break it to you, but you have a massive ego and a tiny wiener. Nobody is clamoring to see your dick. Rather, this tip solves the unfortunate reality of urinal splashback. You know the scenario: After two hours pounding Heinekens at a hot blackjack table, you've built up so much pressure that you're about to piss with the fury of someone with a vendetta against porcelain. Unless you're at one of the few casinos that adorns its urinals with piss pads, you're risking major leg splatter. If you're wearing khakis, you may as well sneak back to your room rather than face the mockery of friends when you return to the table. Don't take the chance. Skip the urinal, head for the toilet, and return to the casino with dry thighs.

- **Use the opportunity as a chance to explore the building.** Most Las Vegas resorts have restrooms that get little use. If you want a truly peaceful experience, find parts of the property not currently in use. During the day, find the restroom near the showroom. At night, head to the conference center. You'll likely have the whole place to yourself. Make yourself comfortable. Sing a little song. Hell, break up the experience by going a little in each stall. The world is yours, and this is your chance to be king or queen of the restroom. If walking to the remote areas of the building is too much work, but you'd like a similar upscale experience, find the high-limit gaming room. JohnH, a writer for must-read website *VegasTripping*, tipped me off to the advantages of high-limit restrooms—they're private and exceptionally clean, and they often feature nicer amenities than standard casino restrooms. Once you get in the habit of pissing in luxury, you'll shun public shitters forever.

TIPPING

When vacationing in Las Vegas, be prepared to tip just about every service industry employee you encounter. Many of them depend on tips for the majority of their income. Failing to tip is like telling them they don't deserve to get paid today. Happy employees provide better, friendlier service, which in turn makes your trip more pleasant. Unless someone provides poor service and ruins your Las Vegas experience, slip them a few bucks and keep the Vegas happiness train rolling down the track.

Because tipping is so subjective, ten people are likely to give you ten different opinions on how much to tip. As with most things, tipping has a sliding scale. Consider the nature of the venue (employees at swanky, high-buck joints will expect more than someone doing the same job in a shithole) and, of course, the quality of service they provide.

Following are some recommended guidelines for average to good service. If you encounter someone not listed here, use your best judgment.

- **Bartenders:** $1 to $2 per wine, beer, and well drinks. Increase accordingly for more time-intensive craft cocktails.
- **Bellmen:** Between $1 and $5 per bag when delivering, checking, and/or retrieving them.
- **Buffet servers:** $2 to $3 per person.
- **Cabbies:** 15 percent.
- **Casino cocktail servers:** $1 to $2 per drink.
- **Casino hosts:** Hosts are usually unable to accept cash, but gifts and gift cards are acceptable.
- **Concierges:** $5 for arranging show tickets or reservations; $20 for sold out show tickets or difficult reservations.
- **Doormen:** $1 to $2 when hailing a cab.
- **Free-shuttle drivers:** $1 or $2.
- **Limo drivers:** 15 to 20 percent.
- **Maids:** $5 per day for a standard room, $10+ for a suite. Tip daily rather than at the end of your trip to ensure the person actually cleaning your room receives the tip.
- **Room service:** Frequently included on the tab. If not, add 10 to 15 percent.
- **Slot attendants:** 1 to 2 percent on hand-pay jackpots; no tip for hopper fills.
- **Spa attendants:** 15 to 20 percent.
- **Table game dealers:** Minimum of $5 to $10 per hour at low-limit tables, either as a straight tip or as a bet for the dealer. Adjust based on amount played, amount won, and dealer's effect on your fun.
- **Valets:** $2 to $5 when parking and retrieving your car.
- **Waiters/waitresses:** 15 to 20 percent.

For many international visitors, the practice of compensating employees in this manner may seem silly, counterintuitive, or simply annoying. However, withholding a $1 gratuity for a cocktail waitress as some grand political statement that you disagree with America's compensation practices isn't going to change the system. All it will do is bum out a waitress and foster negative stereotypes about people from your homeland. Do your best to adapt to our ridiculous tipping system while you're here. Consider it a cross-cultural good-will gesture.

TIME AS CURRENCY

Discovering hidden gems not frequented by tourists is part of the appeal and excitement of traveling. When visiting Chicago, San Francisco, or London, I love exploring different neighborhoods, seeking out local treasures, and wandering beyond the typical tourist attractions. In Las Vegas, however, I am unapologetically a tourist. I spend the majority of my time within walking distance of Las Vegas Boulevard and Fremont Street.

I'm not suggesting you should enjoy Vegas in the same manner I do. The great thing about Las Vegas is the wide variety of experiences available to meet just about every preference. If you find the Bagel Barn on Charleston Avenue irresistible, by all means go there. It's your vacation, so do what you enjoy. I simply encourage you to consider not only the monetary cost of each part of your Las Vegas trip, but also the time expenditure so you don't end your trip feeling like you didn't pack in as much fun as you should have.

Five Hundy listeners often provide recommendations for restaurants, bars, casinos, and other attractions located off the beaten path. However, I have little interest in including most of them in my Vegas plans. It's not that I don't trust the reviews, nor do I fault anyone for making off-Strip destinations part of their Las Vegas fun.

My personal rejection of these recommendations comes from my view of vacation time as currency. As part of each trip, I have a limited amount of money to spend on food, drinks, and gambling. I also have a limited number of hours. My typical Las Vegas trip lasts about five nights. Depending on flight times, I have approximately 140 hours in town. Subtracting sleep and getting ready each day brings my total number of available hours down to about 100. That's not a lot of time. I evaluate every experience—meals, cocktails, and gambling sessions—based not only on monetary cost, but on time value. Some people make spreadsheets to plan and track every moment and movement during their trip. I'm a geek, but I have my limits. Besides, when in Las Vegas, there's no way I would stick to pre-documented plans. However, when faced with a choice, time always plays into my decision.

When considering whether to have breakfast at Du-par's at Golden Gate—located no more than a few blocks from any hotel on Fremont Street—or going to The Egg & I on Sahara Ave., I can't justify the additional time it takes to deal with transportation to and from The Egg and I. It's 13 minutes each way from Fremont Street by car. Adding in time for parking and walking to and from the car, let's say the total round-trip transportation time is 40 minutes, compared to perhaps 10 minutes for Du-Par's. While The Egg & I comes highly recommended and is by most accounts quite tasty, I suspect that I wouldn't find it to be 30 minutes tastier than my other, more convenient option, and I'm not willing to expend the time to find out.

During a guys' trip in 1999, a man sitting next to my brother at a Stratosphere video poker bar touted the benefits of taking the free shuttle bus from Stardust to Sam's Town. "Once you get to Sam's Town, you can take another free shuttle bus pretty much anywhere in the city." It quickly became a running joke that taking the free shuttle to Sam's Town was the best transportation method regardless of where we were going. Free shuttles are great, but I view the time required to take a shuttle from the Strip to Sam's Town and then another one from Sam's Town to Downtown as more valuable than the money I'd save by just cabbing it. Likewise, Sam's Town is known to have better gambling conditions than those found in tourist areas. I can find video poker pay tables that I consider good enough in more convenient locations rather than spending a chunk of my extremely limited time traveling to Sam's Town.

Unlike many large cities, the neighborhoods of Las Vegas simply aren't that compelling compared to the Strip and Fremont Street. That's not to say everything off-Strip is bad. It's just not that much better to justify the time required to enjoy them as part of my 100 hours of Vegas time. If nationwide chains completely overran the touristy areas, I would feel much differently. However, the Strip and Fremont Street areas have so many great options unavailable not only near my home but, in many cases, anywhere else in the world.

I value my limited time as much as my limited dollars, so I choose not to spend that time on experiences comparable or only marginally better than those I would have without using up additional minutes or hours. I like ending each day feeling like I got the most possible time value, and I continue to find the most value per minute around the Strip and Fremont.

LAS VEGAS HEARTBREAK

From 2000 to 2007, Barbary Coast was my home base in Las Vegas. I loved almost everything about the little 200-room hotel nestled among neighboring giants Bellagio, Caesars Palace, Bally's, and Flamingo. Video poker pay tables were some of the best on the Strip. The Victorian Room café served consistently tasty food around the clock at a decent price. Michael's gourmet restaurant offered the best classic Las Vegas dining experience in town. The casino lounge featured legendary impersonator Big Elvis and some of the strangest karaoke performances I've ever seen. Drinks were cheap. Comps were easy to earn. It was perfect for low rollers who appreciated being treated like big shots.

In 2007, the company that is now Caesars Entertainment acquired Barbary Coast, changed the name to Bill's Gamblin' Hall, and immediately began removing just about everything I loved about the joint. Video poker paytables decreased. Victorian Room prices increased. Michael's moved out. Big Elvis took his show to Harrah's, and the oddball karaoke regulars disappeared. Drink prices jumped. Comps tightened up. The building itself was mostly the same, but the personal touch was gone. We didn't just lose a casino; we lost a friend. What happened to Barbary Coast is fairly common. Hotels rebrand, restaurants close, happy hour specials change, and employees change companies.

Few tourist destinations change as often as Las Vegas. This is part of what makes the city great. Change means there are always new hotels, casinos, restaurants, bars, clubs, and shows to check out. However, each of them is typically replacing another hotel, casino, restaurant, bar, club, or show that may have been a beloved favorite.

After experiencing several Las Vegas heartbreaks, I learned an important lesson: Never get attached to anything in Las Vegas. Of course, this is easier said than done. That favorite meal, cocktail, and hotel room creep into the between-trip daydreams that lead us to book the next trip just days after returning home.

Avoiding Las Vegas heartbreak requires a "live in the moment" approach and attitude. Always assume favorite aspects of your Las Vegas trip will be gone next time you visit. If you love something, find time to squeeze it in because it may be the last time you can. Skipping an experience you love, thinking you can always do it next time, is a direct path to Las Vegas regret.

Ever since The Cosmopolitan opened in 2010, the bars featuring video poker have comped players not only wine, beer, and well drinks, but also top-shelf specialty cocktails. Because Michele and I have been known to enjoy a high-quality cocktail or two, we were drawn to Book & Stage. The video poker pay tables were good, and the bartenders were friendly and fun. They excelled at making tasty off-menu drinks based on our specific tastes. Knowing that The Cosmopolitan's cocktail comp practices were generous by Vegas Strip standards, we approached our time at Book & Stage thinking we'd better take advantage of it now. The specialty drink gravy train isn't going to last forever. Unfortunately, the favorable video poker pay tables didn't last long, and some of our favorite bartenders left. In July 2015, Cosmo closed Book & Stage. Surprisingly, the comped top shelf booze continues to flow (for now) at other Cosmopolitan bars. It won't be a surprise when the number crunchers inevitably place restrictions on the types of booze available, however.

Appreciating things while they're available and not assuming they'll be around next time will help ease Las Vegas heartbreak when they're inevitably gone.

Closely tied to Las Vegas heartbreak is the common notion that Las Vegas was better back in the good old days. Interestingly, people's concepts of the Las Vegas glory days typically parallel their early trips. Things they first loved about the city have gone away or become more expensive. They're suffering from a case of Las Vegas heartbreak so acute that they just can't let go.

People love to reminisce about how much better things used to be. "Las Vegas was better when the mob ran the town." The business owners shook down by the mob for protection money probably disagree. "You could get a full steak dinner, including a salad and a baked potato the size of a football for $2." Gasoline used to cost a dime a gallon, and a haircut was two bits. Name something that hasn't increased in price in the past 50 years. You can still find a steak dinner or an all-you-can-eat buffet for under $10, which is a damn good deal. "They used to give gamblers free cigarettes." And a complimentary case of emphysema. Spend enough time in smoky casinos today and you can still pick up the comped emphysema.

Yes, things are different. Some things aren't as great as they once were, and some things are much better. Las Vegas still exists because it keeps changing. Part of the appeal of returning time and time again is that there are always new things to do and see. But that constant flow of newness means accepting the inevitable demise of old standbys. The variety of restaurant, bar, and entertainment options is greater today than ever. The quality of hotel rooms for the price is better than any major city in the country. If you don't allow yourself to get too attached to what Las Vegas was, you'll probably find that you're able to more fully enjoy what the city is today. Skip the Las Vegas heartbreak and you can keep your Las Vegas love affair going strong.

CHAPTER 9

South Strip Hotels and Casinos

L as Vegas's most recognizable and popular landmarks are its many hotels and casinos. In addition to accommodations and gambling, they house a huge selection of restaurants, bars, clubs, pools, nightclubs, shows, and other attractions.

Although no formal boundaries designate which properties fall within the South Strip, Center Strip, and North Strip, for our purposes, the South Strip includes the resorts between Mandalay Bay and Monte Carlo.

Mandalay Bay

www.mandalaybay.com

PLAYERS CLUB: Mlife

UNOFFICIAL THEME: Coppertone SPF 45

Standing at the far south end of the Strip since 1999, Mandalay Bay brings a touch of the tropics to Las Vegas. With a seemingly constant parade of guests in swimwear during the day, the casino sometimes feels more like an ocean-side beach resort than a desert den of debauchery.

Jackpot: Mandalay Bay's signature feature, Mandalay Beach has been the city's predominant family pool complex ever since the hotel opened. This isn't your typical rectangle-shaped, water-filled hole with a few palm trees for ambiance. Mandalay Beach includes three standard hotel pools, several whirlpools, a lazy river, and a 1.6 million gallon wave pool, complete with a sandy beach. Adults seeking a pool environment away from the youthful exuberance of the main pool area can retreat to the

Moorea Beach Club, a neighboring adult pool. Women get in free and are welcome to unleash their sweater puppets in pursuit of a line-free tan. Guys face a hefty cover charge (usually between $50 and $75) because gawking at naked boobage rarely comes free. Mandalay Beach includes bars, restaurants, and the Beachside Casino. Visitors who want to check out the pool complex without showing a room key can get in by saying they want to gamble at the casino. Upon being let in, take a look at the casino and then explore the pool area. Sneaky but effective.

Mandalay Bay carries the tropical theme through to another of its attractions, the Shark Reef Aquarium. Many major cities have some sort of aquarium these days, but Mandalay's is larger and more impressive than most. This sea zoo includes more than 2,000 rare fish, crocodiles, turtles, sharks, and other aquatic creatures in an impressive, sprawling complex. Passes are $18 for adults and $12 for kids.

Not all of Mandalay Bay's noteworthy attractions cater to families and center around its tropical theme. The House of Blues Foundation Room sits high above the Las Vegas Strip at the top of Mandalay Bay. This bar and restaurant features an amazing, open-air view of the casinos to the north. Unfortunately, much like Moorea Beach Club, the views at Foundation Room come with a price—typically a $30 cover charge. Hotel guests may be able to wrangle passes by sweet-talking the concierge.

Tilt: Overlooking the Mandalay Bay wave pool stands a concert stage where touring country, pop, and rock acts perform throughout the summer. General admission tickets run between $35 and $60, depending on the band. Outdoor concerts can be a blast in reasonable climates, but desert temperatures don't drop all that much from their triple-digit highs even after sunset. So the heat can detract from the fun a bit. Also, unless you want to watch the concert while swimming or standing in the water—which may not be a bad idea, given the heat—you won't be anywhere near the stage. Toss in so-so sound quality because it's an outdoor show and a beach environment that inspires socializing, and you've got yourself a recipe for the ever-increasing problem of concert yapping. Audience members chat about their inane shit like their cousin Jen's wedding rather that watching the band they paid $60 to see. Even worse than the dolts holding up phones throughout the show to capture low-quality photos and videos they'll view once, concert yappers are societal scourges. Those of us who actually enjoy music and paid to hear the band rather than to simply say we were there shouldn't have to endure these self-absorbed ass-clowns' pointless chatter. But if you attend a show in an outdoor party venue like Mandalay Beach, you'll probably get an earful. Consider yourself warned.

Luxor

www.luxor.com

PLAYERS CLUB: Mlife

UNOFFICIAL THEME: Identity confusion

The 1990s were a magical time in Las Vegas. The era's megaresorts redefined the Strip's skyline and brought unique, well-defined themes. Paris captured the spirit of France (but without the snobbery and body odor). The Venetian emulated the iconic canals and architecture of Venice. Excalibur paid tribute to medieval times with its enormous, albeit cartoonish, castle. Luxor took its inspiration from Egypt. Defining architectural features include a 30-story pyramid as its main hotel tower and a 110-foot-tall sphinx forming the main entrance. In both concept and execution, the theme in its original form was unmistakable. And yet, in recent years, Luxor has distanced itself from its roots. Others have gone through some minor detheming. Paris ditched the recorded French lessons playing in the restrooms, for example, but the Parisian atmosphere remains mostly intact. Trying to downplay the Egyptian aspect of a pyramid-shaped casino is futile. Even though they removed the robotic camels and some of the decorative hieroglyphics, it's still a pyramid. All Luxor's identity crisis has done is turned the resort into an awkward, middle-aged dad who wears skinny jeans and tries to be pals with his teenage son's friends. The resort would be better served doubling down on its Egypt-inspired roots rather than pretending it's something else.

Jackpot: Luxor's size and structure remain impressive. If looking up at the gargantuan pyramid's peak from the atrium below doesn't wow you, bypassing security by acting like a hotel guest, riding to one of the top floors, and looking over the railing will elicit a gasp. People not only thought that building a giant pyramid-shaped hotel and casino was a good idea, but they made it happen. That's insane! But that's Las Vegas!

Much like the nuttiness of Luxor's physical structure, one of the hotel's shows is kooky in concept but has become a great success story. A muscle-bound ginger whose comedy act centers around pulling wacky, pun-based props from a giant trunk, Carrot Top's show sounds more like the type of Vegas act that shuffles between small, second-tier theaters. Yet, since 2005 he has consistently filled the Luxor showroom and receives rave reviews for having one of the funniest shows on the Strip. Mr. Top constantly develops new props—often tied to pop culture and current events—keeping his show fresh. He's corny, self-deprecating, and, surprisingly, one of the funniest and most popular acts in Las Vegas.

Tilt: Another Luxor entertainer, Criss Angel, hasn't fared as well as Carrot Top. Although technically a Cirque du Soleil show, *Criss Angel Believe* was stripped of most of the traditional Cirque elements following an onslaught of bad reviews early in the show's run. Now a more traditional magic show, *Believe* still gets slammed, but with Angel as the sole target. His performance is light on the grand illusions Vegas audiences expect, instead focusing on Angel talking about himself, exchanging awkward jokes with other cast members, and showing videos of past tricks. Diehard Angel fans who adore his broodiness, Affliction t-shirts, skull jewelry, and arrogant attitude may dig the show, but most will find Angel's most impressive trick is making their money disappear.

Unfortunately, Luxor's problems don't end with Angel's act. The buffet is mediocre, the casino lacks energy, and efforts to make the place feel hip have resulted in a boring space with little personality. Luxor has become flyover country between Excalibur and Mandalay Bay. It's the Nebraska of the Las Vegas Strip, but with slightly less excitement.

Although an impressive structure, the Luxor pyramid is an impractical hotel tower. The novelty of staying in a pyramid-shaped building quickly wears off when the slanted exterior walls lead to horrific flashbacks of the converted attic that served as your bedroom during your teen years. One minute you're staring out the window, watching airplanes land at McCarran, and the next thing you're curled up in the fetal position reliving the first time you got a boner in math class. Even though these rooms are sometimes priced as low as $32 a night, the slightly more expensive tower rooms—located in the two adjoining non-pyramid buildings—have more space and less emotional baggage.

Excalibur

www.excaliburlasvegas.com

PLAYERS CLUB: Mlife

UNOFFICIAL THEME: Childlike wonderment

Looming over the South Strip like the centerpiece of a Legoland Renaissance Festival is Excalibur. The cartoonish, medieval castle façade signals to all that they are in for a… uh… special experience. It's easy to be catty about Excalibur. Much like Circus Circus, the castle sometimes feels more like a playground than a casino. The low-budget, family-friendly nature of Excalibur makes the place feel a tad low-rent. But not everybody wants mixology bars and cutting-edge fusion dining as part of their Las Vegas experience. Excalibur fills a niche and does so quite well. It serves families vacationing on a budget in search of the Las Vegas experience at a discount. Cheap rooms, low-limit table games, and discount dining cater to a segment of Las Vegas visitors not served by new and recently renovated resorts.

Jackpot: Excalibur's design harkens back to a golden age. No, not the Middle Ages. When was the last time you saw an ancient castle with blue, red, and gold turrets? Excalibur is a throwback to the 1990s—the grand era of casino theming previously mentioned. Many neighboring hotels from this era have turned their backs on their original themes. Excalibur, however, continues to embrace its concept. The steakhouse isn't simply called Excalibur Steakhouse, but rather The Steakhouse at Camelot. And the arcade maintains the creepiest, but still themed, name in all of Las Vegas—the Fun Dungeon. If that doesn't sound like Johnny and Susie just boarded an escalator to Molestytown, I don't know what does.

Despite the name, the Fun Dungeon is a surprisingly cool arcade. With a mix of old-style carnival midway games, sports games, and video games, the arcade keeps kids entertained for hours while their degenerate gambler parents piss away the family nest egg at a Three Card Poker table upstairs. Unlike the cramped and sticky Circus Circus midway, the Fun Dungeon is spacious and clean.

Taking the Ren-fest theme a step further, Excalibur's *Tournament of Kings* dinner show serves up large portions of mediocre chicken or Cornish game hen to audience members rooting for their designated country's jousters to triumph. Like most things at Excalibur, it's cheesy, non-glamorous, and family-friendly—the perfect show for this resort. If you've had the inexplicable desire to visit a Medieval Times restaurant but don't have one in your city, *Tournament of Kings* should do the trick. Make sure to tip your serving wench.

Another family-friendly feature, the second-floor Castle Walk Food Court offers one of the most varied fast-food selections on the Strip. Options include McDonald's, Pizza Hut, Schlotzsky's, Popeye's, Cinnabon, Krispy Kreme, and several others. Dining at fast-food restaurants available anywhere in the country is a wasted opportunity during a vacation—especially when so many unique options are available nearby. However, food-court dining fits in well with the Excalibur experience. When traveling on a tight budget and needing nothing more than some quick, relatively cheap options for the whole clan, having a selection of fast-food joints catering to everyone's tastes comes in handy.

Tilt: While no Las Vegas casino carries a theme through 100 percent of its shows, restaurants, bars, and other amenities, Excalibur takes at least one whiplash-inducing turn when it breaks free from its kiddie-friendly, knights-and-dragons roots. Among Excalibur's entertainment options, *Thunder from Down Under* features Australian male strippers. After a long day keeping Andrellica and Stetson occupied, Momma Barb probably needs some entertainment of her own. But greased-up Aussies throwing another jumbo shrimp on Barbie's grill while chanting "no rules, just right" is a weird fit for Excalibur.

The resort's show lineup also includes *The Australian Bee Gees*. I call bullshit. The actual Bee Gees formed and became successful in Australia, so they were the Australian Bee Gees (even if they weren't born there). This would be like a tribute band from Toronto naming itself The Canadian Rush. I demand a law preventing tribute bands from simply slapping the name of a city, state, province, or country in front of the original band's name if the original band first became famous in that location. Besides, half the fun of a tribute band is using or adapting one of the band's song or album titles for the band name. Wouldn't you much rather see a band called Bad Boys Running Wild than The German Scorpions?

Tropicana

www.tropicanalv.com

PLAYERS CLUB: Marquee Rewards

UNOFFICIAL THEME: Sunshine and lollipops

One of the Strip's oldest hotels, Tropicana opened in 1957. The resort had fallen into an embarrassing state of disrepair until a substantial update of the entire property gave it a new lease on life a few years ago. Today, the property is bright, clean, and energetic.

Jackpot: Tropicana has a great South Strip location with quick pedestrian access to neighbors MGM Grand, New York-New York, and Excalibur as well as Luxor and Mandalay Bay via the free tram in front of Excalibur. The hotel's massive renovation in 2011 resulted in comfortable, modern rooms at a reasonable rate. Weekdays are frequently available for under $100, making Trop a great choice for visitors seeking value. Nearby Excalibur and Luxor both offer rooms at lower rates but also lower quality.

Tropicana's pool area also received a much-needed makeover in 2011, but one classic piece of Vegas kitsch—swim-up blackjack—remains. Although many Las Vegas hotels feature poolside gambling, Tropicana is one of the few to offer blackjack without leaving the water. Gamblers can split aces, sip a beer, and take a whiz all at the same time. What a concept!

Tilt: For a hotel the size of Tropicana (approximately 1,500 rooms), the resort offers surprisingly few dining options. Choices include an Italian restaurant (Bacio), a steakhouse (Biscayne), a café, and a food court with a limited selection of burgers, sandwiches, pizza, and teriyaki bowls. The resort announced plans to add more restaurants as part of an eventual Strip-side retail and dining complex expansion. Until its completion—if it even happens—gamblers and hotel guests seeking greater variety are better served next door at MGM Grand.

MGM Grand

www.mgmgrand.com

PLAYERS CLUB: Mlife

UNOFFICIAL THEME: Foot blisters

It may not be shaped like a pyramid or castle, but there's no mistaking MGM Grand, one of the most distinct-looking resorts in Las Vegas. Unlike any other hotel in the city, its unique exterior has lit up the South Strip with an emerald glow since 1993. MGM caters to mid- and high-budget guests with a huge range of room, restaurant, and entertainment options. Offerings start with the tiny but well-appointed West Wing rooms, which sometimes go for as little as $60, and top out with The Mansion, an exclusive hotel-within-a-hotel reserved for big-time celebrities and multi-millionaires. Similarly, dining options range from Nathan's Famous Hot Dogs for a few bucks to Joël Robuchon at several hundred dollars per person.

Jackpot: Mandalay Bay and Flamingo frequently receive props for having fantastic swimming pools, but MGM Grand deserves a spot in the conversation. In addition to four pools and three whirlpools, MGM Grand offers one of the Strip's three lazy rivers (Mandalay Bay and Monte Carlo have the others). There's nothing quite like the smell of one's baking flesh while leisurely floating atop a river of chemically treated piss water on a 110-degree August day. Tube rentals run $16.

Visitors seeking a slightly drier form of relaxation can book a massage and hang out in the spa at pretty much any Strip hotel, but MGM Grand takes wellness to a higher level with its Stay Well rooms. They feature a variety of amenities aimed at clean living. It's like the Betty Ford Center without strict rules, preachy counselors, and depressing group sessions. Antimicrobial linens adorn the beds. The water supply runs through a special filtration system. Custom lighting aims to energize and improve sleep rhythms. Air purification reduces toxins. Shower water includes Vitamin C to soften hair and skin. A lot of this sounds like bullshit aimed at people who embrace every health fad they read about online. (I'm talking about you, self-diagnosed gluten allergy sufferers.) But for guests who need or simply desire a cleaner Las Vegas experience, MGM Grand's

Stay Well rooms fill a niche. Too bad these rooms didn't exist when fabled germaphobe/eccentric nutjob Howard Hughes took up residence on the Strip. He would have loved staying in a room that had self-cleaning coatings on frequently touched surfaces. Although they aren't listed as a standard Stay Well room benefit, the concierge can probably provide urine storage jars by special request.

If your vacation plans call for experiencing the high life in Las Vegas—even just for one meal—it would be tough to top the much-lauded Joël Robuchon French restaurant's 16-course degustation menu. At more than $400 per person (not including booze), this option is a rare treat for foodies to sample the finest dishes from one of the world's greatest chefs. If the thought of 16 courses (or $400) is too intimidating, four-, five-, and six-course prix fixe options are available between $130 and $250. Joël Robuchon is located within The Mansion at MGM Grand, giving common folks willing to splurge for one meal a glimpse of one of the most exclusive hotels in Las Vegas. L'Atelier by Joël Robuchon, a separate restaurant located just off the casino floor is the chef's slightly more accessible and more casual option—also worthy of a visit for special occasions.

Tilt: MGM Grand's massive size makes it one of the most challenging casinos to navigate. Much like Caesars Palace, staying at MGM Grand comes with the assurance that you're going to put more than a few miles on your Adidas. Depending on your room's location, you may require a map, a GPS, or a bag of breadcrumbs to ensure your safe return.

New York-New York

www.nynyhotelcasino.com
PLAYERS CLUB: Mlife
UNOFFICIAL THEME: Large honeycrisps

During the themed casino boom of the 1990s, developers wanted to build a Strip resort that would pay tribute to one the world's most famous cities, mimicking its iconic skyline and bustling streets. However, when customer research showed few people desired to visit a New Delhi themed casino, they went with New York City instead. Opened in 1997, New York-New York pays tribute to numerous familiar landmarks, including the Statue of Liberty, the streets of Greenwich Village, and the skyscrapers of Manhattan. All that's missing are a Billy Joel tribute show, an interactive *Seinfeld* attraction, and an Alex Rodriguez juice bar.

Jackpot: Several Irish pubs dot the Las Vegas Strip, but none are like Nine Fine Irishmen. Constructed in Ireland, disassembled, and shipped to Las Vegas, the bar's decor features rich wood and dark lighting. During the day, Nine Fine feels cozy and comfortable—a welcome refuge from the loud casino. Grab a few shots of whiskey at the upstairs bar and you'll soon feel like you're in Dublin. With Irish bands frequently performing at night, the joint becomes much more loud, lively, and fun.

Tilt: Why New York-New York chose to make its sports book one of the tiniest, most awkward places to watch a game on the Strip is a mystery. You'd think the sports book would try to capture elements of Yankee Stadium, but instead it has all the charm of a second-rate off-track-betting parlor. The wide, shallow space requires anyone trying to watch a game to tilt their heads back to see the monitors above. With so many more comfortable game-viewing options nearby, there's no reason to suffer through the neck-craning views at New York-New York.

Monte Carlo

www.montecarlo.com

PLAYERS CLUB: Mlife

UNOFFICIAL THEME: Ami Dolenz in *She's Out of Control*

Monte Carlo is the plain, semi-nerdy girl in half of the teen comedy movies that came out in the 1980s. She appears boring and is easy to ignore, but if you look beyond the surface and get to know her, she's actually kind of hot. Monte Carlo isn't exactly The Cosmopolitan hidden behind eyeglasses and a hair bun. However, underneath the baggy sweatshirt that is Monte Carlo's bland casino, she's worthy of a second look.

Jackpot: Sandwiched between New York-New York and CityCenter, Monte Carlo straddles the imaginary line between South Strip and Center

Strip. This location makes the hotel an ideal home base for visitors planning to explore both areas by foot. Monte Carlo connects to Aria by a short walkway and to Bellagio by a free tram. This convenient access is ideal for budget-conscious tourists who prefer more lively neighboring casinos. Owner MGM Resorts recently began updating the stale area between Monte Carlo and New York-New York with a new 20,000-seat arena and adjacent outdoor retail and entertainment district, The Park. This new development makes Monte Carlo's already great position on the Strip even more attractive.

With rooms frequently available for as low as $42 per night, Monte Carlo is one of the best hotel values on the Strip. It may not be as modern as nearby Aria or as new as Tropicana, but the location and amenities are superior to comparably priced Luxor and Excalibur.

Visitors craving a more personal, upscale experience should consider Hotel32. Located on the top floor of Monte Carlo, Hotel32 opened in 2009 as a separate hotel within Monte Carlo. Guests have access to limo service to and from the airport (excluded with the lowest-tier studio rooms), a personal concierge, a private lounge with free refreshments, and more modern rooms than those available on lower floors. Hotel32 is a fun splurge for special occasions. Guests begin their trip in style, arriving in a limo, being checked in and escorted to the room by a personal assistant, and finding little cups of fresh fruit on the dresser and bottled water in the fridge. The convenience of Lounge32 makes beginning each day a delight. Grab some fresh fruit, a muffin, and some juice for breakfast and you're on your way.

Another of Monte Carlo's strengths is its pool area. Several years before Mandalay Bay, Monte Carlo was the first Las Vegas hotel to offer a wave pool. Also featuring a lazy river, traditional hotel pool, VIP pool, and volleyball court, Monte Carlo's pool complex is quietly one of the nicest for a mid-priced Strip hotel. It doesn't typically have a high douchebag population like some nearby pools and, although family-friendly, it also isn't overrun with kids to the level of Mandalay Bay.

Monte Carlo also offers a couple exceptional destinations for drinkers. With more than 200 domestic and international bottles and drafts, The Pub is a beer-drinkers paradise. Cocktail connoisseurs will find a hidden gem in Monte Carlo's high limit gaming area: Hit Bar features top-shelf classic cocktails served by some of the friendliest bartenders on the Strip. Monte Carlo bars frequently offer great happy hour discounts as well. Check the resort's website for current times and offers.

Performing on the Strip for more than 15 years, Blue Man Group has become a Las Vegas staple. A popular alternative to the glut of Cirque du Soleil shows featured at other MGM Resorts properties, BMG is quirky, silly fun. Who would ever imagine that a group of guys coated in bright blue Sears Latex High-Gloss Exterior House Paint and playing instruments made from PVC piping would be one of the most consistent draws in town? It sounds like Bob Vila's bad acid trip, but audiences love it.

Tilt: Monte Carlo's biggest fault lies in its mediocrity. It's the Matchbox Twenty, Train, and late-era Goo Goo Dolls of casinos. If Monte Carlo were a color, it would be beige. Much of Monte Carlo actually *is* beige. Perfect. The resort isn't offensive or bad. It's just dull. In a city dependent on excitement and fun, dull doesn't get people in the door. The great aspects of the property previously mentioned are easy to overlook because, on the surface, the casino appears to be devoid of personality.

As development of The Park and its adjacent arena proceed, hotel renovation and rebranding rumors abound. A major facelift for the hotel is warranted, but a significant bump to the currently attractive room rates and the unfortunate loss of some of the property's gems would likely accompany such improvements.

CHAPTER 10

Center Strip Hotels and Casinos

Making up the largest concentration of hotels and casinos on Las Vegas Boulevard, the Center Strip area spans from the multi-hotel CityCenter development to Sands Avenue. This roughly mile-and-a-half stretch includes more than a dozen major resorts. For first-time Las Vegas visitors, I always recommend staying at a Center Strip hotel. It provides the best location for efficient and convenient exploring.

Aria

www.aria.com

PLAYERS CLUB: Mlife

UNOFFICIAL THEME: Cha-cha-cha-changes

When Aria opened in 2009, the resort was underwhelming. The casino felt dark and unwelcoming, and its location at the back of the CityCenter complex, behind the Crystals shopping mall, made it inconvenient. For a new, upscale MGM Resorts property, Aria didn't match the luxury of Bellagio or the more casual fun of upper mid-tier MGM-owned hotels, The Mirage and Mandalay Bay. Based on initial visits, I didn't anticipate spending much time there during future trips. Then, thanks to an unexpectedly generous room offer resulting from some heavier-than-normal gambling I had done at The Mirage, I booked a room and made Aria my home for three nights in August 2011. By then, Aria had already undergone several changes aimed at making the property more inviting. They worked. In fact, the resort has been in a constant state of flux in its first several years, with many bars and restaurants undergoing complete remodels and concept transitions. Aria also brightened up the casino, which made the room feel more vibrant and energetic. Even the initial Cirque du Soleil show, *Viva Elvis*, was dumped in favor of *Zarkana*—a surprising change in a city that hadn't previously seen any Cirque shows fail. Even more surprising was the demise of *Viva Elvis* before Luxor's much-maligned *Criss Angel Believe*. Some casinos stumble out of the gate and need time to find their footing. I'm glad circumstances led me back to Aria after I had pretty much written it off.

Jackpot: Aria loads its rooms with techy goodness, beginning with a delightful discovery before even entering the room. Rather than the usual inserted keycard, Aria uses more modern proximity cards that visitors simply swipe in front of the door. This may not seem like a big deal, but when was the last time your traditional hotel room keycard worked on the first try? Never! In the history of traditional hotel room keycards, nobody has ever successfully entered a room on the first attempt. Bravo to Aria for adopting a better solution. Once inside the room, Aria's lighting, temperature, curtains, television, and music system can all be controlled on the TV or from a universal remote control next to the bed. Guests may choose to wake up from their drunken gambling coma with gentle lighting and the soothing sounds of James Taylor, or with Iron Maiden and all curtains opening to reveal the harsh Las Vegas sun. Either option beats the jolting hotel room clock radio or wake-up call. Rooms also include USB recharging ports and plenty of accessible electrical outlets, eliminating the all-too-common hassle of moving furniture to access a single open outlet.

Guests who stay in suites will find the most pleasant tech in the bathroom. Thanks to magical Toto Washlet seats, suite toilets are also sweet toilets. Until you've benefited from the services of this innovation in hygiene, you simply haven't lived. Your experience begins with a heated seat, ensuring your buns remain toasty throughout your toilet adventure. Once you've completed your business, the real party begins. Using a control panel on the wall, you activate a nozzle that emerges from the seat, gently washing your parts with a spray of water. "Oh, it's a bidet," you may be saying. It's a bidet like an iPhone is a rotary telephone. Sure, it has the functionality of its basic predecessor, but all of the other features are what make it so great. With the Washlet, you can select the water temperature, water angle, and pulsation pattern with the touch of a button. Guys, unless you want your ballbag pummeled, skip the pulsating front wash. That's for the ladies. It makes their girl parts tingle. The rear wash, however, will ensure anyone using it has the cleanest balloon knot in the Southwest. Finish up with a warm stream of air that feels like the gentle breath of 1,000 angels, and you'll be ready to get on with your day. Never has taking a dump been so enjoyable.

Aria frequently offers room rates below neighboring luxury hotels Bellagio and The Cosmopolitan, as well as the often-overpriced Planet Hollywood. Signing up for e-mail offers through Aria's website and checking Mlife rates can yield some surprisingly good discounts, even with minimal casino play. Aria's mix of great tech, comfortable furnishings, excellent service, and quality amenities makes the hotel one of the best upscale resort values on the Strip.

Tilt: The most efficient way to get to Aria from Las Vegas Boulevard is through the Shops at Crystals. This architectural abortion of a shopping mall looks like the aftermath of a tornado hitting an Airstream camper factory. Someone slapped a Prada logo on the front, called it art, and opened for business. Once inside the metallic scrap heap, visitors find the largest collection of inaccessible, high-end retail in Las Vegas. It also features a restaurant inside a giant wooden dick with seating in the scrotum and an information desk at the taint. Hilarious, but—like the rest of Crystals—it proves that architects have depleted every good idea and have resorted to bringing projects to life based on doodles from the back of their fifth-grade math notebooks.

After trekking through Crystals, you'll find that Aria has assembled a respectable restaurant lineup, including Julian Serrano for delicious tapas, Five50 for outstanding pizza, and Sage for artsy-fartsy meat and seafood. Unfortunately, not all restaurants measure up. Even after two remodels in its first five years, The Buffet quality pales in comparison to similarly priced, far superior competitors like The Cosmopolitan's Wicked Spoon and Bellagio's identically named The Buffet. Similarly, Todd English P.U.B. serves mediocre food and has spotty service, redeemed only by one of the Strip's best beer selections. Drink at the bar if you enjoy trying new beers, but skip the food.

The Cosmopolitan

www.cosmopolitanlasvegas.com

PLAYERS CLUB: Identity

UNOFFICIAL THEME: Fedoras and indoor sunglasses

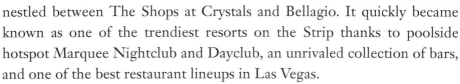

The Cosmopolitan opened in 2010, snugly nestled between The Shops at Crystals and Bellagio. It quickly became known as one of the trendiest resorts on the Strip thanks to poolside hotspot Marquee Nightclub and Dayclub, an unrivaled collection of bars, and one of the best restaurant lineups in Las Vegas.

Jackpot: Few Las Vegas hotels offer guests the ability to enjoy room service outdoors, high above the Strip while watching the Bellagio fountains. Thanks to private terraces on most guest rooms, The Cosmopolitan's rooms are among the most popular on the Strip. Plus, using the mini-bar binoculars, pervy guests may be able to scope out some hot amateur terrace action from other guests, depending on room location. It's a sex safari, all from the comfort of your own balcony! This popular feature comes with a price, unfortunately. Cosmo accommodations command higher rates than comparably sized rooms in neighboring hotels—a not-so-mysterious phenomenon unofficially known as the terrace tax.

Rooms don't provide the only great views at Cosmo. Boulevard Pool overlooks Las Vegas Boulevard from four stories above. One of three pools, Boulevard attracts a young 20s and 30s crowd and offers three levels of lounge space with both open and reserved seating. Arrive early, as it frequently gets crowded. The resort requires a room key to visit the pool area. If you'd like to take a look but aren't staying there, tell the attendant at the bottom of the pool escalator that your room isn't yet ready, but you'd like to see the pool. Most of the time, you'll get access. At night, Boulevard sometimes doubles as an event space, screening classic films on the adjacent Cosmo marquee, and hosting concerts by major touring acts, including Kid Rock, Thirty Seconds to Mars, and Brad Paisley.

The Cosmopolitan has two additional pool areas for those who wish to make the club scene last all day (Marquee Dayclub), or relax in a world in which they can pretend the dayclub scene doesn't exist (Bamboo).

Located next to Cosmo's spa, Bamboo even offers poolside yoga and pilates classes.

Without match, The Cosmopolitan houses the most interesting collection of casino bars in Las Vegas. Each features a different specialty cocktail menu and a slightly different atmosphere, making Cosmo a drinker's haven.

Few hotel lobby bars specialize in complex, sometimes time-consuming versions of classic cocktails, but Vesper does. This can be frustrating for customers who have to wait a couple minutes for their Bud Lights while the bartenders are muddling blackberries for someone else's order. However, cocktail geeks love this bar. Try the hot mule, a variation on the classic Moscow mule with the kick of an angry donkey.

A multi-level bar near the Strip entrances, Chandelier lives within its gigantic namesake chandelier. Each level features its own specialty cocktails. One of the most uniquely Vegas drinks comes courtesy of Chandelier Level 1.5, accessible by stairs or elevator from the casino floor, and open evenings only. The verbena cocktail includes a Szechuan button, which should be thoroughly chewed after an initial sip of the beverage. The flower bud provides an oddly pleasant tongue-on-nine-volt-battery sensation and changes the flavor of the drink.

Cosmo's restaurant lineup is as impressive as its selection of bars. Check the resort's website for current "social hour" dining specials. Favorite Cosmo eateries include:

- **Wicked Spoon:** Cosmo's all-you-can-eat buffet, Wicked Spoon led the trend of offering individually portioned servings instead of traditional self-serve food vats. Although one of the most expensive buffets in Las Vegas at $27 for weekday brunch, $35 for weekend brunch and $38 for dinner, Wicked Spoon's quality exceeds most others as well.

- **Secret Pizza:** So named because it has no signs or other promotion throughout the casino, Secret Pizza is a tiny, walk-up pizzeria located on the third level. Look for the long hallway lined with record album covers. After getting wrecked at The Cosmopolitan's bars, nothing tastes better than a couple slices of Secret Pizza's New York style meatball pizza.

- **Holstein's:** Cosmo's gourmet burger joint, Holstein's has become one of my favorites for its appetizers and boozy shakes. Go-to apps include fried pickles and Philly egg rolls—mini cheesesteaks served up in egg roll form. For all the deliciousness of a childhood breakfast combined with all the wrongness of vodka and ice cream, Holstein's serves the Cereal Bowl shake, made with Fruit Loops, Captain Crunch, and 3 Olives Loopy vodka.

- **China Poblano:** A somewhat odd combination of Chinese and Mexican cuisine from Chef José Andrés, China Poblano offers delicious tacos, noodles, and dim sum. You won't go wrong with the carnitas tacos, lamb pot stickers, and when pigs fly (barbecue pork buns).

- **Estiatorio Milos:** Mediterranean seafood restaurant Milos offers one of the best lunch specials in town. For around $25, diners get a choice of six appetizers, and one of four seafood or chicken entrees, plus a light dessert.

- **é:** A tiny eight-seat room within Jaleo, é offers one of the most special dining experiences in Las Vegas. The restaurant accepts reservations beginning at midnight PST exactly 30 days in advance by e-mailing _reserve@ebyjoseandres.com_. Upon being accepted, diners are required to provide credit card information (no-shows are charged). A 24-course, three-hour dining adventure highlighting the work of Chef Andrés, the meal costs a steep $200-$250 per person.

Wandering around The Cosmopolitan reveals countless surprises. Artwork scattered throughout the property, including high heel shoe sculptures large enough to stand in, human-sized dog statues, and funky wall art, make great photo ops. Several Art-o-Mat vending machines give guests the chance to buy unique, pocket-sized art designed by independent artists for just $5. These little touches make Cosmo quirky and fun.

Tilt: Issues have plagued The Cosmopolitan's hotel operations since the joint opened. Long waits for rooms and shoddy housekeeping continue to annoy guests. Filmed at the hotel, The Killers' "Shot at the Night" music video is a biting documentary exposing the origin of some of these problems. The video follows a Cosmopolitan maid whose responsibilities apparently include not only cleaning rooms but also vacuuming the casino, washing the escalator railings, and wandering around the entire property while pushing her supply cart. The hotel may want to consider having employees specialize a bit more, and perhaps allowing maids to use the back-of-house service elevators. What's worse is the lack of effective supervision and proper discipline. While wandering a hotel hallway, the maid encounters two guys and a gal ready to hit the town. They convince her to jump ship and join them—because most Cosmo guests are just dying to hang out with the person who changes their crusty sheets. When she returns to work hours later, she just stands there and smiles while the boss lady bitches her out. The Cosmopolitan should use the video as a what-not-to-do orientation day training film.

The Cosmopolitan attracts the stylish, young nightclub crowd—who apparently may be inclined to party with their hotel maids. When Marquee nightclub is open, dude-bros wearing sunglasses indoors at night and chicks wearing low-cut black party dresses one size too small fill every corner of the casino. Depending on your perspective at the time, this can be either highly entertaining or highly annoying. Try coping with the chode onslaught by having fun with it. Set an over/under line on how many women you'll see carrying their shoes through the casino in the next 10 minutes, and start counting. When you encounter a Hardy of douches (the official *Five Hundy* terminology of a pack of nightclub bros), try to figure out which one has the unfortunate ugly friend role. There's always one. Stuck in the long cab line? Take delight in the number of women who have trouble climbing into their cabs because of the tightness and shortness of their chosen attire combined with their obvious intoxication. The free entertainment possibilities are endless if you use your imagination.

Some visitors find The Cosmopolitan just a little too precious and hip for its own good. The high-end mixology bars, cutesy art, and bizarre ad campaigns marketing to the "curious class" can be a bit much if you're just looking for a bottle of beer and a slot machine. It's probably over the top to have room service delivered by a waiter wearing a monocle and vintage Soviet Union Navy uniform while you lounge in the hotel's complimentary chinchilla bathrobe. You probably don't need to see formal certification papers documenting that your roasted chicken enjoyed a peaceful life on a Vermont free-range farm that plays Mendelssohn's Symphony No. 5 on a 24-hour loop. And perhaps having an in-room television channel dedicated solely to Charlie Chaplin films dubbed with old Miles Davis records caters to a relatively niche segment of the hotel's clientele. None of this really happens at The Cosmopolitan, but if management reads this book, it's just a matter of time. The place is just that hip.

Planet Hollywood

www.planethollywoodresort.com
PLAYERS CLUB: Total Rewards
UNOFFICIAL THEME: B movies

Following an ownership change in 2007, the former Aladdin became Planet Hollywood. Although the casino hosts the occasional movie premiere, the hotel rooms contain the majority of Hollywood theming. Unlike Hard Rock Hotel, which is designed as a casino version of Hard Rock Cafés, Planet Hollywood Hotel and Casino bears little resemblance to the restaurants carrying the same name. The casino's themed décor consists mainly of large celebrity photos scattered throughout the building.

Jackpot: Each Planet Hollywood guest room highlights a specific movie. Discovering which film is featured and what memorabilia is displayed can be an entertaining part of staying at Planet Hollywood. However, expecting an *Empire Strikes Back* room with a Tauntaun sleeping chamber is a sure path to disappointment. Typically, the featured movies aren't blockbusters, and theming consists of a couple framed photos of movie scenes, a promotional poster, and an actual prop or two displayed inside a case that doubles as an end table.

I have stayed in rooms celebrating such classics as *Cliffhanger*, *Hot Shots Part Deux*, and *Empire Records*. Some panty-sniffing sicko busted open the table in the *Empire Records* room and removed Liv Tyler's underwear, worn in the film. I know what you're thinking, but they were gone when I arrived. The memorabilia in some rooms is more impressive than others.

The *Encino Man* room includes a Lucite chamber containing Pauly Shore and Brendan Fraser.

Planet Dailies has become a go-to choice for dependable late-night dining and breakfast. With a large space on the edge of the casino, this 24-hour café has a huge selection, including burgers, sandwiches, salads, pasta, steak, chicken, and fish. There's rarely a wait to get seated, service is usually good, and the food is a step up from similar style chain restaurants like Applebee's or TGI Friday's.

A quicker, cheaper option for a dependable bite is Earl of Sandwich. A growing international restaurant franchise, Earl offers reliably decent hot sandwiches for under $7 each.

Planet Hollywood also offers some of the cheapest breakfasts on the Strip. Located in the Miracle Mile Shops, La Salsa Cantina, Blondie's, and Cheeseburger at the Oasis have been battling each other for the best breakfast value for the past few years. Each special varies slightly, but for between $3 and $6, you can get a couple eggs and some bacon or sausage. Cheeseburger at the Oasis is a couple bucks more than the others but includes coffee. For more information on the Miracle Mile Shops, see Chapter 15.

One of Gordon Ramsay's restaurants, BurGR is a more affordable option than Gordon Ramsay Steak at Paris, and a tastier, more reliable option than Gordon Ramsay Pub & Grill at Caesars Palace. Although just about every major Strip casino offers a gourmet burger joint these days, and tastes are highly subjective, BurGR rivals the best. Favorite menu items include roasted jalapeno poppers, the Hell's Kitchen burger, and sweet potato fries.

Tilt: With its celebrity-oriented theme, you'd think Planet Hollywood would have a great nightclub, featuring guest appearances by today's hottest celebriskanks and douchetards. Not so. Previous clubs shut down following allegations of questionable practices, so the large, second-level nightclub space has sat vacant since 2013. Given the resort's theme and available space, the absence of a club seems odd.

Bellagio

www.bellagio.com

PLAYERS CLUB: Mlife

UNOFFICIAL THEME: Timeless luxury

Since 1998, Bellagio has graced Las Vegas Boulevard with style, class, and luxury. Although several newer high-end Las Vegas resorts challenge the grand dame of the Strip, several aspects of Bellagio remain unmatched, keeping the hotel atop the city's most elegant destinations.

Jackpot: No free Strip-side attraction will ever top the Fountains of Bellagio. That may be a bold statement about a city that constantly reinvents and outdoes itself. However, the chance of any future hotel dedicating eight acres of prime Strip-front property to something that doesn't directly produce revenue is about as likely as Zombie Bob Stupak rising from the grave to build his Titanic-themed The Boat hotel and casino. Even Steve Wynn, the man who introduced the Fountains of Bellagio, as well as The Mirage volcano, and Treasure Island pirate show (RIP), ditched free Strip-facing attractions when building Wynn and Encore. Fortunately, current Bellagio owner MGM Resorts hasn't yet begun carving out bits of the lake to add another Starbucks or Walgreens to the Strip. So what makes the Fountains of Bellagio so special? Like Las Vegas itself, they provide visitors a grand, over-the-top spectacle. They combine water, lights, and music with the beautiful backdrop of the Bellagio to tug at your heartstrings. The fountains blast water into the air, creating an aquatic fireworks display. Audiences frequently applaud at the end of shows, even though there are no performers to appreciate the accolades. Shows take place every 30 minutes beginning at 3 p.m. during the week and noon on weekends. From 7 p.m. to midnight, shows occur every 15 minutes. A schedule of each day's specific songs is available from the Bellagio concierge, but playing fountain roulette is much more fun. Show up and see what you get. If you're lucky, "Con Te Partirò" (Time to Say Goodbye) or "Hoe Down" (the "beef, it's what's for dinner" song) will be next. If luck isn't going your way, you'll be subjected to Faith Hill's "This Kiss" or Lee Greenwood's audience-pandering crapcicle, "God Bless the USA."

Although most people view the fountains from the sidewalk along Las Vegas Boulevard, some of Bellagio's bars and restaurants provide great views from inside the hotel. Located dead center behind the lake, Hyde lounge and nightclub provides a remarkable view. Most hotel nightclubs serve up loud music, fist-pumping good times, and ridiculously priced bottle service. What sets one club apart from another is often the room itself. With Hyde, Bellagio incorporated the one feature nobody else can emulate—the fountains. Hyde guests have an unmatched, up-close view of the fountain shows while they party. Best of all for those of us who aren't into the nightclub scene, Hyde functions as a lounge from 5 p.m. to 10 p.m. nightly. The indoor/outdoor club relaxes its dress code, ditches its cover charge, and serves delicious (although still expensive at $20 a pop) cocktails to guests wishing to relax and chat while taking in the fountains.

In recent years, several Las Vegas resorts have incorporated fine art into their interior design. Bellagio was the first to make fine art a major element of the hotel and casino. The lobby ceiling features a custom Dale Chihuly sculpture, the French restaurant Picasso is filled with its namesake's works of art, and the Gallery of Fine Art hosts a variety of short-term exhibits. Past gallery shows have highlighted legendary artists including Monet, Van Gogh, Lichtenstein, and Warhol, to name just a few. Admission is $16, with discounts for locals, seniors, and children.

Another of Bellagio's must-see attractions—and a work of art in its own right—the Conservatory and Botanical Gardens brings a bit of nature indoors. Located near the hotel's registration desk, themed exhibits use flowers, plants, trees, and water features to create impressive seasonal displays. The autumn display typically centers around a large cornucopia or old-timey mill. Spring may feature butterflies or a windmill. July 4 includes tons of patriotic imagery, like an oversized model of the Liberty Bell. Although some elements reappear every year or two, the display is never identical to the same season from the previous year. Even if checking out floral displays doesn't seem like the most compelling use of your time in Las Vegas, a 10-minute walk through the conservatory is worthwhile. Much like the fountains, the conservatory takes a Vegas-sized spectacle and makes it elegant and classy.

Tilt: With thousands of guests entering and exiting Bellagio each day, regulating interior temperatures and conserving energy can be a challenge. To help combat the problem, the hotel uses automatic revolving doors, an age-old solution to managing heating and cooling issues near public building entrances. In theory, steps to conserve energy should be applauded. Unfortunately, approximately 87 percent of the general public still hasn't figured out how to successfully maneuver their way through an automatic revolving door. It should be pretty simple. Step into the opening and walk at the same pace as the door is moving until you're in the building five seconds later, then step out. The doors move on their own, so there's no need to push them. If someone pushes the door or gets too close to the door, it stops. This happens at least once during every full rotation. Whether a family of 14 tries to cram into a single open slot or Lanky Larry can't shorten his stride, someone always screws up the pacing, resulting in the door stopping. Immediately after a fountain show, when pedestrians are on the move, it's common to see a dozen or more people lined up, waiting to get through the revolving doors. As a result of this traffic-clogging clusterfuck, I quit using revolving doors years ago, opting for the adjacent standard door most people ignore. I'd feel a slight sense of guilt for contributing to the accelerated decline of our planet if I weren't safely inside the climate-controlled confines of Bellagio with such great speed and efficiency. I've also had a minor fear of being intentionally trapped and gunned down in a revolving door since seeing Carmine Cuneo get picked off that way in *The Godfather*. Granted, I'm probably not a high risk for rotating door assassination, but I'm aware of at least one magician and two authors in the Las Vegas area who are less than thrilled with the manner in which I reviewed their work on my podcast. I also never sit with my back to the door in restaurants, and I frequently travel with a pack of hired goons willing to take a bullet for me. Safety first.

Paris

www.parislv.com

PLAYERS CLUB: Total Rewards

UNOFFICIAL THEME: Bellagio's neighbor

Paris Las Vegas opened in the midst of the themed casino building boom of the late 1990s. Since then, the resort has shed many of its quirky Parisian touches, including street performers, employees greeting guests with "bonjour," and recorded French lessons playing in the restrooms. Despite this, Paris is still heavily themed, with numerous aspects of the property carrying pseudo-French names like Le Village Buffet, Le Bar Du Sport and Le Theatre des Arts. Apparently all it takes to Frenchify anything is to simply add "le" at the beginning. Le lazy, but le effective.

Jackpot: Paris features several architectural tips of the cap to its namesake, including replicas of the Arc de Triomphe, the Louvre façade, and the Alexander III Bridge. The hotel's most iconic structure is its half-sized replica of the Eiffel Tower. Located just feet from Las Vegas Boulevard, the tower has become one of the Strip's most unmistakable landmarks. The tower gives visitors the chance to view the Strip from an 11th story French restaurant and 46th story observation deck. The Eiffel Tower Restaurant's food is good but not exceptional; however, diners pay inflated prices for outstanding views of the Bellagio fountains across the street. The observation deck, dubbed the Eiffel Tower Experience, offers one of the Strip's best views. Compared to other opportunities to pay for an elevated view of the Strip (the High Roller Ferris wheel and the Stratosphere observation deck), the Eiffel Tower makes up for its lower height with a superior location.

Positioned between Planet Hollywood and Bally's, Paris is located in the Strip's sweet spot thanks to its proximity to Bellagio. Not only are the views from the Eiffel Tower outstanding, but many of the hotel rooms face the fountains as well. Everyone who loves a beautiful Strip view first thing in the morning and last thing at night wants to look out upon the Bellagio fountains. If waking up each morning with a gorgeous view improves the quality of your vacation, Paris should be on your short list. Although rooms lack the terraces that contribute to The Cosmopolitan's popularity, rates are significantly lower, offering a more affordable option with a similarly great view.

Location also contributes to the popularity of Mon Ami Gabi, one of the hotel's best restaurants. The food and service are usually great, but dining outdoors on an elevated patio directly across from the fountains really sets it apart. Even when the fountain show isn't active, the entertainment value from passing tourists is top notch. Enjoy breakfast while talking smack about how others are dressed, and play fun Las Vegas games, including Just Up or Still Up?, Spot the Foobs, and Ho or Not a Ho?

Paris also includes the finest of Gordon Ramsay's Las Vegas restaurants. Gordon Ramsay Steak has quickly become my favorite Las Vegas restaurant. When celebrating a special occasion with an expensive meal, Gordon Ramsay Steak has become the go-to choice. As you enter the dining room, your host or hostess will likely take you on a short tour of the restaurant, pointing out the neon sculpture hanging above. Supposedly, the swirly design represents the exact hand movements Ramsay makes when preparing the beef wellington. I just love my gourmet dinner served with a complimentary, double-sized portion of marketing flimflam. Regardless, the beef wellington has become one of a handful of food items—along with Pizza Rock's pizza, Andiamo's meatball, and American Coney's chili cheese fries—that I crave between trips. The flaky puff pastry and melt-in-your-mouth filet often inspire mouth-watering thoughts for weeks after dining there. With a side of mac and cheese, a couple cocktails, and salad, expect to spend at least $100 per person. I've never watched more than a few minutes of any of Ramsay's television shows, so I know him only as the chef who shouts a lot. If being a belligerent dickwad somehow inspires the menu at Gordon Ramsay Steak, keep yelling, Gordo.

Tilt: Caesars Entertainment owns Paris Las Vegas, along with Harrah's, The Linq, Flamingo, The Cromwell, Bally's, Planet Hollywood, Caesars Palace, and Rio. Unfortunately, the company doesn't do the greatest job maintaining its properties. For several years, the symbol of these shabby maintenance practices was the blue Paris balloon marquee. After more than a decade, the blue fabric panels became faded and looked tired. Finally, in 2013—several years and at least one picket-line protest after the marquee began showing its age—Caesars refurbished the sign. With the exception of the company's signature property, Caesars Palace, poor maintenance is the Caesars Entertainment way in Las Vegas. Several years ago, the company remodeled sections of Flamingo, rebranding them as Go rooms. Within a year, stains dotted the new hallway carpet and wallpaper began to peel. More recently, the remaining rooms at Flamingo, the South Tower (now Jubilee Tower) at Bally's, and all of the rooms at The Linq have been renovated. Paris is overdue for a similar facelift. The rooms still include massive armoires—a throwback to the pre-flat-screen TV days, and a telltale sign that a room hasn't been updated in far too many years. If they really wanted to drive home the point, each room would include a VCR. During a 2013 stay, I noticed my room had an ottoman next to the armoire. It didn't have a corresponding chair or match the room's other furnishings. I moved it aside to discover a three-by-three-foot carpet stain where another piece of wooden furniture previously sat. Rather than replace the carpeting, someone simply tried to hide the stain. Good enough. That's one of my biggest frustrations with Paris and the other Caesars hotels. The company considers "good enough" to be good enough.

Bally's

www.ballyslasvegas.com
PLAYERS CLUB: Total Rewards
UNOFFICIAL THEME: No-frills fun

Opened in 1973 as the original MGM Grand, Bally's history forever overshadows the property. On Nov. 21, 1980, one of the worst hotel fires in the nation's history claimed the lives of 85 guests. The tragedy led to much more stringent fire codes, including sprinkler requirements that would have prevented the MGM fire from spreading if they had been in place at the time of the blaze. The hotel became Bally's Las Vegas in 1985. Despite having two towers and nearly 3,000 rooms, Bally's is a fairly unassuming property. It is set farther back from the Strip than other casinos on the east side of Las Vegas Boulevard, and it has neither the theming of Strip casinos built in the 1990s nor the luxury of casinos built in more recent years. The hotel's exterior looks dated and dull. However, what it lacks in glitz, it makes up for with a handful of quirky features worth checking out.

Jackpot: Most Las Vegas casinos have buffets, but none come close to the quality, extravagance, and cost of Bally's Sterling Brunch. Open only on Sundays at BLT Steak, Sterling Brunch serves as much lobster tail, filet mignon, caviar, oysters, and Perrier Jouet champagne as you can suck down. This isn't close to being the largest buffet in Las Vegas, but its selection of uncommon buffet items makes it a special treat for diners wanting an indulgent dining experience. Ask your server about made-to-order items prepared in the kitchen to ensure you're getting the full value. At about $90 per person, arrive hungry and don't hesitate to drink champagne until you black out if you want to get the most for your dining dollar.

Another Bally's gem, the race and sports book resides deep in the bowels of the hotel. Getting to the sports book requires a journey through the casino, down the escalator and past the lineup of hokey shops. Gamblers may need to be in the same physical condition as the athletes they're planning to watch, but at least they'll have a decent shot at getting a seat when they arrive. The room is spacious and, because of its somewhat inconvenient location away from the casino floor, traffic is lighter than other area sports books. The room takes advantage of a remnant from its days as a movie theater—staggered theater seating, a nice and all-too-rare feature when watching games in Vegas.

Visitors seeking mid-priced accommodations with larger-than-average rooms may want to consider staying at Bally's. Between the two towers (Indigo and Jubilee), the hotel has a multitude of room styles and configurations. Basic rooms start at 430 square feet—spacious compared to other hotels in the same price range. Even rooms that haven't been renovated in recent years provide good value for the price.

Another quirky throwback to old Las Vegas, *Jubilee* remains the last of the city's showgirl-laden variety shows. Although it became a disjointed mess when revamped in 2014, the show still offers glimmers of the classic Vegas revues that once were commonplace. If you're able to score discounted tickets and can overlook the lame storyline, *Jubilee's* sparkly costumes, kitschy production numbers, and boobalicious showgirls are still worth checking out.

One additional throwback sets Bally's otherwise ho-hum swimming pool apart from its neighbors. Most Las Vegas hotel pools are waist-deep piss puddles. Bally's Blu Pool, however, plummets to a substantial 12-foot depth. Fortunately for guests who prefer a deep pool, owner Caesars Entertainment's cheapness trumps its lawyers' risk-averse paranoia. So until someone drowns or Caesars decides to turn the pool into a dayclub, even the tallest guests can fully submerge themselves.

Tilt: In early 2015, the Grand Bazaar Shops opened in the space between Las Vegas Boulevard and Bally's main entrance. The complex includes 150 small shops under a series of multi-colored pastel canopies that light up in an allegedly dazzling LED display every hour. I get the feeling this structure was put together using salvaged materials when plans for a Disneyland Easter Village fell through at the last minute. An attempt at a larger, upscale version of the Downtown Container Park, the Grand Bazaar Shops lacks the independent, rough-around-the-edges spirit that makes the container park interesting. Instead of a small handmade jewelry store, Grand Bazaar has a Swatch shop. Instead of a shop peddling unique handmade art, Grand Bazaar features a store selling prints from Disney films. The whole place miniaturizes the most boring aspects of a typical suburban shopping mall in a setting with all the charm of a flea market.

Caesars Palace

www.caesarspalace.com
PLAYERS CLUB: Total Rewards
UNOFFICIAL THEME: Size matters

When arriving at Caesars Palace, there's no confusion about where you are. The iconic fountains and replica statues of Greek and Roman gods may be a couple tipoffs. But it's the hotel name in bright orange letters plastered across the top of not one or two, but three separate Strip-facing towers, in addition to the marquee and the entrance from the Las Vegas Boulevard pedestrian overpass that signal you're visiting a property with no interest in subtlety.

Caesars Palace introduced the themed megaresort concept to Las Vegas in 1966 and continues to execute it better than any of its competitors more than 50 years later. The architecture, tower names (Forum, Roman, Palace, Augustus, and Octavius), showroom and shopping mall facades, artwork, and numerous other touches make Caesars Palace unmistakable, cohesive, and unique.

Legend has it that "Caesars" has no apostrophe because developer Jay Sarno wanted all guests to feel like they were Caesars, regardless of their origin, profession, or economic status. I suspect this story is one of the earliest examples of Las Vegas public relations bullshit. Most likely the apostrophe slipped through the cracks or simply looked less appealing in the logo mockups, so Sarno decided to exclude it and come up with a creative PR spin. The problem is that even if the "we're all Caesars" idea is accurate, the property should be called "Caesars' Palace." If Sarno were around today, he'd probably chronically use the wrong versions of "your" and "there" on Twitter too.

Jackpot: The poolside snack bar at Caesars Palace is named Snackus Maximus. Other than perhaps Excalibur's long-gone Lance-A-Lotta Pasta, no Las Vegas restaurant has had a better theme-related name in recent history. Celebrity sightings of Biggus Dickus and his wife, Incontinentia Buttox, are common at Snackus Maximus. There's a certain art in bastardizing the English language in this manner to fit a theme while maintaining familiarity. Done poorly, it comes across like your semi-racist Uncle Kenny, who thinks you can just add "el" or "los" to the beginning and "o" to the end of any word to convert it to Spanish. "I'd like el turkey sandwicho and los chipos with a small lemonado, por favor." Paris took this approach by adding "le" to everything. Caesars Palace makes it work a bit more gracefully.

Caesars Palace maintains a long tradition of popular entertainment options. One of the best showrooms in town, the Colosseum usually features headliners catering to Baby Boomers. Since opening in 2003, the Colosseum has been home to resident performers including Bette Midler, Cher, Elton John, Rod Stewart, Shania Twain, Mariah Carey, Jerry Seinfeld, and Celine Dion—Caesars Palace's signature performer. In recent years, Caesars has also hosted *Absinthe*, a raunchy circus-style variety show performed in a large tent in front of the hotel. No Las Vegas show receives more consistent audience raves than *Absinthe*. With the exceptions of prudes, religious zealots, and people who fear curse words, everybody loves *Absinthe*, making it one of the safest entertainment bets in town. Avoid the front rows unless you want to be part of the performance.

Tilt: Because Caesars Palace has expanded numerous times over the past 50 years, adding several hotel towers and the Forum Shops mall, the property layout is a sprawling clusterfuck. Guests should be assigned a personal navigator (Sherpus Navigatus) and fully equipped pack mule (Donkus Assistus) to ensure a safe and efficient journey. During my last visit, I stumbled over the skeletons of three ill-prepared tourists who misplaced their map, became disoriented, and ultimately perished on the 16th floor of the Octavius Tower without reaching their destination—the Field of Dreams store, where football legend Dick Butkus was signing autographs. Godspeed, Bears fans.

In 2013, Caesars Palace completed renovations of its outdated Centurian Tower, rebranding it as Nobu Hotel—a separate hotel within the Caesars Palace complex. Although Nobu is well-designed and luxurious, placing a Japanese-themed boutique hotel in the midst of an otherwise cohesive Roman-empire-themed resort makes about as much sense as having Pizza Hut cater a Civil War reenactment. Even though everyone already knows the whole thing is a sham, when the people responsible for carrying out the theme don't even fully commit, how can guests be expected to buy into it? "Here at Caesars Palace, we're all Caesars... except the people staying in the Nobu Hotel. They're Hirohitos."

The Cromwell

www.thecromwell.com
PLAYERS CLUB: Total Rewards
UNOFFICIAL THEME: Rooftop oontz

Surrounded by towering monstrosities including Flamingo, Bally's, Caesars Palace, and Bellagio, The Cromwell's unassuming 11-story building almost gets lost, despite its location on one of the busiest intersections in Las Vegas. At a time when many hotels purport to offer a boutique experience, The Cromwell is one of few true boutique hotels in the city. It contains fewer than 200 rooms and offers guests several small but pleasant perks, including complimentary sangria delivered to the room shortly after check-in, and a coffee and tea station outside the elevator on the casino level. Rooms are compact but elegantly designed, making exceptional use of limited space.

Jackpot: At many Strip resorts, getting from a hotel room to the street includes a long walk to the elevator, a seemingly lengthy wait for an elevator to arrive, stops on several other floors, and a walk through a large casino and past several shops before finally arriving outside. Because of The Cromwell's tiny footprint, guests leaving their room are rarely more than three or four minutes from the street. This may seem like a minor convenience, but after experiencing it, you'll find the long treks at other hotels to be excessively daunting.

The Cromwell has a relatively tiny casino, one restaurant (Giada), and a few bars, but they are all secondary features compared to the hotel's centerpiece, Drai's Beach Club and Nightclub. This rooftop club's gorgeous design and amazing views appeal to even those of us who don't otherwise care about the club scene. Hotel guests get free admission and can enjoy the space without the party during weekdays, when it functions as the hotel pool area. Add Drai's After Hours, the early-morning club located below the casino, and The Cromwell offers an around-the-clock party during warm-weather months, when the beach club is open.

Tilt: Unfortunately, the around-the-clock, club-centric aspect of The Cromwell comes with a price. The loud bass thump from the rooftop permeates many of the hotel rooms. Traffic noise from Flamingo Road can be disruptive as well. Light sleepers should request a room near the back, facing north. The problem with many north-facing rooms, however, is the view. When converting the building from Bill's Gamblin' Hall, additional support was needed to handle the weight of the new rooftop pool complex. This support came in the form of a massive wall on the north side of the hotel, near Las Vegas Boulevard. As a result, many of the rooms face a wall. If a view is important, request a near-Strip, south-facing room. You may see the Bellagio fountains, but you'll also likely hear the previously mentioned club noise pounding from above.

Flamingo

www.flamingolv.com
PLAYERS CLUB: Total Rewards
UNOFFICIAL THEME: Neon and stomach cramps

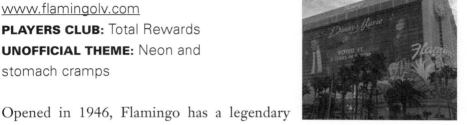

Opened in 1946, Flamingo has a legendary history—much of it clouded by myths. The image of mobster Bugsy Siegel having a vision of what would become the Las Vegas Strip, which inspired him to build the Flamingo, is Hollywood myth. Bugsy took over the hotel when construction was well underway. However, his inability to control spending and the hotel's bungled grand opening are likely part of what led to his murder in 1947. Although nothing from the original 77-room hotel remains, a memorial plaque near the wedding chapel commemorates Bugsy's ownership. Today, Flamingo includes four hotel towers containing more than 3,500 rooms.

Jackpot: Near the Bugsy plaque, Flamingo offers a unique refuge from the madness of the Strip. The hotel's Wildlife Habitat is home to a variety of fish and birds, including ducks, swans and, of course, flamingos. Turtles sunning themselves on the habitat's rocks provide a calming environment for gamblers coming to grips with their ill-advised decision to place a grand on a 16 seed over a 1 seed in the NCAA men's basketball tournament. Don't bother whining to the koi. Fish don't give a shit about your problems.

Just beyond The Wildlife Habitat is one of the nicer pool areas on the Strip for a hotel in Flamingo's lower to moderate room rate range. Over the past several years, Flamingo has been trying different tactics to maximize use of this space. For a while, the smaller of two pools was a topless, adults-only pool. When the topless pool trend tapered off, Flamingo changed gears again. Now, the small pool is the family-friendly Beach Club Pool. The large Lagoon Pool is the Go Pool, open only to ages 21 and up. It seems Flamingo is attempting to turn it into a pseudodayclub with DJs cranking the oontz and go-go dancers shaking their asses. Don't be surprised if this concept turns out to be short-lived. Many of Flamingo's guests aren't cut out for a Cosmopolitanesque pool experience. Still, Flamingo's pool grounds are lush and inviting, making the hotel a worthy consideration for budget travelers who enjoy some time in the sun.

Flamingo also provides a glimpse of the days when colorful neon signs lined Las Vegas Boulevard. Unfortunately, most of them have been replaced by modern LED video screens, which are effective but not nearly as cool. Flamingo's giant orange, red, and pink neon feathers are among the few iconic Strip neon signs still welcoming visitors.

Tilt: One of my few self-imposed rules in Las Vegas is to never dine at Flamingo. I've given their restaurants several chances, but no more. I'm done. I've experienced slow service and soggy fries at the cafe; bland, flavorless everything at the buffet; and nuclear orange artificial cheese goo at Carlos' 'n Charlie's. Fool me once, shame on you. Fool me twice, shame on me. Fool me a third time… well, that's on me again, but I was drunk. That's it though. I draw the line at three foolings.

The food at Margaritaville gets consistently high marks, and everybody seems to be having a great time there. However, I refuse to subject myself to a voluntary ear-raping by Jimmy Buffett's *Socks, Sandals, and Sunshine* album while trying to enjoy some volcano nachos.

Another reason I avoid food at Flamingo is the presence of cockroaches. Several years ago while enjoying drinks at Bugsy's Bar with friends, a two-inch-long cockroach leisurely strolled across the bar. We pointed this out to a bartender, who shrugged and brushed the roach onto the floor, signaling that its presence was neither rare nor problematic. Until that point, I assumed the bar's name honored Bugsy Siegel. Unfortunately, cockroaches have been seen in Flamingo hotel rooms as well, as reported in a 2012 Fab Room review from *VegasTripping*, so my experience wasn't a one-off aberration.

The Linq

www.thelinq.com

PLAYERS CLUB: Total Rewards

UNOFFICIAL THEME: Airport Concourse B

Anchored by a shiny, new outdoor promenade of shops and restaurants leading to the High Roller Ferris wheel, The Linq is a newly renovated, rebranded hotel and casino built on the architectural bones of longtime dumpy but fun casinos Imperial Palace and O'Sheas. Briefly named The Quad in 2012 before taking on The Linq name as part of a 2014 hotel upgrade, this property is pleasant, but much more sterile and generic than most of its competitors. If located in almost anywhere else in America, The Linq would be the nicest casino in the state. However, in Las Vegas, it's just boring.

Jackpot: The Linq Promenade, High Roller, and renovated casino opened in 2014. Among the highlights are:

- **O'Sheas:** A tribute to the former Strip-side Irish bar and casino by the same name, the smaller, relocated version has less character than its namesake. However, it is still a hit among the beer pong crowd that inhabited the original location in its last few years. Gambling options include low-limit blackjack and bartop video poker. O'Sheas offers a respectable selection of as many as 60 beers, and drink specials are common. Even when the rest of the casino is sleepy, O'Sheas is lively and energetic.

- **Brooklyn Bowl:** Modeled after the original New York location by the same name, this multi-purpose entertainment venue has quickly become one of the best Strip locations to check out national touring musical acts. With a capacity of 2,000, Brooklyn Bowl has featured concerts by acts including Jane's Addiction, Wu-Tang Clan, The Avett Brothers, and The Roots. Bowling is available on 32 lanes for $25-$30 for 30 minutes (plus $5 shoe rental fee per person). Skip the restaurant. The food is underwhelming.

- **3535:** This casino bar's focus is infused liquors. Featured drinks include thin mint, made with Mint-Oreo-infused vodka;

pig newton, made with bacon-infused bourbon; and cocorita, made with coconut-infused tequila. Drinks are $13, but gamblers snaring one of the few video poker machines pay just $2.

- **Tag Sports Bar:** Another casino bar, Tag's main attraction is beer. With more than 300 options, unique beer cocktails, and self-serve draft tables, Tag has quickly become the best casino bar for beer drinkers in the city.

- **Hash House a Go Go:** With several Las Vegas locations, Hash House serves up grotesquely large portions of American comfort food. Their breakfast scrambles and hashes are perfect hangover killers after a night of boozing.

Tilt: Looming behind the hotel, The Linq's most prominent attraction is the High Roller Ferris wheel. The public relations reps hate when people refer to it as a Ferris wheel rather than an observation wheel, but tough shit. It's a Ferris wheel. As Las Vegas attractions go, the High Roller is fine—not horrible, and not great, just fine. With rides lasting about 30 minutes, the 550-foot-high wheel offers some nice views of the center Strip once you ascend above the adjacent parking garages. However, if you have a high Strip-facing hotel room in the area, your window view likely beats it. There's nothing noteworthy to see to the east of the Strip, so if your room faces Caesars Palace or the Fountains of Bellagio, skip the High Roller. If you decide to ride it, discounts should be relatively easy to find. Because the High Roller hasn't attracted the anticipated crowds, diamond and seven stars Total Rewards members can get free passes, as can Total Rewards credit card holders. Some Caesars properties are offering passes along with hotel room offers, and casino employees have been known to pass out free drink tickets redeemable with a ticket purchase. Searching online for current deals and asking casino employees if they're aware of any discounts may be worthwhile.

One popular High Roller ticket package includes riding in a pod with an open bar for a few extra bucks. As a result, some riders attempting to get their money's worth approach the High Roller as a challenge: How much booze can they suck down in 30 minutes? Many have found between six and eight to be reasonable with nothing more than an empty bladder, a can-do attitude, and a generous tip for the bartender.

Among The Linq's restaurants is Guy Fieri's Vegas Kitchen and Bar. The *Diners, Drive-Ins and Dives* host's restaurant should be called Hey, What's in the Fridge? because it serves bar food that seems to incorporate every ingredient within the chef's reach. Appetizers include the guy-talian fondue dippers—crispy breadsticks wrapped in pepperoni and covered with shaved parmesan cheese, served with fondue sauce topped with chopped tomato, basil, and sausage. The burger selection includes the mac-n-cheese bacon burger—exactly what it sounds like. Order fries and you'll receive a mishmash of waffle fries, shoestring fries, home fries, and crinkle fries. Rather than giving diners a choice or simply offering one type, Guy's throws everything together. Fieri's flavor rampage makes the Taco Bell menu seem subtle and nuanced. Stoners and junk food aficionados love this place. However, if you just want a decent burger or sandwich that hasn't been violently assaulted with flavor, you can do better just about anywhere on the Strip.

Harrah's

www.harrahslasvegas.com
PLAYERS CLUB: Total Rewards
UNOFFICIAL THEME: Dullsville

Harrah's opened in 1973 as Holiday Casino and was rebranded following an ownership change in 1992. For many years, the hotel was part of the Holiday Inn chain, and the whole place still feels that way—casual, comfortable, and clean with no flash, flair, or zing. The property isn't particularly objectionable, but it lacks excitement. The most lively part of the hotel is the Carnival Court, located outside, between Harrah's and The Linq.

Jackpot: Harrah's is home to one of the city's most legendary lounge acts—Big Elvis. Performing on the Las Vegas Strip since 2002, Pete "Big Elvis" Vallee draws audiences intrigued by the novelty of an impersonator who makes Vegas-era Elvis seem svelte. However, he isn't some overweight hack who just grew out his sideburns, bought a jumpsuit, and learned a bunch of Elvis tunes. This guy absolutely nails Elvis's voice and style. You'll be hard-pressed to find a more entertaining tribute to The King in Las Vegas. Best of all, his show is free in the Piano Bar most weekday afternoons.

Tilt: In the center of the casino at Harrah's stands a creepy statue of Buck and Winnie Greenback—a fictional tourist couple who just struck it rich at Harrah's. Sporting green pants covered with dollar symbols, a white leather jacket with a giant dollar bill on the back, and a Harrah's cowboy hat, Buck is carrying a suitcase bursting with cash. Based on the outfit only an insane serial killer would wear, I'm pretty sure the suitcase also contains a severed human head. Winnie is wearing a low-cut, belly-revealing top and tight yellow pants. Her purse is also bursting with cash. Although masquerading as Buck's wife, it's obvious that Winnie is a $20 Texas truck-stop hooker. A little-known second Greenback statue portraying Buck burying Winnie's body in a shallow grave in the desert was created at the same time as the one displayed at Harrah's. Its whereabouts are unknown.

The Mirage

www.mirage.com

PLAYERS CLUB: Mlife

UNOFFICIAL THEME: Fabulous Germans in paradise

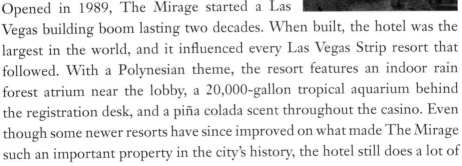

Opened in 1989, The Mirage started a Las Vegas building boom lasting two decades. When built, the hotel was the largest in the world, and it influenced every Las Vegas Strip resort that followed. With a Polynesian theme, the resort features an indoor rain forest atrium near the lobby, a 20,000-gallon tropical aquarium behind the registration desk, and a piña colada scent throughout the casino. Even though some newer resorts have since improved on what made The Mirage such an important property in the city's history, the hotel still does a lot of things well.

Jackpot: Why put a volcano replica in front of a hotel and just yards from Las Vegas Boulevard? For one, this is Las Vegas, where "why not?" is a more apt question. The Mirage volcano ensures the hotel appears in just about every television show and movie set in Las Vegas. If there's an establishing shot showing the Las Vegas Strip, The Mirage volcano nearly always make the cut. It has become an iconic landmark and a must-see free attraction. The four-minute, Strip-side fire, water, and light show choreographed to a percussive soundtrack by The Grateful Dead's Mickey Hart erupts nightly at 8 and 9 p.m., with an extra 10 p.m. show on weekends.

Another impressive spectacle, *The Beatles Love* combines the acrobatics, dancing, and over-the-top production values of Cirque du Soleil with the classic songs of The Beatles. Unless you're one of the ten people on the planet who dislikes The Beatles, *Love* won't disappoint. The storyline incorporates bits of the band's history and lyrics, but like most Cirque shows the perfectly timed choreography of dozens of performers is equally captivating.

Before Cirque overtook the city's entertainment scene, two names were synonymous with Las Vegas—Siegfried and Roy. Unfortunately, in 2003, Montecore the tiger turned Roy into a mid-show chew toy, ending the magicians' reign as kings of The Mirage. Even though their show has become another chapter in the Las Vegas entertainment history books, a couple attractions from the Siegfried and Roy era remain. Next to the sidewalk in front of the hotel, a large bronze statue of the magicians and one of their tigers makes a great setting for cheesy tourist photos. What better Christmas card backdrop than the gigantic craniums of two flamboyant Bavarians and their beloved white tiger? If mere statuary only whets your appetite for another dose of Siegfried and Roy's world, several animals from their exotic cat menagerie live in the Secret Garden and Dolphin Habitat. For about $20, guests can visit the mini-zoo to see a variety of tigers, lions, panthers, leopards, and bottlenose dolphins. Many years ago, while awaiting the start of a tour of the Secret Garden, I was treated to one of my favorite unintentionally comedic Las Vegas moments. The tour guide rattled off a few basic rules: don't attempt to feed the animals, stick to the sidewalks and observation areas, and don't smoke. From the back of our group rose the gravelly, two-packs-a-day-since-1975 voice of a nicotine angel, who expressed her dismay at having limitations being placed on her fun. "Well, this better be a good habitat." For moments like that alone, I love Las Vegas. And fortunately for Selma, it was a good habitat.

For visitors who prefer eating animals over watching them play, nap, and poop, The Mirage has amassed an impressive collection of restaurants, covering all the Strip casino essentials. Cravings Buffet offers a selection on par with similarly priced buffets (Planet Hollywood and Paris), but with slightly better quality. Plus, unlimited beer and wine are included at no additional charge—a rarity on the Strip. BLT Burger offers one of the best gourmet burger options in town. Its menu features more than a dozen specialty burgers and some amazing spiked milkshakes. The I-80 burger (bacon, BBQ sauce, caramelized onions, and cheddar cheese) with a grandma's treat milkshake (Maker's Mark, caramel, and vanilla ice cream) makes my ample tummy gurgle with joy. Pantry offers dependable, but overpriced comfort food (burgers, fish and chips, fried chicken) and 24-hour breakfasts, while Carnegie Deli stuffs diners with oversized sandwiches and legendary cheesecake—much like the New York original location. Preparing meat in wood-burning ovens and on charcoal grills, Tom Colicchio's Heritage Steak is among the best celebrity-chef steakhouses in Las Vegas. The steaks are delicious, and the spicy onion rings are among the best in town.

Tilt: Featuring a small indoor bar and a larger outdoor patio on the Strip, Rhumbar offers fantastic tropical drinks, cigars, and hookah. Unfortunately, it also features an unadvertised concession fee. The operator adds this mystery charge as though it's a required tax. Other Strip establishments that charge this fee, ranging from 3 percent to 5 percent, include Cabo Wabo Cantina (Planet Hollywood), Señor Frog's (Treasure Island), Double Barrel Roadhouse (Monte Carlo), Hexx (Paris), and Casa Fuente (Caesars Palace). Fees usually appear on the bill as "CSF" or "CNF," and menus may or may not disclose the fee in tiny print, depending on the bar/restaurant. This practice is deceitful and lame.

Another bummer at The Mirage, the hotel has plastered the exterior of the top several stories of the hotel with advertisements for *The Beatles Love*. As I already mentioned, it's a fine show, worthy of a splashy marketing campaign. However, these window wraps, common throughout Las Vegas, suck for guests. They obscure otherwise stunning views with a net-like cover. Forget about getting any decent photos from your room window. You may as well take them through a spaghetti strainer because you'll get the same effect. What's especially unusual about The Mirage wrap is its location at the top of the hotel, where the property's suites reside. So guests paying a premium for their rooms are treated to sub-premium views.

Casino Royale

www.casinoroyalehotel.com

PLAYERS CLUB: Casino Royale Players Club

UNOFFICIAL THEME: Slumming it

Tired of upscale mixology bars, fancy gourmet restaurants, and casinos that feel more like museums? Head to Casino Royale, the tiny hotel and casino dwarfed by next-door neighbors The Venetian and Harrah's. Casino Royale's hotel stands just four stories high with only 154 rooms and 22,000 square feet, making it among the Strip's smallest casinos. Despite its size, Casino Royale offers a surprisingly large variety of mediocre chain restaurant options, including Outback Steakhouse, Denny's, White Castle, Subway, Noble Roman's Pizza, and Cinnabon.

Jackpot: Casino Royale serves up some cheap alternatives to surrounding megaresorts. The casino frequently offers low table game limits, including $5 blackjack, $3 craps, and 50-cent roulette. For years, Casino Royale has sold bottled Michelob and Michelob Light for $1, and other drinks are just a buck or two more. The casino is free of pretense, promising a cheap buzz and a reasonable chance to stretch a small gambling bankroll.

Tilt: For more than 15 years, Casino Royale has proudly boasted that the Travel Channel named it the world's #1 best place to strike it rich. This honor was part of a show that first aired in 2000, based on the casino offering 100x odds on craps bets. Even when the maximum odds bet shrunk to 20x for several years, Casino Royale continued to proclaim its #1 status. I can't blame Casino Royale. That show was probably the last mention the place had on national television. And unless the Travel Channel produces a show on the top 10 weirdest casino odors, it's unlikely to receive another #1 ranking any time soon.

Speaking of odors, Casino Royale is home to the only White Castle west of Missouri. If you're excited about visiting the Las Vegas White Castle, you most certainly don't live in an area served by the fast-food chain, you're super drunk, or both. Sober people who have easy access to White Castle tend to stay away because the food isn't particularly good, and the burgers may induce diarrhea. They aren't called sliders for nothing. That said, when adequately hammered, a dozen little White Castle burgers taste like manna from hangover heaven.

Casino Royale also boasts the highest grossing Denny's restaurant in the world. Denny's is fine for what it is. The restaurant serves cheap diner food quickly. But when you're on vacation, do you really want to waste a meal at a restaurant you can have any day of the week at home? The Strip and Fremont Street have hundreds of dining options, and for the same price or just a few bucks more you can expand your horizons and have a new experience unavailable elsewhere.

The Venetian/The Palazzo

www.venetian.com **and** www.palazzo.com

PLAYERS CLUB: Grazie

UNOFFICIAL THEME: Corporate dorkwads and tomato sauce

Much like other themed resorts, The Venetian provides a sterile, Disneyfied version of the city that inspired it. Stroll cobblestone streets and dine at St. Mark's Place without being pestered by pigeons, or take a gondola ride without exposure to atmospheric canal stink. (If you experience atmospheric canal stink, shower immediately. If the condition persists, see a doctor post haste.) Opened in 1999, The Venetian includes several architectural nods to familiar Venice landmarks, including Rialto Bridge, Piazza San Marco, and St. Mark's Campanile. Adorned with frescos, marble, and plenty of pseudo-gold plating, parts of the building look more like a cathedral than a hotel or casino. In 2007, The Palazzo opened as a separate but complementary hotel and casino connected to The Venetian.

Jackpot: The Venetian/Palazzo restaurant lineup is massive, with more than three dozen options between the two hotels and Grand Canal Shoppes. Celebrity chefs who have leased their names to restaurants here (in other words, don't expect to see them on property) include Buddy

"Cake Boss" Valastro, Emeril Lagasse, Mario Batali, and Wolfgang Puck. Standouts include Thomas Keller's Bouchon for its popular brunch and Emeril's Delmonico Steakhouse for great meat. Public House offers one of the best beer menus on the Strip, but the food is hit-or-miss. While most of the dining options skew upscale, food courts in the mall and casino offer several fast-food choices. Oddly enough, despite its variety of restaurants, neither The Venetian nor The Palazzo offers a buffet—a rare omission on the Las Vegas Strip.

In addition to Delmonico and another restaurant, Table 10, Emeril has also created the menu for the massive Palazzo sports book/bar, Lagasse's Stadium. The food is decent enough sports bar cuisine, but above all else Lagasse's offers an amazing space for watching any game. The room includes table, couch, lounge, bar, and countertop seating, some of it arranged in stadium-style tiers. The room seats 500 and includes more than 120 screens. Despite the large capacity, demand is high for seating during major events. Contact the restaurant in advance for reservations and food/beverage minimum details.

At 650 and 720 square feet respectively, The Venetian and The Palazzo hotel rooms provide an abundance of space for square footage junkies. Although labeled as suites (because Las Vegas hotels have successfully bastardized the term to mean absolutely nothing), each room's living area and bedroom flow together, separated only by a short wall and a couple stairs. Still, the extra space makes the rooms ideal for lounging or working— common here because of the attached Sands Convention Center.

At a time when many Las Vegas resorts have deemphasized themes, The Venetian and The Palazzo have not. Visitors to the Grand Canal Shoppes can enjoy/endure street performers, including living statues, singers, and hourly "Streetmosphere" performances, including costumed opera singers in St. Mark's Square. Some of these acts are more annoying than entertaining, but I give credit to owner Las Vegas Sands for keeping street performers because they contribute to the theme even though they don't directly contribute to the bottom line.

For about $19 per person, guests who are trying to capture the full Venice experience can take an indoor or outdoor gondola ride, complete with a singing gondolier. The rides last only about 10 minutes, however, so you may want to skip the boat ride and just enjoy watching them glide past.

Because they have an abundance of performance space—three theaters and a showroom—the resorts usually have several different entertainment options of varying quality. Among recent resident shows is *Human Nature: The Motown Show*. If you dig classic Motown music, definitely see it. An Australian boy band may not be the logical act for a Motown tribute show, but these four guys don't disappoint.

Tilt: Las Vegas brings in a lot of conference business, so seeing people wearing nametag-adorned $99 Joseph A. Banks suits occurs pretty much everywhere on the Strip. Because The Venetian includes the large Sands Convention Center, the property frequently has a higher concentration of corporate dorkwads than other area hotels. I have a certain illogical contempt for these people. It makes little sense—I've been one of them several times. Still, when I'm wandering through a casino and pass a group of people wearing nametags, I disdainfully think, "corporate shmucks." They're not doing anything especially annoying, other than wearing nametags and spewing corporate buzzwords outside of the actual convention center. Perhaps overhearing people talk about "paradigm shifts" and "synergy" jolts me out of my blissful vacation haze and reminds me of the world I'm trying to escape for a few days. So, if you have an aversion to blowhard conventioneers like I do, The Venetian and The Palazzo may not be your ideal hangouts.

Another factor that may offend some visitors is The Venetian's scent. Most Las Vegas resorts pump in scents to enhance the theme and mask less appealing odors. Much like colognes and perfumes, these scents appeal to or repulse people in a variety of ways. Since opening, The Venetian's scent has always seemed cranked up a little higher than many others, although Flamingo and Aria are close. I used to enjoy the scent simply because it was uniquely Vegas. Upon returning home from a trip, I could still catch a whiff of the smell in my clothing before tossing them in the washing machine—a last olfactory reminder of Las Vegas. Now, I'm a little more sensitive to strong scents, so I find it more annoying than enjoyable. If you have a particularly sensitive sniffer, The Venetian and The Palazzo may not be ideal places to spend your time.

Treasure Island

www.treasureisland.com
PLAYERS CLUB: TI Players Club
UNOFFICIAL THEME: Generic mediocrity

Some Las Vegas hotels inspire dreams of staying there forever. Your room feels more comfortable than home, the service makes you feel like a celebrity, and you can't imagine ever tiring of the restaurants. Treasure Island is not that hotel, nor does it try to be. Treasure Island is the place you stay because it's located near the hotels you'd like to call home, but it's cheaper. Treasure Island is unapologetically middle-of-the-road, offering a basic version of everything but with few frills. The name of the players club is TI Players Club. That's the same level of creativity and imagination that permeates the property.

Jackpot: Surrounded by more upscale hotels, including Wynn, Encore, The Palazzo, The Venetian, and The Mirage, Treasure Island is a great value in an otherwise pricey neighborhood. If the underwhelming casino and restaurant lineup don't hold your attention, escaping to a nicer resort couldn't be easier. A free tram takes visitors to The Mirage approximately every 10 minutes.

When Phil Ruffin acquired Treasure Island from previous owner MGM Resorts, he inherited the original Las Vegas Cirque du Soleil show, *Mystère*. Although Cirque shows are a matter of personal preference, people who typically like Cirque rave about *Mystère*. Packed with impressive acrobatic stunts, colorful costumes, and plenty of Cirque's signature what-the-hell-was-that weirdness, *Mystère* has dazzled and entertained at Treasure Island since 1993. No matter how good this show may be, however, there's no excuse for including a full-grown man in a diaper, imitating a baby. That shit is just plain creepy.

Tilt: Treasure Island has all the personality of a suburban shopping mall, complete with the requisite Starbucks just feet from the Strip. Nightlife options include Kahunaville (a generic version of Margaritaville), Señor Frog's (an outpost of the Mexican party bar), and Gilley's Saloon (a cowboy bar best known as the inspiration for a movie nobody under the age of 40 has seen)—all perfect options for 30- and 40-somethings still trying to recapture the magic of their college spring break trip to Cancun.

From 1993 until 2003, Treasure Island featured bad-ass, staged pirate battles between two ships in Buccaneer Bay, the cove between the hotel and Las Vegas Boulevard. It was one of the few redeeming aspects of the short-lived family-friendly push of the 1990s. When the hotel stripped many pirate-themed elements from the hotel, including the rad skull and crossbones marquee, it recreated the free Strip-side show as Sirens. Featuring choreographed dancing in place of its action-packed predecessor, the show sucked. But still, free show. In 2013, Sirens was killed off, and corporate pirates claimed a chunk of Buccaneer Bay for use as a CVS convenience store.

NONGAMING HOTELS

Few things feel like Las Vegas as much as that moment when you leave your hotel room, get on the elevator, and seconds later find yourself in the middle of the action—music blaring, slot machines singing, and dice players cheering. For novice Las Vegas visitors, staying in a hotel without a casino is like living in your parents' house while going to college. You're missing out on the full experience, and in both cases that experience may involve getting drunk, passing out, and having your friends draw dicks on your face. However, once you've become a Las Vegas veteran and the novelty of the full Las Vegas experience has dulled a bit, nongaming hotels are worth considering.

Visitors seeking some refuge amidst the overall madness will appreciate having a Fortress of Solitude when they need a break. Without casinos or nightclubs on site, these hotels maintain a lower energy level than their bustling neighbors and feel more like luxury hotels in other major cities. Returning to your hotel allows you to flip a switch, turning off Las Vegas for a while without straying too far from the action. Many of these hotels also offer a great bang for the buck—more space and additional amenities, frequently including a kitchen. While the restaurant scene in Las Vegas is far too great to waste time whipping up your mom's legendary slow-roasted garlic chicken in your hotel room, a fridge for beverages and leftovers, and a microwave to warm those leftovers can come in handy. Because many of these rooms are actually timeshare condos that function as hotel rooms when owners aren't using them, they frequently include a washer and dryer, making them exceptional options for lengthy trips. Several nongaming hotels are located on or within an extremely short walk of the Strip.

Delano
www.delanolasvegas.com

Formerly THEhotel, Delano adjoins Mandalay Bay. The hotel operates its own café, coffee shop, bar, spa, and pool. Because the hotel elevators are mere feet from the casino floor, Delano feels like a Mandalay Bay hotel tower rather than a separate hotel.

Elara
www.elaralasvegas.com

A Hilton Grand Vacations timeshare property connected to Planet Hollywood via the Miracle Mile Shops, Elara opened in 2009. The hotel includes its own pool, lobby bar, and fitness room. Elara is part of the Hilton Hhonors loyalty program. Unfortunately, staying here will likely result in future solicitations to buy a timeshare.

Four Seasons
www.fourseasons.com/lasvegas

Occupying the top five floors of Mandalay Bay, Four Seasons has quick-and-easy access to the casino. However, Four Seasons amenities, including Charlie Palmer Steak, Veranda Italian restaurant, lobby bar, spa, and pool, are a bit more secluded. As with Four Seasons hotels in other major cities, this location excels at exceptional, personal service. For example, guests have access to the hotel's car service for free transportation anywhere within three miles.

Hilton Grand Vacation Suites at Flamingo

www.hilton.com/lasvegas

Located behind Flamingo, this HGV timeshare property includes a pool, deli, and fitness room. Guests may also use Flamingo's pools, which are just steps away. Exhibitionist guests should request a room on a low floor so they can get their rocks off by flashing riders on the passing monorail. As with Elara, expect timeshare pitches during and after your stay.

Mandarin Oriental

www.mandarinoriental.com/lasvegas

Located between The Shops at Crystals and Monte Carlo, Mandarin Oriental offers swanky rooms and unmatched service. Among its finest features are hidden gems Mandarin Bar and MOzen Bistro. Located on the 23rd floor, Mandarin Bar boasts one of the best views on the Strip. MOzen Bistro functions as an Asian restaurant for lunch and dinner and serves an outstanding American breakfast and brunch. The hotel also offers a French restaurant, tea lounge, spa, pool, and—like Four Seasons—complimentary car service.

The Signature at MGM Grand

www.signaturemgmgrand.com

Each of three Signature towers located behind MGM Grand offers its own swimming pool. They share a deli (tower 2), lounge (tower 1), and coffee shop (tower 1). Towers 1 and 3 have fitness rooms. The indoor walk to MGM Grand takes just three to five minutes, depending on the tower. Because MGM Grand is so massive, the walk from The Signature to the Strip takes more like 15-20 minutes.

Trump International

www.trumphotelcollection.com/las-vegas

Sitting near the back of Fashion Show Mall, Trump International features surprisingly stylish accommodations, despite carrying the stamp of gaudiness—Donald Trump's name. Unfortunately, the isolated location not far from active railroad tracks makes a stay there inconvenient and possibly noisy. Trump has a restaurant, pool, and spa. The hotel provides a guest shuttle to Wynn and Caesars Palace.

Vdara

www.vdara.com

Nestled behind The Cosmopolitan, Vdara offers the benefits of a nongaming hotel but just a five-minute walk to Bellagio, Aria, or Cosmo. The hotel, which opened in 2009 as part of MGM Resorts' multi-property CityCenter development, offers a spa, salon, pool, deli/coffee shop, and lobby bar. Shortly after opening, Vdara made news when pool loungers received significant burns from the sun's reflection off the hotel. Umbrellas now protect guests from the otherwise dangerous Vdara Death Ray.

CHAPTER 11

North Strip Hotels and Casinos

Venturing north along Las Vegas Boulevard begins well enough as you encounter Wynn and Encore—two of the most luxurious resorts on the Strip. Unfortunately, after that you'll encounter a no man's land of dirt lots, shady strip malls, unfinished construction projects and only three other casinos—Circus Circus, SLS, and Stratosphere. Developers have announced plans for a few new resorts and other projects on the north end of the Strip. Until they become reality, it's a little bleak north of Sands Avenue.

Wynn/Encore

www.wynnlasvegas.com
PLAYERS CLUB: Red Card
UNOFFICIAL THEME: Rich guy fanciness with a splash of crazy

No single person in recent history has put his mark on Las Vegas Boulevard like Steve Wynn. Building The Mirage in 1989 sparked a 20-year boom and set a new standard for Vegas megaresorts. With Bellagio, he brought a level of elegance never before seen on the Strip. When he built Wynn and Encore, he doubled down on luxury but made it feel more fun and inviting. Where Bellagio sometimes comes across as stuffy and stodgy, Wynn and Encore feel bright, lively, and welcoming.

Jackpot: Wynn, which opened in 2005, and Encore, which followed in 2008, pride themselves on providing personal service in a full-scale Las Vegas resort setting. To test their capabilities, I encourage guests to call the front desk from their rooms with odd requests. If it's 3 a.m. and you ask to have your bathtub filled with mayonnaise, Wynn should be able to meet your needs. Of course, the joke may not seem quite as funny when you're greeted with a $4,500 condiment charge at checkout. Regardless, expect an abundance of smiles and "good mornings" as you walk through the hotel. These small gestures may not seem like a big deal, but they set the tone for a pleasant visit.

Tucked behind Wynn and Encore sits the Wynn Golf Course, the Strip's only public course (the nearby Las Vegas Country Club is accessible only to members). Strip-adjacent land is a valuable, precious commodity, so using 137 acres as green space for golf doesn't make sense for most property owners. At $500 a round per player, Wynn squeezes plenty of revenue from the land, however. I'm not a golfer. I experience enough frustration without voluntarily subjecting myself to the irritation of trying to club a tiny ball into a cup-sized hole two blocks away. Whenever I see travelers lugging their Volkswagen-sized golf bags through an airport, I question whether the inconvenience is worth it. I have a difficult time believing most of these people play at a level that necessitates using their own equipment over rentals. That said, if someone ponies up $500 for a round of golf, he probably wants his beloved clubs to share in the experience. Hell, for $500 I'd understand if he wanted to lug along his dead father's corpse to show that son of a bitch that he amounted to something. Unfortunately, the Wynn Golf Course prohibits corpses. It's listed in the course rules, right under No Bare Feet.

Wynn and Encore offer some of the city's best fine dining options, including several with outdoor patio seating. Nothing at Wynn comes cheap, so expect to rack up some hefty dining charges when staying there. Most of the restaurants receive consistently positive reviews, but the quality carries a substantial price tag.

The Country Club overlooks the golf course's 18th hole waterfall and remains one of the Strip's hidden gems. Jazz brunch on Sundays may not offer filet mignon, lobster tails, and caviar like Bally's Sterling Brunch, but for $65 (vs. $90 at Bally's), the value is excellent and the atmosphere is far better. For lunch, The Country Club offers a small selection of salads, sandwiches, burgers, and steaks. Averaging about $18 for a sandwich or burger, the prices are comparable to Wynn's Terrace Point Café, but in a nicer setting.

Nobody matches Wynn and Encore for vegan dining options. Thanks to Steve Wynn's adoption of a vegan diet several years ago, all Wynn and Encore restaurants offer vegan menu items. Unlike most restaurants, where vegan diners get stuck eating steamed vegetables with a side of steamed vegetables, Wynn and Encore restaurants offer variety and quality to carnivores and plant-munchers alike. This is great news not only for vegans, but also for their non-vegan travel companions, who otherwise may have to limit their choices to accommodate their high-maintenance friends. I know, my vegan readers, that the high-maintenance comment seems a little harsh, but there's something you should know. Your friends and relatives won't admit it to you because they love you, but your vegan lifestyle drives them nuts. It's not that they don't respect your choice (although they probably don't), but they hate having to either dine at the Hay Hut or listen to you complain about how limited vegan options are at most restaurants. Well, thanks to Steve Wynn, in Las Vegas, everybody can happily dine in harmony, free of eye rolls.

If you've been to Las Vegas in the past decade, you may have noticed a nightclub or two. As hotel operators seek to diversify their revenue sources, they've discovered that club kids don't piss away their money in the casino like their parents and grandparents. However, they don't think twice about dropping a grand on bottle service while pumping their fists to DJ Skydmarx's sick beats. Wynn and Encore capitalize on this trend with a dayclub—Encore Beach Club—and three nightclubs—Tryst, XS, and Surrender. The level of luxury and design that makes Wynn casinos a visual delight does the same for the property's clubs. They also book big-name DJs, including Lil Jon, Ryan Lewis, Diplo, and Zedd to bring the oontz. As a result, Wynn and Encore continue to attract the fickle, what's-new-is-hot crowd even with several more recent options down the Strip.

Those of us who enjoy our alcohol in a more subdued environment can grab a seat at the Encore Lobby Bar, Parasol Down, or Sinatra and order one of the Strip's most delicious cocktails, the Sinatra smash. Made with Gentleman Jack whiskey and muddled blackberries, the smash is sweet and delicious with a boozy kick. Although named after Frank, Old Blue Eyes wouldn't be caught dead with this fruity crap. He was a real man, who drank his whiskey with a splash of water. For us modern-day pussies who were raised on Bartles and Jaymes wine coolers, Mike's Hard Lemonade, and fruity cocktails, a Sinatra smash refreshes and delights.

Tilt: Like several other Las Vegas hotels, Wynn Las Vegas offers a European-style pool. Hotels use "European-style" because it sounds classier than "topless." They don't want to convey the image that they're hosting free-for-all titty carnivals. They're hotel pools, not strip clubs. For a while, topless pools were all the rage. Even lower-end hotels like Flamingo dabbled with the concept. Many soon found their clientele wasn't interested in publicly displaying their lady mounds and promptly ditched their topless pools. Wynn's remains. Fantastic. I applaud any effort encouraging more public breast display. My beef with the Wynn topless pool is its location next to the hotel's conference center. As a result, most companies holding events there insist the hotel shut down the topless option while they use the conference space. I suppose they want to prevent fistfights for window seats and ensure the audience focuses on the speakers instead of the jugfest outside. But think of poor Ella and Cristina from Spain, who arrive in town with the goal of achieving a perfect, line-free tan, only to have their Vegas dreams dashed because the Northern Arizona Dental Society's annual MolarCon is in town. It doesn't seem fair. I demand justice for Ella and Cristina!

The topless pool debacle is the least of Wynn's water-related atrocities. Steve's previous hotels featured fun, free attractions—the Bellagio fountains, The Mirage volcano, and Treasure Island pirate battle (RIP). At Wynn, he built the Lake of Dreams, which includes shows every 30 minutes throughout each evening. Unlike previous attractions, the Lake of Dreams cannot be viewed from the street. Visitors need to enter Wynn. The best views require a seat at one of several restaurants or the Parasol Down patio. The shows range from somewhat odd to full-blown what-the-fuck? One involves two balls (Steve Wynn's balls), floating across the water and eventually giving birth to a smaller ball. Others star a large, mechanical frog that lip-syncs "What a Wonderful World," "Low Rider," and "Friends in Low Places." They're moderately entertaining because it's baffling that the guy behind the greatest spectacle on the Las Vegas Strip—the Fountains of Bellagio—thought this was a good idea.

Speaking of what-the-fuck, Wynn has been known to spend millions on well-known pieces of art. Some have appeared in his casinos, including a bizarre $28.2 million purchase he made in 2014. Artist Jeff Koons designed the six-and-a-half-foot sculpture of Popeye. Yes, Popeye. The cartoon character. For $28.2 million. Really. I don't get it either. Steve Wynn has a degenerative eye condition causing him to lose his vision, but paying $28.2 million for a Popeye statue makes me wonder if he's losing his mind too. As you're reading this, I'm putting the final touches on an eight-foot-tall sculpture of Alice the Goon. Steve should expect a phone call as soon as it's on the auction block. I'm willing to part with it for a mere $24 million.

Unlike the limited topless pool availability, ridiculous Lake of Dreams shows, and silly Popeye statue, another negative aspect of the Wynn properties could truly ruin your time there. Countless guests have reported the pounding nightclub noise being so loud they were unable to sleep. Artwork and furnishings in the rooms rattle. Because club operations extend well into the early morning hours, this is a problem for any guests not interested in staying out all night. This problem is not exclusive to Wynn and Encore, but most Strip and Downtown hotels with noise issues aren't high-end, luxury resorts. Nobody wants to pay for a Las Vegas hotel room that isn't property suited for its primary use—banging hookers sleeping. But when you're paying luxury hotel rates at a property that boasts about the comfort of its guests, the problem is even more maddening. If you value sleep and plan to stay at Wynn or Encore, insist on a room facing the golf course.

Circus Circus

www.circuscircus.com

PLAYERS CLUB: Circus Players Club

UNOFFICIAL THEME: Night terrors

"The Circus-Circus is what the whole hep world would be doing Saturday night if the

Nazis had won the war. This is the sixth Reich. The ground floor is full of gambling tables, like all the other casinos… but the place is about four stories high, in the style of a circus tent, and all manner of strange County-Fair/Polish Carnival madness is going on up in this space."—Hunter S. Thompson, *Fear and Loathing in Las Vegas.*

Long before Las Vegas attempted and ultimately failed to rebrand itself as a family destination in the 1990s, there was Circus Circus. Opened in 1968, the North Strip clownstrocity is a casino built for children. How many types of wrong is that? Of course, laws prevent children from gambling or even lingering on the gaming floor but, make no mistake, kids are everywhere. And much like many of the young children running around Circus Circus, the whole place seems a little sticky and a little stinky. The casino almost always stays busy though, so apparently cheap rooms, family-friendly attractions, and first-time tourists who don't know any better are enough to keep the money flowing.

Jackpot: For visitors who bring their kids to Las Vegas, Circus Circus has more activities to keep them busy than any other resort. The hotel's star attraction is The Adventuredome. The massive indoor theme park has two roller coasters, a swinging pirate ship, and a variety of spinning rides sure to induce vomiting after a buffet lunch (not that the Circus Circus buffet needs the help). In addition to the rides, The Adventuredome includes laser tag, mini-golf, rock climbing, bungee jumping, midway games, and an arcade.

In a resort filled with oddities, one of the most amusing features is a small, two-story section of the casino (first level) and midway (second level) that rotates. This area was formerly a bar made to look and function like a merry-go-round (as seen in the movie adaptation of *Fear and Loathing in Las Vegas*). Today, the upper portion holds a snack bar called the Horse-A-Round Bar. Below sits the Hank's Look Around Café of casino slot banks. This unique feature oozes wonderful cheesiness.

The Steak House at Circus Circus consistently receives rave reviews as one of the best old-school restaurants on the Strip. For diners seeking a solid steakhouse experience with a touch of old Vegas charm, this is the place for you.

Tilt: One key problem with Circus Circus is the theme. When was the last time someone enjoyed a circus? I'm not talking about Cirque du Soleil or some modern performance art billed as a circus. I'm referring to the real deal—elephants, lion tamers, and—worst of all—clowns. I grew up in the 1970s and '80s. By that time, circuses had been relegated to elementary-school-class-trip-level entertainment. Kids were dumped off by the busload with little if any supervision. I remember wandering the concourses at the St. Paul Civic Center in 1985, scoping out girls from other schools, before eventually giving up and just going home. My friends and I didn't even bother locating our seats. That's how much circuses suck. Seventh graders would rather spend the afternoon watching *Partridge Family* reruns at home than sitting through a live circus performance. I can't imagine circuses were that much more popular in the late 1960s, when Circus Circus opened. And yet, there it stands, a monument to an entertainment form built on animal abuse and pedophiles in grease paint.

Located on the second floor, a carnival midway overlooks the casino. Anyone whose resume includes blowing up balloons by aiming a water pistol at a clown's mouth, tossing rings over the end of Coke bottles, or throwing basketballs into undersized hoops will love this place. Although, in theory, a quaint throwback to a simpler time, the claustrophobia-inducing midway is sensory overload at its worst—and this is Las Vegas, where sensory overload is not only welcomed, but encouraged.

I have an odd mixture of respect and pity for the free carnival act performers appearing in the midway daily. It takes gigantic balls to swing on a trapeze or walk on a tightrope—even if there are safety nets below. However, I doubt any of these toned, highly trained athletes aspired to perform over a bank of Texas Tea slot machines when they were competing in the NCAA gymnastics finals a few years earlier.

My respect and pity turn to fear and repulsion when faced with another admission-free entertainment option. The Circus Circus marquee frequently includes three words so frightening that seeing them makes my testicles climb into my abdomen: "Free clown shows." First off, of course they're free. Nobody is paying for that shit. Second, clowns are creepy as fuck. They make kids cry and adults repress memories. I don't know a single person who thinks clowns are funny or entertaining. And yet, there they are in every parade (another activity that seems well beyond its useful entertainment value) and on stage every afternoon at Circus Circus. I appreciate that Circus Circus commits to the theme. However, they don't force heavily sedated animals to do tricks under the threat of an ass-kicking—another staple of traditional circuses. So maybe it's time to throw in the makeup-smudged towel on the clown shows too.

SLS

www.slslasvegas.com

PLAYERS CLUB: The Code

UNOFFICIAL THEME: Monkeys and failure

SLS Las Vegas must offer discounted room rates to young men with severe corneal ailments. What else would explain the large percentage of dudes wearing sunglasses indoors? Oh, that's right, this place is competing with The Cosmopolitan for the Best of Las Vegas Award for the Strip's preeminent chode factory. Seeing four of the nine check-in clerks assisting fedora-adorned dude-bros during my first visit to SLS confirmed the place is indeed attracting its desired clientele, described by an SLS executive as "the tribe."

Jackpot: Despite a heavy emphasis on nightlife, there's plenty to like about SLS, even for those who aren't fans of nightclub culture. The hotel and casino are filled with weird, quirky, fun design choices. From the chandeliers to the blackjack table felts to the dealer vests, monkey images are everywhere at SLS. The lobby bar is even called Monkey Bar. There doesn't seem to be any obvious reason the property has an unofficial simian theme, but who doesn't love monkeys? There's also no good explanation for Saam, the statue greeting guests at the main entrance. Looking like the cycloptic bastard lovechild of the Pillsbury Doughboy and SpongeBob's buddy Patrick Star, Saam defies logic but has become one of the North Strip's most popular photo ops. Design elements scattered around the casino also pay tribute to the location's former tenant, Sahara. A chandelier includes old S-shaped door handles, and the former hotel's logo appears on a small section of the casino carpeting.

Newer Las Vegas casinos including Downtown Grand and SLS feature open ceilings with exposed ductwork. The marketing spinsters proudly tout this recent trend as "industrial chic" design. In reality, it's simply a way to save a bunch of money on construction. Both properties are built on the bones of previous resorts—Downtown Grand using Lady Luck and SLS using Sahara. Although the SLS ceilings are sparse, they incorporate a handful of unique features. Like a horizontally tipped version of newer Strip-size hotel marquees, the LED video screen above the casino bar displays colorful screensaver-style animation, including some with 3D effects. A twisty, white, neon light installation near the players club booth is reminiscent of a similar red neon piece at Gordon Ramsay Steak in Paris Las Vegas. The Ramsay neon supposedly depicts Chef Ramsay's hand movements when creating his signature beef wellington. Although no such story has yet emerged regarding the SLS neon, I believe it mimics SLS founder Sam Nazarian's hand movements while "air DJing" at the casino's Foxtail nightclub.

Several SLS restaurants are transplants from Los Angeles, including Umami Burger. The burgers at Umami are decent but not better than any number of other gourmet burger joints on the Strip. However, this location's adjacent beer garden is an under-appreciated gem. Enjoying a cold beer or cocktail outdoors, yards from the Strip, just feels right. The only real downside to the beer garden is picnic table seating, which serves no benefit over traditional tables and chairs—with one possible exception. Watching nightclub girls in short skirts attempting to swing their legs over the picnic table benches without giving the whole bar a full noochie view can be highly entertaining. The beer garden serves food from Umami as well. Skip the burgers and order some fries or tater tots. The dipping sauces are outstanding.

Tilt: An unfortunate downside of being constructed on the bones of Sahara is the minuscule size of the standard SLS rooms. Although designed to get the most use out of the space, the rooms are awkwardly laid out and so cramped even those wackadoos who have adopted a "tiny-house lifestyle" would feel claustrophobic. The Story Superior room bed is located in the center of the room. The bathroom consists of three compartments—shower, sink, and toilet—accessible via sliding mirror doors behind the bed. The television is mounted to a side wall, rather than the wall at the foot of the bed. The closet consists of an open metal frame sitting in one corner. A minibar fills another corner. Illuminated frames surround both the bed and sofa. The ceiling consists of exposed, rough, unpainted concrete. With no lower-tier room available, calling these rooms "superior" comes across as a tad disingenuous. Fortunately, larger rooms feature more straightforward, comfortable layouts. Do yourself a favor and pay for the upgrade.

Another oddity at SLS awaits in the casino men's room. Located above each urinal a mounted plaque states, "You must be at least 21 years of age with proper identification to be served alcohol. Anyone found using, buying, selling, or possessing illegal drugs will be ejected from the property and subject to arrest. Any lewd or lascivious behavior will result in the immediate removal of all involved from the premises." Well, thanks for the condescending lecture. Underage drinking, drug consumption, and naughty touches may plague nightclubs, but is the blanket warning to every dude throwing a whiz in the casino restroom really necessary? I'm fairly certain the octogenarian two urinals down, prattling on about how much he misses Sahara, doesn't need to be told he'll get the boot if he tries to sell me some molly. (And based on the sputtering sound coming from his direction, I'm guessing he mourns the loss of a forceful piss much more than he misses Sahara.) Besides, doesn't this sign imply that anything not covered under the listed rules is completely fine? Apparently setting fire to the blackjack dealer who keeps throwing me 13s and 14s is perfectly acceptable as long as I keep my dick in my pants and don't have a joint in my pocket.

Unfortunately, until North Strip redevelopment occurs, SLS's biggest problem, its location, will remain. Stratosphere and Circus Circus are the nearest neighbors, and they aren't drawing enough traffic to help SLS. If announced plans for new hotels in the area pan out, the North Strip will transform by the end of the decade. Until then, SLS is an inconvenience. Hotel guests should plan on having a car, racking up cab fees, or depending on the monorail to get around.

Stratosphere

www.stratospherehotel.com
PLAYERS CLUB: Ace Play
UNOFFICIAL THEME: Phallic symbols

Located at the far north tip of Las Vegas Boulevard stands the iconic, ever-protruding Stratosphere. Opened in 1996, Strat is best known for its most visible feature—the 1,149-foot-high tower, topped with a restaurant, lounge, observation deck, and thrill rides.

Jackpot: Like a lighthouse beckoning drunken thrill-seekers, Las Vegas's tallest erection is a novelty you won't find anywhere else. Plenty of cities have observation decks—many including restaurants and bars—but only Stratosphere features four thrill rides, including:

- **Big Shot:** Riders harnessed to their seats shoot 160 feet into the air to the highest point on the Stratosphere tower. Riding the Big Shot in 1998, I set a whole new standard in cursing upon the ride's launch. I'm pretty sure other riders have dedicated the past 15+ years to figuring out what "motherfucking shitsucking fuckcocking ass" means.

- **Insanity:** Seated on a spider-like contraption that dangles over the edge of the tower, riders rapidly spin around. The seats achieve a 70-degree angle so riders face downward while spinning. Great for long-distance projectile vomiting!

- **Sky Jump:** Individually strapped to a cable from the tower platform, riders rapidly descend to the ground below. Think of Sky Jump as a vertical zip line. Although it feels much more controlled than a bungee jump or skydive, Sky Jump still gives riders a taste of leaping more than 100 stories to their death but without the pesky death part.

- **X-Scream:** Seated in a roller coaster car on a long platform, a group of riders slide over the edge of the tower. The platform tilts downward, making them feel like the car will plunge off the edge of the tower. It's scary but still feels safer than most Las Vegas cab rides.

Simply visiting the indoor/outdoor observation deck requires a $20 fee. Rides cost an additional $15, except Sky Jump, which costs $120. Strat also sells several discounted tower/ride packages.

Located in the Stratosphere tower pod, just below the observation deck are Lounge 107 and Top of the World. An upscale bar, Lounge 107 offers specialty cocktails for around $15 and a selection of appetizers. Visit in the early evening to take advantage of happy hour specials and avoid the DJs that begin later at night. Because Lounge 107 does not have a cover charge and foregoes the $20 observation deck admission, having a round of drinks during happy hour is the value-seeker's best bet for taking in Strat's views. A fine-dining restaurant, Top of the World has the added twist of rotating slowly, giving diners the full 360-degree view from the tower in about 80 minutes. The food is decent, but diners pay a premium for the view. Salads, steaks, and cocktails for two will total more than $200.

Tilt: Just like SLS, Stratosphere's location sucks. Guests should rent a car or use the monorail unless they plan to spend the majority of their time at Strat and SLS. The neighboring area to the north includes a lot of pawn shops, check-cashing businesses, and rent-by-the-hour motels, so visitors should avoid strolling to the Pawn Stars shop or making the nearly two-mile trek to Fremont Street by foot unless getting mugged is on their bucket list.

NO PRIVACY FOR THE NAKED

With the exception of a relatively niche handful of German scheisse porn connoisseurs, people would rather not be privy to the bathroom practices of others. And yet, in recent years, Las Vegas hotel room designers have treated the bathroom as though it's part of the city's entertainment experience. It began when Rio included a small window from the bedroom into the shower. Others have followed suit with similar privacy-be-damned features. Flamingo's Go rooms have sliding, frosted-glass bathroom doors with no locks. The Cosmopolitan and SLS suites include floor-to-ceiling windows between the bedroom and shower. The Cromwell's rooms include full-length two-way mirrors from the bedroom into the shower.

Such whimsical features may be acceptable for visitors traveling with a significant other. However, that girls' weekend celebrating your friend Darlene's 50th birthday will take a tragic turn if open access to the shower gives you a glimpse of her lightning-bolt-shaved pube patch. And let's not even discuss the ramifications of these rooms when traveling with teenagers.

The Go room doors aren't transparent, but they still provide little privacy. Frosted glass leads to unintentional shadow puppet shows, and because Flamingo isn't known for its attention to detail, sometimes the doors malfunction, sliding open a couple inches on their own. That's a delightful little surprise when you're trying to squeeze out last night's all-you-can-eat prime rib dinner.

Far too often the minimal privacy protection—in the form of a curtain or blinds—is located on the outside. Shouldn't the naked person control access? Even when traveling with a spouse, giving control to the person in the bedroom can lead to problems. Feeling playful, you may decide to pull back the curtain at the exact moment your hubby is aggressively taking a soapy washcloth to Buttcrack Boulevard. I don't care how solid your relationship is. Seeing your partner scour Trouble Valley like he's trying to separate baked-on tomato sauce from a lasagna pan is the beginning of the end of any relationship.

When it comes to bathroom design, hotels should take the opposite approach. Next time I stay at Wynn, I want to turn on the television in the bathroom and be greeted by Steve Wynn's warm voice: "Welcome to your bathroom here at Wynn Las Vegas. If you're like most people, you enjoy a peaceful, private experience when using this space. When designing each of our luxurious guest suites, we spared no expense to ensure your comfort and privacy. Each restroom was constructed using state-of-the-art soundproofing materials and the only panic room technology endorsed by Jodie Foster. My hotel may be known for its surprises, but I guarantee your bathroom experience won't be one of them."

CHAPTER 12

Near-Strip Hotels and Casinos

S everal off-Strip casinos reside within a short walk, or shuttle, monorail, or cab ride from Las Vegas Boulevard. They either cater to the tourist market or are convenient enough to the Strip that tourists make up a significant portion of their business. Following are thoughts on several of them. If you're bummed out because I didn't include a specific casino you enjoy (Silver Sevens or Palace Station, for example), here's a little trick to make yourself feel better. While reading the Gold Coast section, simply replace references to "Gold Coast" with the name of your locals casino of choice. Problem solved.

Hard Rock

www.hardrockhotel.com
PLAYERS CLUB: Backstage Pass
UNOFFICIAL THEME: Rock and/or roll

Over the past three decades, Hard Rock Café locations have sprouted up in pretty much every city that has an airport. Apparently many tourists love spending $18 for a mediocre hamburger enjoyed under Mike Reno's red headband from the "Working for the Weekend" video. So why not expand that concept to hotels and casinos?

For the six people who have never been inside a Hard Rock establishment, let me clarify one point. The term "hard rock" does not accurately describe the type of music typically highlighted there. You're just as likely to hear Chicago's "25 or 6 to 4" as you are Mötley Crüe's "Wildside" blasting through the casino. Memorabilia spans the past

60 years or so of popular music, including the Rolling Stones, Prince, Madonna, Spice Girls, Rihanna, Slipknot, and Katy Perry.

Jackpot: As a result of the vast memorabilia collection, Hard Rock's casino significantly differs from any other in Las Vegas. Looking at rows of signed guitars and platinum albums gets old quickly, but the larger displays contain more interesting items—outfits worn in music videos and rare pieces of stage-used equipment. Hotel rooms may have a couple framed band photos, but they aren't themed like Planet Hollywood's. You won't find a signed Wild Mick Brown drum head hanging above the shitter. Room 658 was the location where The Who bassist John Entwistle died, and room 248 was allegedly where Kevin Federline knocked up Britney Spears. So, those rooms are unofficially themed, but in a super creepy way.

Because Hard Rock's theme focuses on music, the property foregoes a traditional showroom in favor of The Joint, a 4,500-capacity live music venue. The Joint hosts touring acts and, in recent years, short-term residencies from Guns 'n Roses, Mötley Crüe, Kiss, Journey, and Def Leppard. A separate venue holding up to 650 people, Vinyl also features touring musical and comedy acts. Together, they make Hard Rock one of the city's best live music destinations.

Hard Rock also maintains one of the nicest pool complexes in town. With multiple levels of lounge, daybed, and cabana seating, beach sand, and way more trees and greenery than most Vegas hotel pool areas, Hard Rock's pools—including one that is heated and open all year—are much more luxurious than the cement holes found at many Las Vegas resorts. On weekends during the summer, the pools are overtaken by Rehab. Before Encore Beach Club, Wet Republic, and Marquee, Rehab started the Las Vegas dayclub trend. A drunken, debaucherous party, Rehab fills Hard Rock's pools with scantily clad babes and greased-up meatheads consuming massive amounts of alcohol all day long. If you don't mind partying in a pool filled with enough sunscreen, piss, and assorted other bodily excretions to challenge even the strongest filtration system and chlorine application, give Rehab a try.

Tilt: As a hotel with a rock and roll theme, you might think Hard Rock would be a 24-hour frat party. Think again. Not only are you unlikely to see someone chuck a Zenith though his room window, but you may get busted by security for trying to bring a liter of Ketel One to your room. The Hard Rock food and beverage policy says, "The Hard Rock Hotel & Casino prohibits coolers; boxes; bags; or other containers for the purpose of transporting food and beverage on property. In addition, all outside food and beverage is also prohibited... Hard Rock Hotel reserves the right to confiscate any items considered a violation of this policy without compensation." What the hell? Apparently Dean Wormer runs Hard Rock. Other hotels have similar policies; however, Hard Rock is one of the few known to enforce it. Reports of guests with coolers and grocery bags being stopped on their way to the elevators, and others having their luggage searched for contraband have repeatedly sprung up over the past several years. So if you're planning a raging throwdown, book elsewhere. Red Solo cups are not welcome.

Ellis Island

www.ellisislandcasino.com
PLAYERS CLUB: Passport
UNOFFICIAL THEME: Cheap and sleazy

Longtime Las Vegas visitors love to bitch about how expensive the city has become compared to when they began visiting. "I remember when the Stardust coffee shop had a $1.95 prime rib special." Well, you can't get a Mars bar for a quarter anymore either. You also used to live comfortably on a household income of $12,000 a year. It's called inflation. Suck it up and deal. There's no reason Las Vegas would be immune to the same economic conditions as the rest of the country. While it's rare to find a gourmet feast for pocket change, meals below $10 haven't completely faded from existence. Some of these specials require an adventure, so grab your switchblade. We're heading to Ellis Island. This tiny dive of a casino connected to a Super 8 hotel behind Bally's may not look like much, but it contains a few surprises.

Jackpot: One of four restaurants, the 24-hour Ellis Island Café serves up dozens of breakfast, sandwich, burger, and pasta dishes for between $3 and $9, with nothing over $15. Because ordering not-so-secret off-menu specials is fun, the steak special has been a popular draw for years. For $8, diners get a "filet-cut" steak (whatever the hell "filet-cut" means), salad, potato, veggie, and beer. It's a ton of food and a great value. You may not get a Delmonico-quality cut of meat, but it's not a chunk of shoe leather either. To get the $8 price, you'll need a players card and a coupon from the players club kiosk, obtained after gambling at least $5.

Ellis Island brews six beers and a root beer on site. Free when gambling or just $2 at the bar, this is some surprisingly good brew. Craft beer fans can combine a visit to Ellis Island with stops at Downtown's Banger Brewing, Chicago Brewing Company, and Triple 7 Brewpub for a nice little Las Vegas craft beer tour.

After downing a few of those beers, you'll probably feel like singing. Fortunately, Ellis Island is the place for that too. Karaoke kicks off nightly at 9 p.m. and goes well into the early hours of the morning. Once plentiful on Las Vegas Boulevard, nightly karaoke has all but disappeared in the past few years, leaving the near-Strip Ellis Island as the most convenient option. Consisting of locals and tourists alike, the clientele is generally fun and supportive, regardless of your talent level.

Tilt: Located on Koval Lane near Flamingo Road, just one block—a long block—from Las Vegas Boulevard, Ellis Island is a five-minute stroll from the lower level Bally's exit near the food court. However, the walk can seem a little sketchy at night. Whenever I venture to Ellis Island after sundown, I feel like there's a 50/50 chance of getting stabbed. If you do choose to make the trek, pick up a 40-ouncer of malt liquor to pour out in honor of Tupac at the intersection of Koval and Flamingo, where he was shot.

The Westin
www.westinvegas.com
PLAYERS CLUB: Max Rewards
UNOFFICIAL THEME: Excitement-free wagering

Have you ever wanted to gamble in a Westin Hotel lobby? Now you can! The Max Casino at The Westin, located a block east of The Cromwell on Flamingo Road, captures all the atmosphere of a Kansas City airport-adjacent convention hotel. Take any generic hotel bar in America and add gambling. That's The Westin's Max Casino.

Jackpot: When all of the nearby Strip casinos are busy, and you need a break from the crowds, you may very well find some peace and quiet at The Westin.

Tilt: Have I mentioned that this place is boring? Because it's really boring.

Stage Door Casino
UNOFFICIAL THEME: Winston smoke and desperation

One block off-Strip, behind The Cromwell sits Stage Door Casino. You've probably seen it from a cab or the monorail. It's the shabby, one-story building with the marquee proudly proclaiming, "We have 13 years left on our lease." Stage Door offers refuge from the Strip and one of the cheapest buzzes around.

Jackpot: At its heart, Stage Door is a dive bar. Drink specials often include $2 shots of Jagermeister, $2 bottled Pabst Blue Ribbon with a shot of whiskey, $3 hot dog with a Budweiser, and $4 shots of Patron. Steps away at The Cromwell, you'll be hard pressed to get a drink for under $10. Cheap drinks attract... let's say "characters." As a result, you're likely to encounter a colorful slice of Las Vegas while hanging out at Stage Door. Take all advice, theories, and general information overheard in this casino with a grain of salt, because most have little basis in reality.

Tilt: As the sign indicates, Stage Door is technically a casino. However, the slot machines are notoriously tight, and the video poker pay tables are bad even by Strip standards. The casino encourages late-night gambling by paying double on royal flushes between 1 a.m. and 9 a.m., but you'll likely go bust well before hitting one. You're better off bellying up to one of the two bars and paying for your booze. Air filtration isn't a thing at Stage Door, so asthma sufferers beware.

Gold Coast

www.goldcoastcasino.com
PLAYERS CLUB: BConnected
UNOFFICIAL THEME: Oxygen tanks

Most Strip resorts offer essentially the same amenities. They include a steakhouse, a buffet, a 24-hour café, a couple bars, a nightclub, a spa, conference space, a theater, and some shops—pretty much everything a tourist needs to have an enjoyable, memorable experience. Casinos catering to Las Vegas locals take a different approach than those aimed at tourists. They focus on value and convenience. You'll find cheap dining, favorable gambling conditions, and amenities including movie theaters, pharmacies, and bowling centers. Many Las Vegas locals often make it a point to mention that they don't gamble, and yet casinos catering to locals do a brisk business. It must be the bowling.

For tourists who want a taste of the local casino experience without venturing far from the Strip, Gold Coast meets your needs. Located on Flamingo Road about a mile west of Las Vegas Boulevard, Gold Coast shuttles visitors to and from the Bally's tour bus entrance about every 30 minutes. So, there's no need to pay for a cab, deal with a rental car, or waste a significant chunk of time traveling to the outer edges of the Las Vegas Valley. And, with The Palms and Rio just a five-minute walk away, if you get bored at Gold Coast—and you probably will—you can conveniently explore a couple other slightly off-Strip properties.

Jackpot: Like many locals casinos, Gold Coast doesn't try to impress guests with visual flash. You're not going to find go-go dancing blackjack dealers there. You will, however, find plenty of $5 blackjack, rows of video poker machines with better pay tables than those on the Strip, and a breakfast buffet for under $6. These joints depend on value to bring customers back week after week and, in many cases, day after day. So everything at Gold Coast is relatively cheap. Bowling is only $3 during the day and $1 after midnight.

Sometimes spending time on the Las Vegas Strip reminds those of us who are no longer in our 20s that we're no longer in our 20s. Spend an hour at The Cosmopolitan on a Saturday night, surrounded by skinny girls and buff dude-bros, and you might start to feel like your better days are behind you. A trip to Gold Coast will have you feeling youthful in no time. Even guests in their 60s decrease the median customer age at this joint. Players club points are redeemable for Medi-Alert subscription credits. "Help, I've been sitting at this Wheel of Fortune machine for three hours, and I can't get up." How long until an enterprising casino developer opens an adjacent nursing home? I can't believe this hasn't happened yet.

Tilt: Despite their bang-for-the-buck, locals casinos just don't feel like Las Vegas. They lack the excitement—the pulse—of Las Vegas Boulevard and Fremont Street. So as much as I appreciate the value, the great gambling conditions, and cheap food, they generally bore me. Just like when I visit casinos near my home or in other parts of the country, I frequently want to leave within an hour or two. They don't get my heart racing like the full-on Las Vegas tourist experience. Whenever someone asks why I love Las Vegas, I talk about the city as my escape from reality. I don't feel that sense of escape at Gold Coast and other off-Strip, local-skewing casinos. They do what they do quite well, and they have an obvious place in the Las Vegas market. But for those of us who unapologetically embrace our role as escapist tourists, locals casinos simply don't provide much of a thrill.

Rio

www.riolasvegas.com
PLAYERS CLUB: Total Rewards
UNOFFICIAL THEME: Sadness carnival

Las Vegas casinos' popularity ebbs and flows over time. What's hot today may very well be stale in a few years. Rio exemplifies this trend. When it opened in 1990, the property was an instant hit with locals and tourists. The larger-than-average buffet featured several food stations rather than the traditional extendo-row of slop troughs. The property was the first Strip-area hotel with suites as standard rooms. And the Masquerade Show in the Sky—a Mardi Gras parade suspended from the casino ceiling—contributed to a party atmosphere that permeated Rio. Time has not been kind, however. Many buffets eventually co-opted Rio's layout and matched or surpassed its quality. The hotel became yesterday's news. The sky parade's drawing power dwindled until it was discontinued in 2013. There hasn't been much reason to visit the red-headed stepchild of Caesars Entertainment's Las Vegas empire in recent years.

Jackpot: At 600 square feet and larger, Rio's hotel rooms provide ample space for interpretive dance exhibitions, yoga parties, or orgies. So if you're planning on getting a little weird during your Vegas trip, Rio may be a good option. Because the location is less convenient than comparable hotels on the Strip, you'll get more for your money, even if the rooms are a tad outdated. Although a Las Vegas hotel room is used mainly for sleeping, and arguably needs little more than a bed and a bathroom, having extra space makes for a more pleasant stay.

Tilt: As much as I appreciate Rio offering large rooms, I take issue with its bastardization of the word "suite." In any other city, a hotel suite includes multiple rooms—at a minimum one bedroom and a living room. Rio's standard suites include a combo bedroom/living room—the equivalent to a master bedroom in a home. Thanks to this redefinition, many Las Vegas hotels have followed suit, slapping the word suite on any room that is either slightly larger than average or simply nicer than the standard rooms.

Rio's cocktail servers aren't just waiters and waitresses. They're also entertainers. Rio calls them "bevertainers." They deliver beverages and act as entertainers, thus "bevertainers." In the immortal words of David St. Hubbins, "It's such a fine line between stupid and clever." Every hour or so, the casino cranks up the music, the cocktail staff climbs onto mini-stages, and gamblers are "treated" to a free song-and-dance number. I'm all in favor of free casino entertainment. I miss the days when cheesy lounge acts serenaded me while I pissed away my cash on Buccaneer Gold slot machines. However, I'm a fan of separated roles in the casino. Employees should be allowed to focus on their core competencies. Let the singers sing and the servers serve. I don't want burgeoning songstress Jillian fumbling the dance steps to "Crazy in Love" because she's thinking about my Corona Light any more than I want Kyle the security guy whipping up a batch of fettuccine alfredo at the Carnival World Buffet. I'm sure lovely Jillian is perfectly capable of delivering my beer and lighting up the world with her smile, however… Oh, who am I kidding? Any delay in the speedy delivery of my drink annoys me. I don't want to be bevertained. I just want my damn beer.

The Palms

www.palms.com

PLAYERS CLUB: Club Palms
UNOFFICIAL THEME: Former glory

When it opened in 2001, The Palms immediately became the hottest resort in Las Vegas. The hotel hosted MTV's *Real World*, brought in the day's popular celebuskanks, like Paris Hilton, and drew the Los Angeles club crowd to nightclubs Ghostbar and Rain. The place had buzz. Simultaneously, the casino offered great gambling odds and promotions to pack the machines and tables with Las Vegas residents. The Palms figured out a formula for attracting local gamblers during the day and party-hungry tourists at night—a rare combination. The resort expanded, adding a Playboy-branded hotel tower with more nightclubs, and a condo tower, Palms Place. Unfortunately, the tumbling economy led to an ownership change, newer nightclubs stole away the party crowd, the Playboy partnership dissolved, and the once loud Palms buzz became an inaudible flicker. Today, Ghostbar remains, but other club space has fallen dormant. Like neighboring Rio, the casino's glory days have passed.

Jackpot: Much like Gold Coast, The Palms offers the benefits of a locals casino with a location less than a mile from the Strip. Video poker players can find tons of machines with 99 percent and higher payback without having to journey far from Las Vegas Boulevard. Rooms start as low as $39, and even 1,200-square-foot Palms Place suites are frequently priced below $200. Good luck finding those prices on the Strip for rooms anywhere nearly as nice as those at The Palms. Nove Italiano, Alize, and the awkwardly named N9ne Steakhouse receive rave reviews for fine dining, and The Pearl Theater offers an intimate 2,500-capacity concert venue, mostly used for throwback acts from the 1970s and 1980s.

Tilt: Like all off-Strip casinos, The Palms's location makes it mildly inconvenient. Although the resort feels more modern than its immediate neighbors Rio and Gold Coast, there's little to warrant a special trip unless you just want to get away from Las Vegas Boulevard and explore a little without expending too much time. Once novel for being a rare off-Strip casino that acted more like a Strip casino, The Palms has been surpassed by other locals casinos (M Resort and Red Rock Resort, for example). Even the dayclub and nightclub scene that The Palms once dominated has shifted to the Strip, leaving the resort behind with just Ghostbar, several shuttered club spaces, and memories of its former heyday.

Westgate

www.westgatelasvegasresort.com
PLAYERS CLUB: Players Club
UNOFFICIAL THEME: What's old is new again

Opened in 1969 as the International Hotel before becoming the Las Vegas Hilton in 1971, Westgate has a fascinating history. Elvis Presley resurrected his career and forever became associated with Las Vegas thanks to more than 600 sold out shows there in the 1970s. The hotel appeared as the Whyte House Casino in the James Bond film *Diamonds are Forever*. And a tragic 1981 fire— coupled with an earlier fire at the original MGM Grand—contributed to more stringent fire safety measures nationwide.

In the years just before Westgate's 2014 purchase of the resort, it experienced a rough patch. After ownership changes and the end of a licensing deal forced the property to abandon the Hilton name, it became LVH: Las Vegas Hotel. The lack of creativity demonstrated with the generic name carried through to other elements of the resort as well. Amidst rumors the hotel may not survive much longer, Westgate became its unexpected savior. Immediately upon taking over ownership, the company began a series of major upgrades aimed at improving and modernizing the hotel and casino.

The largest off-Strip hotel, with more than 3,000 rooms, Westgate caters heavily to timeshare owners and business travelers attending events at the neighboring Las Vegas Convention Center. Fortunately, the hotel includes a monorail stop, giving guests relatively cheap and easy access to the Strip.

Jackpot: Westgate's casino includes one of the best sports books in the city—the SuperBook. The massive room occupies more than 30,000 square feet with two dozen large screens and another five dozen smaller monitors. Like much of the property, aspects of the SuperBook were showing their age, but Westgate's renovations have modernized the technology and improved the overall experience.

Throughout Westgate's history, the casino has maintained elements of its late 1960s origins. Chandeliers, sconces, and other design elements define classic Vegas style. Whether all of these elements survive the latest round of renovations remains to be seen. However, some of the resort's other updates suggest Westgate's management appreciates the resort's history, so it's likely many of the unique, old-school touches will remain.

What better way to take advantage of Westgate's storied past than by bringing back Elvis? The resort has partnered with Graceland to open the Elvis estate's second permanent exhibit. Much like the original Graceland exhibit in Memphis, Tenn., *Elvis: The Exhibition* displays vehicles, stage outfits, and tons of assorted other Presley memorabilia. In addition, couples can get hitched in the Graceland Wedding Chapel.

Tilt: Being a timeshare property, Westgate views anyone walking through the door as a potential timeshare owner. Although the sales reps staffing the lobby haven't been quite as aggressive as the timeshare hawkers on the Strip, they will try to convince you to sit through a sales presentation with the promise of $100 in gambling credits and a couple free buffets. The 90-minute presentation may run closer to three hours, and you will likely be pressured and made to feel like you did something wrong if you decline to buy one. Timeshares are notoriously bad investments, and the sales tactics are sleazy.

CHAPTER 13

Downtown Hotels & Casinos

The massive resorts and iconic attractions most associated with Las Vegas reside on the Strip. But the heart and soul of Las Vegas live on Fremont Street. The city's history lies in the cracks of well-worn bars. It glows from neon signs. And it hums from the din of gamblers pressing their luck. In a town known for imploding its past and replacing it with the next big thing, Downtown remains a reliable, old friend.

That's not to say Downtown Las Vegas has completely avoided change. For more than 20 years, a massive LED canopy has covered Fremont Street, displaying light shows every evening. In 2014, a 12-story faux slot machine was added, housing the base of a zip line. And in the past several years, dozens of new restaurants, bars, and retailers have fueled Fremont Street's resurgence. The relatively recent additions keep Downtown vibrant without completely sweeping away the past.

Compared to their sprawling competitors on the Strip, Fremont Street hotels and casinos are compact, cozy, and unpretentious. They focus on gambling, dining, and drinking over clubbing and shopping. Finding decent gambling odds is relatively easy, and food, drinks, and accommodations are relatively cheap. This is classic Las Vegas—a little gritty, a little loud, and a lot of fun.

All of Downtown's noteworthy hotels and casinos are located on a half-mile stretch of Fremont Street or within two blocks north.

Main Street Station

www.mainstreetcasino.com

PLAYERS CLUB: BConnected

UNOFFICIAL THEME: Choo-choo trains

Located two blocks from the action of Fremont Street, Main Street Station is one of Downtown's gems. With its high ceilings, rich woods, stained glass, and chandeliers, the building looks and feels more like a Victorian-era train station than a hotel and casino.

Jackpot: Antiques and historical artifacts add to Main Street Station's unique ambiance. Unlike many Las Vegas casinos, which mimic history with replicas, Main Street displays actual antiques from the Figaro Opera House in Paris, the Coca-Cola Building in Austin, Texas, and Kuwait Royal Bank. The registration and bell desks distribute free guides to the collection. The most noteworthy piece is a large chunk of the graffiti-covered Berlin Wall installed behind the casino men's room urinals. Seeing the wall in person evokes memories of the defining moments of a generation—the 1987 speech by President Ronald Reagan that changed the world forever. Reagan commanded, "Mr. Gorbachev, tear down this wall," unzipped his pants, whipped out Little Ronnie, and sprayed the Berlin Wall with the uncontrolled ferocity of an unmanned fire hose. At least I think that's how it went down—I'm not a historian. Anyway, male visitors can reenact that moment, however they remember it, at Main Street Station.

Despite having limited dining options, Main Street Station's two restaurants are dependable and relatively cheap. The Garden Court Buffet may not match the quality and selection of top Strip buffets, but it's the best buffet choice Downtown. Breakfast and lunch are under $10, and dinner isn't much more except on Fridays, when it features an expanded seafood selection. The hotel's only other dining option, Triple 7 Restaurant and Microbrewery offers one of the most varied menus in the area, including salads, sandwiches, burgers, pizza, sushi, steaks, ribs, seafood, and pasta. Portions are large, quality is excellent, and prices are reasonable. Triple 7 brews its own beers, also served at Boar's Head Bar.

Tilt: Las Vegas is home to an off-Strip, locals chain of Station Casinos with names like Texas Station, Sunset Station, Palace Station, Santa Fe

Station, and Boulder Station. One might logically deduce that Main Street Station is part of this chain and its players club. This, however, would be false. Boyd Gaming owns Main Street Station, so it is part of the BConnected loyalty program. Las Vegas is good at name-related confusion. Downtown Grand and MGM Grand are also unaffiliated, and the Public House restaurant at Luxor has no connection to the Public House restaurant at The Venetian.

California

www.thecal.com

PLAYERS CLUB: BConnected

UNOFFICIAL THEME: Getting lei'd

Since shortly after opening in 1975, California Hotel & Casino has catered to Hawaiian visitors. Offering affordable air and hotel package deals and heavily marketing to visitors from the islands has made The Cal an unofficial Las Vegas home for tourists from the 50th state.

Jackpot: California restaurants specialize in Hawaiian delicacies, including oxtail soup, rice bowls, and all things Spam. Most of the world would just as soon choke down a can of Fancy Feast as a can of Spam, but islanders treat it like manna. Many Hawaiian visitors who prefer familiar cuisine from home even when they're on vacation keep this niche a success for The Cal. Regardless, the abundance of Hawaiian offerings is also great for visitors who love island food but rarely or never travel to Hawaii.

Tilt: Although named after Nevada's closest neighbor to the West, California's theming has evolved into a Golden State/Aloha State hybrid. A few restaurants and bars are named after California references (Redwood Bar and Grill and San Francisco Bar), while meeting rooms have Hawaiian names (Ohana and Maile). The Cal could do so much more with its theme. With a loving nod to many Californians' inexplicable addition of "the" before freeway numbers ("the 405"), The Cal could do the same with hotel room numbers. "I'm staying in the 1027." Security guards could dress like Ponch and John. The pool could be rebranded as an adults-only topless pool named Silicon Valley. The possibilities are endless.

The Plaza

www.plazahotelcasino.com

PLAYERS CLUB: Royal Rewards

UNOFFICIAL THEME: Shattered dreams

Opened in 1971, The Plaza sits across Main Street from the west end of the Fremont Street Experience. Plagued for years by a rancid sewage smell, The Plaza has masked the odor with a strong perfume scent since undergoing a major renovation in 2011. Despite high hopes that came with much-needed upgrades, the hotel has struggled to keep shows, restaurants, and bars afloat, resulting in an underused theater, limited dining options for a hotel of its size, and vacant floor space.

Jackpot: When the Fontainebleau hotel project on the Strip stalled and its owner sold off the unused furnishing, The Plaza was one of the bargain hunters acquiring new décor at a significant discount. As a result, the hotel now offers 1,000 modern, updated rooms for as little as $45 a night.

Despite the closure of multiple restaurants in the past few years, The Plaza still has a few good options:

- **Oscar's:** The second-floor steakhouse occupying the iconic glass dome above the main entrance, Oscar's carries the name of legendary mob attorney and former Las Vegas mayor Oscar Goodman. The space appears in several movies, including *Casino*, and once housed the hotel's swimming pool. Unfortunately, the Fremont Street Experience canopy and the Slotzilla zip line's landing pad across the street ruin a once-impressive view. When dining at Oscar's, skip the steak in favor of fish or chicken with salads and sides.
- **Hash House a Go Go:** Like its other locations off-Strip and at The Linq, Hash House a Go Go serves up huge portions of comfort food. Although some customers report the quality at this location doesn't match the others, it's still a decent bang for the buck for diners who value massive quantities.
- **Pop Up Pizza:** Located on the edge of the casino floor, Pop Up Pizza offers thin-crust pizza for just a few bucks a slice. It's

a cheap and tasty option when walking to the superior Pizza Rock seems daunting.

Tilt: Despite glimmers of promise since the 2011 upgrades, The Plaza hasn't lived up to its potential. The best aspects are outdone by better alternatives nearby. Oscar's is a cool room, but there are far better steakhouses—Andiamo at The D, Vic and Anthony's at Golden Nugget, and Triple George Grill at Downtown Grand. Hash House is decent, but not as good as Du-par's across the street (or even other Hash House locations). Pop Up Pizza is dependable, but it doesn't touch Pizza Rock's quality.

The casino is spacious but lifeless. Even on weekend nights when Fremont Street is bustling, the casino frequently lacks energy. Factor in the overpowering perfume scent pumped in to mask The Plaza's mysterious natural odor and the casino simply doesn't make for an enjoyable environment.

Beer Garden has a decent selection of beers, but the bar feels like part of The Plaza's food court. Outdoor seating includes the novelty of live grass, a rarity in the desert. However, its view of the den of sadness that is Las Vegas Club makes even the otherwise enjoyable al fresco seating a bit depressing.

Las Vegas Club

www.lasvegasclubcasino.com
PLAYERS CLUB: Royal Rewards
UNOFFICIAL THEME: Despair

Operating as Las Vegas Club at its current location on the corner of Fremont and Main for more than 60 years, this casino has deteriorated into a shell of what it once was. Since 2013, the hotel towers have been closed. Virtually all of the retail and restaurant space has been abandoned for even longer. Although the casino remains open, part of it has been walled off for use as a makeshift souvenir shop, and the owner has aspirations to convert it to a CVS drugstore.

Jackpot: Table limits are low, and drinks at the casino bar are cheap.

Tilt: Everything else. Spending time at Las Vegas Club can have one of two effects. You may leave feeling better about yourself because even though not everything in life is perfect, at least you don't spend all your day working in this dump. Or, Las Vegas Club could take you to a very dark place as you think, "What has my life become that I'm voluntarily hanging out here?" If you begin to have these thoughts, immediately flee to La Bayou, where you'll be plied with so much alcohol that you'll promptly black out and forget your Las Vegas Club visit ever happened.

Golden Gate

www.goldengatecasino.com
PLAYERS CLUB: Club 1906
UNOFFICIAL THEME: Shrimp cocktails and shrimpy rooms

Opened in 1906 and renamed Sal Sagev in 1931, Fremont Street's first hotel became Golden Gate in 1955. Although recently renovated, the hotel contains many nods to its storied history. Golden Gate displays old-timey slot machines and other relics near the registration desk, and a plaque at the end of the casino bar reminds guests that members of the Rat Pack drank and gambled there.

Jackpot: Golden Gate's 24-hour café, Du-par's features a huge menu, including breakfast, burgers, pot pies, steak, fish, meatloaf, chicken, salads, and sandwiches available around the clock. The food comes out quickly and always hits the spot. I'm baffled by how one kitchen can churn out such a variety of food and do all of it well. Du-par's has earned its reputation for the best pancakes on the planet. Granted, few people have tried all the pancakes on the planet. However, after eating Du-par's pancakes, there's little reason to go elsewhere. Hot, fluffy, and buttery, they are the perfect end to any night or the perfect start to any day. Request some of Golden Gate's homemade jam to turn your pancakes into a fruity treat. Du-par's is also home to the classic shrimp cocktail—a Las Vegas tradition.

Tilt: Golden Gate's 106 original hotel rooms are tiny by today's standards. When hotels were built 100 years ago, customers were smaller and didn't expect more space than needed to sleep and shower. Although

Golden Gate has done a fine job modernizing its rooms, not much can be done to modernize the size. The hotel's 16 suites, added in 2012, better serve couples and solo travelers who want a little more space.

La Bayou

www.facebook.com/LaBayouCasino

UNOFFICIAL THEME: Rapid intoxication

With no hotel, restaurants, or blackjack tables, La Bayou offers only two reasons to visit— slot machines and free-flowing booze. Upon entering the casino, you'll be handed a string of Mardi Gras beads and a raffle ticket by two women dressed like they just returned from a taping of *Let's Make a Deal*. Let the party begin.

Jackpot: Smaller than many casino restrooms, La Bayou has rightfully earned a reputation as the quickest place on Fremont Street to catch a buzz. It's not unusual for three different cocktail waitresses to ask for your drink order before you even insert money into a slot machine. And they return often. Toss $20 in a Wheel of Fortune machine, play slowly, and stumble out 20 minutes later with a smile on your face, alcohol in your bloodstream, and a song in your heart. The slot inventory at La Bayou rarely changes, so you will likely find a few classics, such as Wild Cherry Bonus Pie three-reel slots.

La Bayou's daiquiri bar offers 26 different flavored frozen drinks in a variety of zany novelty glasses. So, if you've ever wanted a plastic football full of rum and sugar, for $16 all your dreams can come true.

Tilt: Don't bother waiting around for the raffle, designed to get gamblers to stay and play longer. The last time the jackpot hit, the Fremont Street Experience canopy was still illuminated by kerosene lanterns.

Mermaid's

www.facebook.com/MermaidsCasino

UNOFFICIAL THEME: Diabetes

Mermaid's is a larger version of its sister casino, La Bayou. Almost everything is the same:

- Upon entry, two women in fugly costumes offer free beads and a ticket to a drawing.
- The casino contains only machines—no table games.
- It closes each night from 1 a.m. to 9 a.m.
- The cocktail service is fast and furious.
- The bar offers a variety of frozen drinks in novelty cups.

Jackpot: One major feature differentiates Mermaid's from La Bayou—it includes a simultaneously awesome and frightening snack bar. Did you inadvertently schedule your Las Vegas visit while your hometown county fair is being held? Fear not! The Mermaid's snack bar offers all the artery-clogging, grease-dripping treats you may have otherwise missed. Highlights include chocolate-covered bananas, deep-fried Oreos, and deep-fried Twinkies for 99 cents each.

Tilt: If you keep leading this lifestyle, you're going to die soon.

Binion's

www.binions.com

PLAYERS CLUB: Club Binion's

UNOFFICIAL THEME: Remnants of greatness

A stroll through Binion's offers glimpses of and tributes to the casino's long-gone glory days. The casino carries the name of iconic former owner Benny Binion, the lawless Texan who founded Binion's Horseshoe in 1951. The Gallery of Champions displays photos of every World Series of Poker main event winner from 1970 through 2004, when the company now known as Caesars Entertainment acquired rights to the tournament and moved it. An autographed poker table on display near the poker room includes the signatures of dozens of poker pros and commemorates the last WSOP hosted by Binion's. If the casino's dark wooden walls and whiskey-soaked bartops could talk, they would tell stories of gamblers who won their fortunes only to lose it all back, and of cheaters who were dragged to a secluded back room, never to be seen again.

Jackpot: Another tip of the cap to Binion's bygone era is the $1 million display. A plexiglass case on a poker table contains a stack of currency totaling $1 million. Visitors can pose behind the display and pick up their free souvenir photo a few minutes later. In an age when everyone carries a camera at all times, you wouldn't think getting a free photo would be much of a draw. However, the novelty of standing behind $1 million, and the tradition of stopping in Binion's for the souvenir keep the display alive.

Tilt: Unfortunately, the many bits of history scattered throughout Binion's serve more as reminders of better days rather than making visitors feel like they're part of an ongoing tradition of greatness. Minor renovations have modernized the café and added outdoor bars, but it's difficult to ignore the vacant hotel, closed since 2009. Large chunks of space on the casino level go unused or are occupied by out-of-place, low-rent "amenities," like discount t-shirt vendors. The main casino area can be fun, and the café offers some decent, cheap food, but the farther you wander within Binion's, the less appealing the old joint becomes.

Even the 24th floor Top of Binion's Steakhouse fails to capitalize what could be a classic Las Vegas dining experience. Worth a visit only for a strong cocktail at the bar and perhaps a look at the old-school steakhouse décor, the restaurant has recently gained a reputation for spotty service and hit-or-miss food quality. This may have been easy to overlook before Downtown had several better options. The 24th-floor location would be great if there was anything noteworthy to see. Unfortunately, unless you're especially turned on by the phallic Stratosphere tower, the Strip view is too distant to be impressive, and the Downtown views are more impressive from the street.

Golden Nugget

www.goldennugget.com/LasVegas

PLAYERS CLUB: 24k Select Club

UNOFFICIAL THEME: A taste of the Strip

Evaluating Downtown Las Vegas hotels typically requires a different set of criteria than used when judging Strip hotels. Unlike their Las Vegas Boulevard counterparts, the hotels on and around Fremont Street simply aren't full-service resorts. Most of the pools (for those Downtown hotels that even have one) pale in comparison to even mediocre Strip hotel pools. Downtown fitness rooms are typically barebones, and spas are nearly absent from Fremont Street. Many standard hotel rooms that are considered very nice with the qualifier "for Downtown" would be simply average on the Strip.

Golden Nugget is the exception. A full-service, all-the-bells-and-whistles resort, Golden Nugget is undeniably the nicest Downtown Las Vegas hotel. Opened in 1946, Golden Nugget's series of owners have consistently maintained, expanded, and upgraded the property, ensuring it offers all of the amenities Las Vegas visitors want. With the most recent major renovation in 2009, the Nugget is home to 2,400 rooms—more than double any other Downtown property. Visitors accustomed to the comforts of major resorts on the Strip but looking to explore Downtown won't find a better option than the Nugget.

Jackpot: Golden Nugget includes four hotel towers built between 1977 and 2009. Because rooms in new towers nearly always outshine their older counterparts, Rush Tower features the swankiest standard rooms at the Nugget. Of course, the room rate reflects this. Fortunately, all of Golden Nugget's rooms are well-maintained and comfortable. Even standard Carson Tower deluxe rooms are modern and clean, and they book for around 30 percent less than those in the Rush Tower.

Without question, Golden Nugget features the best pool area Downtown, and one of the coolest in all of Las Vegas. Built surrounding a 200,000-gallon aquarium, the pool gives swimmers the chance to get up close and personal with sharks and a variety of other fish. A three-story translucent water slide shoots swimmers through the middle of the shark tank. Guests seeking a bit of seclusion from the family-friendly main pool can escape to The Hideout, a more laid back experience on the deck above the tank. The Hideout has a much smaller pool, its own bar, and lounge chairs renting for $25 per day.

Golden Nugget also has the largest variety of casino bars in Downtown Las Vegas. Excluding restaurant bars, they include:

- **Gold Diggers:** The only nightclub on Fremont Street, Gold Diggers is much more casual and welcoming than what you'll find on the Strip. With a relaxed dress code and a lot less pretense, Gold Diggers attracts a more diverse clientele than you'll find in Strip nightclubs too. You can dance if you want to (you can leave your friends behind), but if that's not your scene, grab a seat in the lounge or out on the patio overlooking Fremont Street. Gazing down on the freak show below rarely disappoints. Gold Diggers sometimes charges a cover, but arrive early and you'll probably get in free.

- **Rush Lounge:** Open only at night, Rush Lounge offers live bands and plenty of bar and lounge seating.

- **Sports Bar, International Beer Bar, and Claude's Bar:** These are typical casino video poker bars.

- **H2O Bar and The Hideout Bar:** Conveniently located on the first and third levels of the pool area, these bars offer frozen drinks, beer, and cocktails during regular pool hours.

- **Ice Bar:** Located just outside of the pool area, Ice Bar includes one of the best vodka menus in Las Vegas.

- **Bar 46:** Just a few steps from Fremont Street, Bar 46 is an oval casino bar with its own gaming area. Always lively and fun, this is my favorite bar at Golden Nugget. I always meet interesting and fun people here and have never had a bad time.

- **Stage Bar:** An outdoor walk-up, Stage Bar offers limited seating with views of Fremont Street Experience's First Street Stage.

A standard amenity on the Strip and otherwise absent Downtown, Golden Nugget offers a full-service spa. With whirlpools, saunas, a large workout room, and a full selection of massages and other spa services, nobody else on Fremont can pamper guests at the same high level as Golden Nugget.

Tilt: Despite being owned by a company specializing in restaurants (Landry's) and having more dining options than any other Downtown hotel, Golden Nugget's restaurants disappoint. On paper, it seems Golden Nugget offers something for every palette—seafood, Italian, Mexican, Asian—but few of them measure up. The buffet is mediocre (even by Downtown standards), and the café is a chain restaurant, Claim Jumper. The only standouts in Golden Nugget's dining lineup are Vic and Anthony's, which receives consistently good reviews as one of Downtown's best steakhouses, and Red Sushi, which has some of the best happy hour food specials on Fremont Street.

Unfortunately, as Downtown's only Strip-quality resort, Golden Nugget also features Strip-quality gambling conditions. Unlike at other Downtown casinos, gamblers are unlikely to find favorable video poker pay tables or low-limit table games at the Nugget. Expect $10 and higher blackjack minimums, compared to $3 and $5 at neighboring properties.

Four Queens

www.fourqueens.com

PLAYERS CLUB: Royal Players Club

UNOFFICIAL THEME: Oldness

Like several Fremont Street properties, Four Queens feels a little tired. Open since 1966, the well-worn hotel and casino could use a facelift, but visitors who prefer a little grit with their Las Vegas experience will love it. Cramped slot machine aisles, smoky air, and sticky bar tops remind guests they're not gambling at Wynn or Bellagio. Like most of its Downtown neighbors, Four Queens offers low-limit table games and decent video poker odds. Hotel rooms are comparable to similarly priced low-budget Downtown properties.

Jackpot: Tucked away a few steps below the casino level at Four Queens is Hugo's Cellar, one of the last old-style gourmet restaurants in Las Vegas. Female guests receive a red rose, waiters wear tuxedos, and the aura of a more formal, classy era fills the air. Dining at Hugo's feels like a step back in time to the 1960s. Entrees (steaks, seafood, chicken, and chops) average around $50 and include tableside-prepared salad, choice of veggies, and chocolate-dipped fruit. Portions are large, and service is outstanding. For a special occasion or a romantic dinner, Hugo's Cellar is a perfect hidden gem.

Tilt: When I first checked in at Four Queens for a stay several years ago, I noticed the housekeeping staff had provided several pairs of earplugs along with the traditional amenities of shampoo, conditioner, and soap. I thought it was a nice touch to help light sleepers. Later that evening, however, I discovered that earplugs were necessary for just about anyone except Marlee Matlin to sleep there. My room overlooked the 3rd Street stage, where a band loudly serenaded me with Bon Jovi covers until 1 a.m.

Unfortunately, this problem isn't unique to my particular room or even to Four Queens. A large number of rooms at Fremont Street hotels face either the concert stages or the Viva Vision light show, which also features loud music. Even guests at Downtown Grand—a block removed from Fremont Street—have had issues with the volume. Because the hotels are old, soundproofing isn't so great. Unless you're planning to stay up every night until things quiet down—sometimes as late as 2 a.m.—request a room on a high floor, facing away from Fremont Street and the stages.

Fremont

www.fremontcasino.com
PLAYERS CLUB: BConnected
UNOFFICIAL THEME: Meh

Opened in 1956, the Fremont Hotel and Casino has become the Chili's of Las Vegas hotels. There's nothing especially great about it, but also nothing particularly objectionable. Pretty much every other hotel and casino on the Strip and in Downtown has some noteworthy feature and some aspect that is exceptionally annoying. Fremont, however, walks the line of mediocrity. The rooms, casino, and restaurants are average. Come to the Fremont, you'll have a reasonably okay time.

Jackpot: Having a difficult time figuring out whether anything at

Fremont is exceptional or different, I asked *Five Hundy by Midnight* podcast listeners for help. As expected, most of the responses from Fremont fans cited things like great service, convenient parking, and easy comps. All of these are reasonable reasons to enjoy a hotel and casino, but not factors that significantly set it apart from other Downtown properties. Howard Park from Washington, D.C., provided a response that made the most sense: "The Fremont hasn't changed in over 20 years. Binion's has changed for the worse. The D changed for the better. Las Vegas Club has become much worse. Fremont? Exactly the same." In a town where nothing stays the same for long, there's something to be said for consistency and stability. Many people like things the way they like them, and change bums them out. Fremont may be the perfect hotel and casino choice for them.

Tilt: In late 2014, owner Boyd Gaming announced plans to update some of the restaurant options at its Downtown Las Vegas casinos. They began by replacing Pasta Pirate at The Cal with California Noodle House. If similar updates occur at Fremont, the whole two decades with essentially no major changes thing goes out the window.

Downtown Grand

www.downtowngrand.com

PLAYERS CLUB: My Points

UNOFFICIAL THEME: Floundering

A complete remodel of Lady Luck, a hotel and casino that shuttered in 2006, Downtown Grand opened in October 2013. Since that time, adjustments have been constant as the casino works to attract customers. Despite being located just one block from Fremont Street, Downtown Grand gets about as much foot traffic as the Bellagio art gallery during National Finals Rodeo week. As a result, Downtown Grand has slashed restaurant hours and increased promotions. New resorts always fine-tune as they figure out what's working and what's not. Whether Downtown Grand succeeds in attracting visitors remains to be seen. Main Street Station has a comparable location—perhaps even a little worse—but benefits from cross-promotion with other Downtown Boyd Gaming properties (California and Fremont)

and its continuous operation since 1977. An independent hotel and casino, Downtown Grand doesn't have this advantage.

Jackpot: Despite stumbling out of the gate, Downtown Grand isn't without some nice features. Second only to Golden Nugget's shark tank pool, Downtown Grand's rooftop pool deck is one of the area's most comfortable. The pool deck includes a bar, tons of lounge chairs, cabanas, a fire pit, blackjack, and a performance stage for DJs and bands. Attempts at giving the pool deck a dayclub vibe, complete with bottle service, are misguided and probably won't survive. Such concepts thrive on the Strip but don't fly in budget-conscious Downtown. However, the rooftop pool is the ideal option for Downtown guests looking for an alternative to the Nugget but not wanting to settle for the low-rent cement holes found at the few other Downtown properties that offer a pool.

Two Downtown Grand restaurants are among the best not only Downtown but in all of Las Vegas. Located across Third Street from the casino and main hotel tower, Pizza Rock blows away all other pizzerias in Las Vegas. Them may be fighting words, as the number of pizza joints across the city has exploded in the past few years. However, none match Pizza Rock for variety and quality. Baked in four different ovens, pizza styles run the gamut from New York style and classic Italian to California and Chicago cracker thin. Proprietor Tony Gemignani's claim to fame, the Margherita won a bunch of awards and tastes great. However, other options are more flavorful and filling. For the best experience, skip the by-the-slice counter option in favor of a freshly made pie. If dining with a group, choose from the Romana pizzas, large, rectangular, multi-sectioned pies—like three pizzas in one. Make sure to check the website for current specials, as Pizza Rock's happy hour frequently features exceptionally cheap food and decent drink discounts.

Nestled next door to Pizza Rock is Triple George Grill, a restaurant that matches the quality of many upscale steakhouses but in a more casual environment. Steaks average around $30, with salad, seafood, chicken, and pasta dinner entrees averaging $18. Although Triple George is an outstanding dinner option, value seekers will love the lunch menu. Many sandwiches and salads run less than $10, with comfort food entrees (pot roast, chicken pot pie, fettuccini alfredo) priced around $15. For a special treat, ask your server if the off-menu chicken Parmesan sliders are available. An unofficial holdover from the original Mob Bar location connected to Triple George, these delicious mini-sandwiches are melt-in-your-mouth perfection.

Tilt: Speaking of Mob Bar, Downtown Grand completely screwed the pooch when it moved the popular bar out of its original location on Third Street in favor of a larger space tucked away in a corner of the hotel. Because the new location faces the neighboring Mob Museum, it makes sense in theory. However, it didn't work. Coupled with other changes, including the addition of dueling pianos and the elimination of food, Downtown Grand killed the place. The bar is now used only for special events.

Downtown Grand also wastes its outdoor space. A patio built for outdoor table games is rarely open. The three outdoor walk-up windows for sports bets, drinks, and food also get no use. In fact, the deli on the other side of the food window closed after just a few months in business, so the food window is useless unless the restaurant reopens. It's as if by building these outdoor features, Downtown Grand's management just assumed people would show up. This isn't *Field of Dreams*, motherfuckers. The casino should exercise its ability to close down Third Street between Stewart and Ogden, build a stage and book bands to play nightly. Roll out a bar and sell $3 drinks, open a few $3 blackjack tables, and sell hot dogs for $3 each. This would generate pedestrian traffic from Fremont Street, take advantage of Downtown's party atmosphere and begin building brand recognition and loyalty. Instead of operating a nice property that still caters to Downtown value-seekers, Downtown Grand tried competing with Golden Nugget—and failed.

The D

www.thed.com

PLAYERS CLUB: Club D

UNOFFICIAL THEME: Tinnitus

Opened in 2012 after a remodel and rebrand of Fitzgerald's, The D features two distinct casinos. On the first floor, table game dealers dance to blaring Katy Perry and Lady Gaga hits. On the second floor, the clank of quarters dropping into slot machine trays competes with Frank Sinatra, The Beach Boys, and Billy Joel hits from the past.

Jackpot: The D's second-floor Vintage Vegas casino is home to one of only two Sigma Derby machines in Las Vegas (the other is at MGM Grand). This casino rarity is a throwback to the days long before video slot machines with vibrating chairs. Up to 10 players sit around a table containing a miniature horse track (because a full-size horse track wouldn't fit). Betting between one and 20 quarters on projected first- and second-place combinations, gamblers cheer for five plastic horses galloping around the track. Winners are paid based on odds posted before each race begins. The game is a little silly, a little stupid, and a lot of fun. It serves as a perfect showcase piece to The D's classic casino floor.

Located around the corner from Sigma Derby is the most impressive of The D's four restaurants. Joe Vicari's Andiamo Italian Steakhouse has quickly become one of the best restaurants Downtown has to offer. Whether you order a steak, the veal osso bucco, or pasta, start with the grande meatball. I dream about the meatball. I also dream about trains going through tunnels. The meatball dream is my favorite though. Dinner for two with drinks will average around $150 to $200.

A more budget-conscious meal is available on the first level at American Coney Island. Serving up Detroit-style coney dogs and chili cheese fries, American Coney is an ideal place to grab a bite after a night of boozing on Fremont Street. A semi-secret menu item, American Coney's FiveHunDog is named in honor of the *Five Hundy by Midnight* podcast. Originally offered during the Vegas Internet Mafia Family Picnic hosted at The D in 2013, the FiveHunDog includes two dogs covered in chili, mustard, and onions, in a single bun.

The first-floor bar, Longbar is an ideal place to watch televised sports. The quantity, size, and placement of Longbar's TVs make it a huge upgrade over other casino bars for taking in a game. At most casino bars, televisions are mounted high so everyone at the bar can see them. Depending on your seat, you're nearly always looking up or at an angle. Longbar's row of TVs is mounted just above the back of the bar, so no neck craning is required.

Tilt: The biggest bummer about The D is the music volume in the first-floor casino. When cranked up at night, the loudness makes it nearly impossible to have a conversation without yelling. I get that loud music adds to the party atmosphere and perhaps gets the dancing dealers to shake their asses a little harder, but if "Party Rock" was brought down to just below the level of a jet-engine roar, I could fall asleep later without the Emergency Broadcast System tone ringing in my ears. Also, get off my lawn, you damn kids.

Another part of The D's party vibe that gives me mixed feelings are the flair bartenders. Unless I'm at a mixology bar and there's some hard-core fruit-muddling going on, I want my drink served as efficiently as possible. I don't need a bunch of flippy shit delaying delivery of my Captain and Diet. I'm getting parched and losing my buzz while Tom Cruise and Bryan Brown are exchanging witty quips and chucking Smirnoff bottles back and forth. Cocktails and dreams, my ass. Where's my drink? That said, once I have a significant buzz, I become entranced by the bartenders' bottle acrobatics. These guys are pros, and they know how to entertain. So, I offer a million-dollar idea to Longbar and flair bars around the world. At Brazilian steakhouse chain Fogo de Chão, diners each receive a round disk the size of a drink coaster. One side is green and the other is red. When they want more meat brought to them, they flip the disk to green. When they don't, they flip it to red. The same concept could easily work for flair bars. When I display the red side of my coaster, pour my drink quickly and without dramatic enhancement. When I feel like seeing a little razzle-dazzle with my drink order, I'll flip it to green. Fogo de Chão that shit. Everybody wins.

El Cortez

www.elcortezhotelcasino.com
PLAYERS CLUB: Club Cortez
UNOFFICIAL THEME: White Diamonds by Elizabeth Taylor

Located two blocks east of the end of the Fremont Street Experience, El Cortez epitomizes what many people love about Downtown casinos—low limit gambling with great odds, cheap but delicious food and booze, and friendly service from longtime employees.

Jackpot: One of the oldest hotels in Downtown, El Cortez finds itself in one of today's trendiest areas of the city—Fremont East. Just a few years ago, visitors walking from the Fremont Street Experience to El Cortez encountered empty storefronts, panhandlers, and many shades of shady characters. Today, the storefronts are filled with bars and restaurants, bar-hoppers, and only the occasional panhandler.

Going strong since 1941, El Cortez embraces the charm and grit of old Las Vegas without getting stuck in the past. This balance means that visitors will find plenty of classic coin-dropper video poker machines with favorable pay tables and the latest video slots. It means bar patrons can get a great old fashioned or caramel appletini. It means hotel guests can choose an original room above the casino, accessible only by stairs, or a Cabana Suite with a vibrant, modern design.

Catering to tourists and locals alike, El Cortez offers great value. The casino frequently features quarter roulette, $3 craps with 10x odds, and $3 and $5 single, and double deck 3:2 blackjack—long-gone relics in most Las Vegas casinos. A few hours of casino play typically result in monthly mailers offering two-for-one meals, 2x to 5x players club point multipliers, and discounted or free room nights. Even without the mailers, meals and hotel stays are cheap.

Among the three casino bars at El Cortez, The Parlour Bar & Lounge is a little-known Downtown treat. Although the actual bar has only seven stools, lounge seating provides space for a few dozen people. Free entertainment includes a lounge pianist performing instrumental classics from the Rat Pack era, an Elvis impersonator, and karaoke. Designed with rich colors and comfortable leather furniture, Parlour Bar feels a little swanky, but never snobby. It's the sort of place that inspires guests to order martinis and manhattans, relax, and pretend it's 1958.

In addition to a variety of no-frills pavilion, vintage, and tower rooms, El Cortez offers a couple options with more modern designs. Located in the main tower, several 600-square-foot designer suites feature unique themes, including a 1950s rec room, and mobster-era Vegas. These rooms are frequently available for under $100. Located in a separate tower behind the main hotel tower, the El Cortez Cabana Suites are modern boutique hotel rooms. In hotel parlance, "boutique" means super small but with fun, quirky designs. Indeed, the El Cortez Cabana Suites fit this description. Despite their small footprint, the Cabana Suites are designed to take full advantage of available space. Not an inch is wasted. Painted in bright green, these rooms are modern, hip, and fun. Guests who want a little extra square footage should opt for a junior suite or super suite (still small, but with more breathing room than the deluxe rooms), for just a few bucks more. Cabana Suite rooms are frequently available for as low as $30 during the week and $60 on weekends.

Tilt: Many Las Vegas hotels pump scents into the air to mask cigarette fumes and other unpleasant odors. Unfortunately, El Cortez fills its casino with a fragrance you last encountered at the McDermott-Quinn Funeral Home for Aunt Wilma's memorial service. Like an industrial blast of White Diamonds by Elizabeth Taylor, this sweet, flowery scent is sure to make any church-going octogenarian feel right at home. Casino operators likely go through an extensive evaluation process when choosing an appropriate scent. I suspect El Cortez managers looked at the number of oxygen tanks propped up next to slot machines and decided to go with Eau de Funerale to help customers begin acclimating to their final destination before taking a permanent dirt nap.

CHAPTER 14

Dining and Drinking

"Man shall not live on bread alone. He also needs a medium-rare steak and a cold Chimay every once in a while."—Stupak 4:4* This oddly specific, moderately sexist bible passage rings truer than ever in Las Vegas. The world's favorite desert wonderland has become a haven for magnificent dining and drinking choices. If you enjoy splurging on expensive gourmet dinners, the city provides a multitude of options. If you prefer more casual burger and pizza joints, you'll never go hungry in Vegas. If you like to stuff your face with as much food as possible for a single price, no destination can match Vegas. And when it comes to the alcoholic arts, cocktail, beer, and wine drinkers alike can discover numerous locations to quench their boozy thirsts.

DINING

Despite the huge variety of dining options in Las Vegas, the Strip's resorts aren't always restaurant trendsetters. In many cases, they mimic each other's success. As a result, just about every major Strip resort includes its version of certain types of restaurant. For a long stretch of the city's history, this meant every casino had a 24-hour café and a buffet. Today, you can walk through the doors of nearly any property on Las Vegas Boulevard and also find a steakhouse, a burger joint, and a pizza place.

CAFÉS

Most Las Vegas casinos offer some form of dining around the clock. The most common 24-hour casino restaurant is the café. Good casino cafés are unpretentious and dependable. They're a logical place to begin the day and often a necessary final stop before hitting the sack.

So what makes a great casino café?

- **Breakfast around the clock:** In Las Vegas, your day may just as easily begin at 1 p.m. as 6 a.m. Thus, 24-hour access to eggs, pancakes, and bacon is a must. Every decent casino café meets this basic requirement.

- **Variety:** Many of us end our day drunk and hungry in a casino café. We don't know what we want, but we know we need to eat something or face a crippling hangover in a few hours. Offering breakfast, sandwiches, burgers, salads, soup, comfort food, and miscellaneous specialty menus (3 a.m. kung pao chicken, anyone?), cafés cater to all but the pickiest customers. Can't decide? Mix and match. There's no shame in ordering a shrimp cocktail, a cup of chili, meatloaf, a side of bacon, and a slice of apple pie in a Vegas café.

- **Speed:** I always marvel at how one kitchen can produce such a huge variety of menu options so quickly. Within about 15 minutes of ordering, you'll be filling your mouth hole, whether you ordered a turkey club or fish and chips. It's not like these are Mexican restaurants, which can produce 120 menu items with the same seven ingredients. A café's food storage capacity must be huge, and the organization in the kitchen has to be perfect to crank out orders so efficiently.

- **A little grit:** Although some modern casino cafés feel like any Applebee's restaurant, the best ones are a little rough around the edges. The menus are worn, the booths have seen better days, and the waitresses have put up with too much bullshit to feign amusement at your lame jokes. Don't mistake gritty for dirty. Nobody wants dirty. It's just a little tarnished. As Strip casinos have become more corporate, most of the grit has disappeared from their cafés, but you'll still find it on Fremont Street.

Many times, the best 24-hour café option is the one closest to your hotel room. All considerations other than convenience take a backseat when you need food immediately. When you have a little more flexibility, these cafés are worthy of a visit.

- **Du-par's (Golden Gate):** With classic shrimp cocktails and arguably the best pancakes on the planet available around the clock, Du-par's has become my go-to café choice Downtown.

- **Hash House a Go Go (The Linq):** If you value quantity over quality, Hash House is a solid option. That's not to say the food is bad, but patrons remember the visuals—the trough of pasta and foot-tall stack of chicken and waffles—more than the taste of the food.
- **Peppermill:** Although not located in a casino, this around-the-clock café just north of Encore is the prototypical American diner with a splash of Vegas neon. Portions are large, the food is decent, and the location is ideal after stumbling out of the neighboring Fireside Lounge.
- **Planet Dailies (Planet Hollywood) and Grand Lux Café (The Venetian):** Presenting a modern take on the classic casino café, Planet Dailies and Grand Lux have large menus, good quality, and huge portions.

BUFFETS

No dining option is as closely associated with Las Vegas as the all-you-can-eat buffet. Although some Strip casinos, including The Linq, New York-New York, and The Venetian shun the tradition of offering a buffet, most major resorts continue to offer unlimited quantities of food for a single price. Caesars Entertainment has taken the buffet concept a step further by selling a Buffet of Buffets pass, giving customers access to five of its buffets for 24 hours for a single (frequently increasing) rate. Pricing begins at $50 (higher on weekends or with the addition of the company's more expensive Rio and Caesars Palace buffets).

In general, higher priced buffets offer better quality and greater variety of foods not found at mid-tier and low-priced options. However, just like with its hotel rates, Caesars Palace wildly inflates its buffet price, making it one of the worst all-you-can-eat values in the city. The quality and variety are great, but not great enough to justify a dinner price of more than $50—between $10 and $20 higher than the better-quality Bellagio, The Cosmopolitan, and Wynn buffets. Planet Hollywood and The Mirage are dependable, and Aria is dependably disappointing. Paris excels at breakfast—largely because of its made-to-order crepes—but its lunch and dinner selections are mediocre. Treasure Island, Monte Carlo, and MGM Grand are generally mediocre as well, while Flamingo and Circus Circus are notoriously awful.

For a reliable, current list of buffet prices, visit www.lasvegasadvisor. com/buffets.cfm.

If you decide to eat at a buffet—particularly a high-end buffet—having a strategy will help you get your money's worth from the meal. Following are tips to maximize your buffet value.

- **Take it easy on the first pass:** Some people like to scope out the entire buffet before selecting any items. This isn't a bad idea. However, having chosen to eat at a buffet, there's a decent chance you don't have that much self-control. You're ready to load up—research be damned. Keep portions small so you can sample a lot of items and figure out what you want to really load up on during your second pass. It may be difficult to temper your enthusiasm upon seeing a giant vat of macaroni and cheese. But you'll be grateful you took only a little when you encounter the shrimp trough ten steps later.

- **Skip the bread:** Las Vegas buffets try to get those of us who love carbs to load up on dough-based items. They're cheap and fill us up quickly, minimizing stomach space for more expensive items like prime rib. Buffets usually position bread at the beginning of the buffet line or with the salad bar and include options like pretzel bread rather than just boring, extremely resistible dinner rolls. Just say no to the dough.

- **Avoid the pizza too:** The more you love pizza, the more disappointed you'll be by the pizza offered at even the finest buffets in Las Vegas. It's never good. Ever. Vegas buffet pizza falls between grade school cafeteria pizza and Pizza Hut's so-bad-we-filled-the-crust-with-liquid-cheese pizza. In fact, the readers of *VegasTripping* voted "any buffet pizza" as the worst Las Vegas pizza in the 2015 Trippies Awards (www.vegastripping. com/trippies2015).

- **Be different:** Just about every time I've ever dined at a Las Vegas buffet, there's one guy in the place who loads up an entire plate with crab legs. This fucker elaborately stacks them like he's practicing for some sort of seafood Jenga competition. He unapologetically loves crab legs and doesn't care who knows it. That's fantastic—but it's *always* crab legs. Just once, I'd like to see someone with a similar public display of love for something else. So when you find that item you love, make a special trip back to the line just for that. Some people may stare disapprovingly as you stroll back to your table with a pyramid of sausage links, but I will salute you. While you're having fun, why not go full-on Richard Dreyfuss and construct a replica of Devil's Tower out of a full plate of mashed potatoes too?

STEAK

You're in the city of excess, pissing away last month's earnings in the casino, challenging your liver's capabilities, and inhaling more smoke than Snoop Dogg. You may as well thumb your nose at your cardiologist and enjoy a thick, juicy t-bone. Fortunately, you'll have no trouble finding a good chunk of beef in Las Vegas. You could order a cheap steak from the casino's café, but the full steakhouse experience is much more Vegasy. Waiters in formal attire mix salads tableside, ply you with stiff drinks, and encourage you to order way too much food. No, you don't technically need an order of calamari before ingesting half a cow, but Jimmy the waiter insists. He's been serving customers in Las Vegas since 1957 and just told you a funny story about the time he nearly spilled a manhattan on Ol' Blue Eyes, so you can't resist taking his suggestion. It's easy to drop a few hundred bucks in a steakhouse, so choosing a winner is important. Steakhouses that consistently receive positive reviews from *Five Hundy* listeners include:

- Andiamo (The D)
- Craftsteak (MGM Grand)
- Delmonico (The Venetian)
- Gordon Ramsay Steak (Paris)
- Heritage Steak (The Mirage)
- Prime (Bellagio)
- The Steak House (Circus Circus)

- SW (Wynn)
- Triple George Grill (Downtown Grand)
- Vic and Anthony's (Golden Nugget)

BURGERS

Las Vegas has become the land of the $16 burger. Dress up some ground beef with roasted tomato, arugula, and some obscure euro-cheese you've never heard of, and you've got yourself a gourmet burger. You'll also have a choice of fries—regular, truffle, or sweet potato—but they'll cost you an extra $8. Make sure to add a boozy shake for another $9. Check, please! You just racked up a $60+ lunch tab for burgers, fries, and shakes for two people. Oh, Vegas. Is there any method you haven't developed for taking our money while we walk away smiling? You won't have any trouble finding a gourmet burger joint on the Strip, although they haven't yet infiltrated Fremont Street. When Downtown, you can find some delicious (and cheap) basic burgers at the Binion's and El Cortez's cafés. Pizza Rock (Downtown Grand) has a small selection of outstanding burgers—unexpected for a pizza joint. Popular gourmet burger options on Las Vegas Boulevard include:

- BLT Burger (The Mirage)
- Burger Bar (Mandalay Bay)
- BurGR (Planet Hollywood)
- Holstein's (The Cosmopolitan)
- Stripburger (Fashion Show Mall)

PIZZA

In 2010, The Cosmopolitan opened with its not-so-secret Secret Pizza restaurant—located on the third level, at the end of an album-cover-lined hallway with no signage. Although certainly not the first pizzeria in Las Vegas, it received raves and has spawned more than a dozen new pizza places on the Strip and Downtown in subsequent years. They typically offer full pies and pizza by the slice, with an emphasis on New York thin crust options. Without question, the three pizza joints garnering the most raves from *Five Hundy* listeners are: Pizza Rock (Downtown Grand) for its quality and huge variety of styles, prepared in four different types of ovens;

Secret Pizza (The Cosmopolitan) for its basic, slightly greasy, hangover-preventing pizza by the slice; and Five50 (Aria) for a great variety of interesting signature pizzas with unusual ingredients, including ghost chili salami and truffles. Other decent options include:

- 800 Degrees (Monte Carlo and SLS)
- Pin-Up Pizza (Planet Hollywood)
- Pop Up Pizza (The Plaza)

DRINKING

Whether you're a longtime *Five Hundy* podcast listener or know me only by what you've read in this book, you've probably figured out that I like to have an occasional cocktail or beer. It's true. I enjoy the effects of alcohol. Podcasting hero Chris Hardwick describes drinking as "pouring smiles on your brain." I like to keep my brain drenched in smiles while I'm in Las Vegas. If you have the urge to write me an e-mail warning me of the dangers of over-consuming alcohol, don't bother. Nobody sucks down a long island iced tea thinking it's packed full of essential vitamins and nutrients. I've never asked a bartender what percentage of my recommended daily allowance of riboflavin is contained in a 10 ounce Delirium Tremens. I'm boozing, not juicing, so settle down. The point is this: booze is a fun component of my Las Vegas vacations.

If you're genetically inclined to make bad decisions after sipping a Sinatra smash or 10, you may want to skip this section. I'm in no way encouraging anyone to participate in an activity that could lead to jumping behind the wheel of your Honda Accord, tooling down the Strip, and t-boning a police car at 11 a.m. Know your limits and act accordingly. And that's one to grow on.

Now, for those of us blessed with a healthy liver and a favorable genetic disposition, let's talk about drinking in Las Vegas.

The rise of craft cocktail and craft beer culture has leveled the playing field amongst drinkers. Not so long ago, only wine connoisseurs could blather for hours about "hints of birch wood," "fruity finishes," and "subtle undertones." Today, cocktail and beer drinkers are just as likely to sniff their drink before tasting, and drone on about beverage complexity. Bartenders specializing in craft cocktails educate their customers about the nuances of mixology, pointing out the benefits of double straining and proper ice consistency. Brewpub bartenders offer suggestions based on customers' preference for IPAs vs. Belgians vs. stouts. They explain the effects of pairing specific hops with specific malts, and the types of beer best matched with different foods. It's a fun time to be a drinker.

IF YOU GAMBLE, BOOZE WILL COME

It's no secret that the people who run casinos want your money. Plying you with free alcohol is among their many tactics for getting it. Even if you have a super-attentive bartender or waitress who ensures your glass is never empty, that booze won't cost the casino more than a buck or two an hour. If it keeps you happy and firmly planted at a machine or table, the potential profit far exceeds the costs. Plus, alcohol impairs your judgment, leading some people to make bad decisions, like placing higher bets, ignoring optimal strategies, or dining at the Flamingo buffet.

Depending on how you approach your time in the casino, free alcohol may be a welcome fun-enhancer or an evil temptation. Some players' ultimate goal is minimizing the casino's edge. They play perfect blackjack and video poker strategies, shun sucker bets, and never consume alcohol when gambling. At least they can take advantage of free water, juice, and soda, remaining hydrated while playing. Then there are the rest of us. Although we certainly want to win, we put more focus on the overall casino experience. We like to combine our vices—gambling, boozing, and smoking. We want to win, but playing with a tasty buzz adds to our perceived entertainment value. In other words, drinking while gambling is fun.

There are a few things to keep in mind when it comes to free casino booze.

- **Tip your waitress a buck or two per drink.** When playing table games, tipping with chips instead of cash is perfectly acceptable. Tips make up the majority of her pay, so don't be the cheap fucker who throws two quarters on her tray and expects a hand-written thank-you note. Besides, you'll likely get much better service from a happy waitress than from one who thinks you're a dick.

- **If you're playing at the bar, don't be shy about asking the bartender about proper protocol.** Asking, "Are drinks comped for players?" will result in all the information you need. The majority of bars expect you to put in at least $20 and play max coins (five coins per bet). A few casino bars do not comp drinks, so it's always good to ask when you're playing somewhere new. If you play one coin at a time in an obvious attempt to drink as much as possible for as little play as possible, you'll likely get charged. They've seen it a million times. You aren't nearly as clever as you think. Upon serving your drink, the bartender will likely place a receipt in front of your machine—frequently in a glass. Don't make the mistake of thinking you're being charged and leave the amount of money printed on the receipt. If you owe money, the bartender will ask for it. Tip a buck or two a drink.

- **You're probably not going to get top-shelf liquor.** Expect the generic version of whatever booze you order. Playing at a bar, I once looked at the receipt for my Captain Morgan and Diet Coke and noticed it said Admiral Nelson and Diet Coke. Close enough. How different could one sailor-based spiced rum be from another? If you're a beer drinker, ask what type of bottled beer is available. If the casino serves only tap beer (which is pretty rare these days), don't be surprised if you get an unrecognizable brew unless you're sitting at a bar, where you see them fill the glass. Many years ago at the late, great Barbary Coast, when the cocktail waitresses came to the bar to have orders filled, the bartenders would line up several glasses and turn on all the taps. It didn't matter what type of beer players ordered. They were unwittingly playing beer roulette. Of course, Barbary's tap beer always tasted unusually skunky, so it was all similarly bad regardless of the brand.

- **Some bars will comp the good stuff.** Again, don't be shy about asking your bartender whether she can comp specific brands. Unlike on the casino floor, you'll see her mix the drink, so there won't be any question what you're getting. A few bars—most notably the video poker bars at The Cosmopolitan—comp even their specialty cocktails. And in recent years, some bars are offering a wider selection of beers than the traditional Coors, Miller, and Bud choices. The Linq's Tag Sports Bar has a particularly nice selection.

- **Drink service sometimes sucks.** Depending on the day and time, casinos may not have enough cocktail waitresses working to provide adequate casino coverage. As a result, service can be spotty. If you've been playing for a while and haven't seen a waitress, asking your dealer, a pit boss, or a floor person if a waitress is available may help. Cut the waitress some slack. She's likely a victim of the casino's attempt to cut costs by having too few waitresses cover the entire casino.

NON-GAMBLING CASINO DRINKING

Sometimes you may want to have a few drinks without gambling. Fear not. Las Vegas has a multitude of options to meet your alcohol cravings.

Casino Bars: Just because a bar includes video poker doesn't mean you have to play. They'll gladly accept your money in exchange for beverages. Most standard casino bars include a few TVs showing sporting events, making them good options for keeping an eye on the status of your sports bets. The Cosmopolitan's Chandelier Bar (first level) and Bond are among the most noteworthy casino bars for cocktail drinkers. They use top-shelf liquor and fresh ingredients. It's always a good sign when you see a bartender muddling fruit. While most casino bartenders specialize in pulling taps and slinging rum and Cokes, most Cosmo bartenders specialize in craft cocktails. Tell them what types of alcohol or flavors you prefer, and they can make something off-menu to meet your tastes.

Lounges: Las Vegas lounges used to be small rooms on the edge of the casino floor where live bands played late into the night. Although some may still feature a jazz combo, piano player, or small band, many have either a DJ or no live entertainment. And while some remain open to the gaming floor, others are more defined spaces, isolated from the casino. Some have a small dance floor, but unlike nightclubs, the energy level is more relaxed, and the focus is more on conversation than partying.

Many Vegas lounges focus on craft cocktails. Vesper and Chandelier at The Cosmopolitan, along with Bound at The Cromwell do amazing things with fresh fruit, bitters, and miscellaneous creative ingredients (such as marshmallows and cookie crumbs). For an only-in-Vegas experience, order a verbena at Chandelier 1.5 (discussed in Chapter 10). Another Chandelier 1.5 specialty, the fire-breathing dragon includes a raspberry frozen in liquid nitrogen. Chewing the berry causes smoke to come out of the drinker's nose. Other outstanding lounge options include Hyde at Bellagio (before 10 p.m., when it becomes a nightclub), Mandarin Bar at Mandarin Oriental, and Parasol Up/Down at Wynn. Specialty cocktails typically run about $12 to $20.

Wine Bars: With its dozens of upscale restaurants, Las Vegas makes it pretty easy to find a decent bottle of wine. A few, however, offer exceptional wine-by-the-glass menus, extensive collections, or unique experiences catering to wine lovers.

- **Aureole (*www.charliepalmer.com/aureole-las-vegas*):** This Mandalay Bay seafood restaurant from Charlie Palmer boasts a wine collection of more than 50,000 bottles, including nearly 10,000 stored in a four-story wine tower accessed by levitating "wine angels." A daily happy hour features $6 wine by the glass.

- **Double Helix Wine & Whiskey Lounge (*palazzo.double-helixwine.com*):** Located at The Palazzo, Double Helix offers more than 50 wines by the glass, wine flights, and signature wine cocktails, plus an appetizer menu from Emeril Lagasse.

- **Hostile Grape (*www.themresort.com*):** Located off-Strip at M Resort, Hostile Grape's selection of more than 150 self-serve wines via 26 Enomatic stations using pre-paid tasting cards makes it worth a special trip for wine lovers wanting to sample a large selection of wines.

- **La Cave Wine and Food Hideaway (*www.lacavelv.com*):** A Wynn Las Vegas bar and restaurant from Michael Morton, La Cave serves light fare and offers more than 250 bottled wines and 50 wines by the glass.

- **Wine Cellar & Tasting Room (*www.riolasvegas.com*):** Designed to look and feel like an ancient wine cellar, this gem hidden below the Masquerade Village casino at Rio features a $10 million wine collection, more than 100 wines by the glass, and a huge bar. The Wine Cellar is arguably Rio's most impressive attraction.

Beer Bars: Not so long ago, if you wanted a beer in Las Vegas you were typically limited to mass-produced domestics—Budweiser, Miller, Coors—and perhaps Heineken or Guinness as imports. Fortunately, as the craft beer craze grew nationwide, Las Vegas quickly adapted. Today, even basic casino bars often have obscure and varied beer options. Brew connoisseurs seeking large beer selections have a multitude of options.

- **Burger Bar (Mandalay Bay):** Two dozen taps and 100+ bottled and canned beers. *www.burger-bar.com*
- **Rí Rá Irish Pub (Mandalay Bay):** 16 taps and 100+ bottled and canned beers. *www.rira.com*
- **Pub 1842 (MGM Grand):** Two dozen taps and 40+ bottled and canned beers. *www.michaelmina.net/restaurants/las-vegas/pub-1842*
- **The Pub and Keg Room (Monte Carlo):** 80+ taps and 200+ bottled and canned beers. *www.montecarlo.com/restaurants/the-pub-and-keg-room.aspx*
- **Todd English P.U.B. (Aria):** 65+ taps and 30+ bottled and canned beers. *www.toddenglishpub.com*
- **Holstein's (The Cosmopolitan):** Two dozen taps and 100+ bottled and canned beers. *www.holsteinslv.com*
- **Gordon Ramsay Pub & Grill (Caesars Palace):** Three dozen taps and 60+ bottled and canned beers. *www.caesarspalace.com/restaurants/gordon-ramsay-pub-and-grill.html*
- **Tag Sports Bar (The Linq):** 300+ bottled and canned beers.
- **Yard House (The Linq):** 140+ taps. *www.yardhouse.com*
- **Public House (The Venetian):** Two dozen taps and 150+ bottled and canned beers. *www.publichouselv.com*
- **Park on Fremont (Fremont East):** 14 taps and 36+ bottled and canned beers. *www.parkonfremont.com*

Las Vegas also offers a small, but tasty selection of local craft beers.

Those worth sampling include Banger Brewing Company at Neonopolis (*www.bangerbrewing.com*), Chicago Brewing Company at Four Queens (*www.fourqueens.com/dining/chicago_brewing_co*), Triple 7 Restaurant and Microbrewery at Main Street Station (*www.mainstreetcasino.com/dine/triple-7-restaurant-and-microbrewery*), and Ellis Island Brewery at its namesake casino behind Bally's (*www.ellisislandcasino.com/brewery*). Sin City Brewing Co. (*www.sincitybeer.com*) has three Strip bars serving its five varieties, but the quality pales compared to the other four options.

Sports Bars: Las Vegas is a haven for viewing televised sporting events. Most casinos have a bar connected to or just steps from their sports books. A few of them offer the full sports bar experience, including chicken wings, nachos, and other munchies. Lagasse's Stadium at The Palazzo exceeds all others. Not only is betting available on-site, but the massive complex also includes bar, lounge, and multi-level table seating, and food by Emeril Lagasse. The place gets packed on NFL Sundays and during major events, so make reservations and expect minimum food/beverage purchases. For a more traditional sports bar experience, try Blondie's (*www.blondieslasvegas.com*) in the Miracle Mile Shops at Planet Hollywood. Decent food, beer pong, and hot waitresses dressed like cheerleaders make Blondie's a lot of fun. Another decent option is The Pub and Keg Room at Monte Carlo, which has a large space, 35 screens, and an extensive beer selection.

Piano Bars: If you love singing along with "Piano Man," "Sweet Caroline," and "Don't Stop Believin'" performed by piano players who spend as much time shilling for tips as entertaining, Las Vegas can meet your needs. Popular dueling piano bars include New York-New York's Bar at Times Square, Harrah's Piano Bar, Napoleon's at Paris, and Eastside Lounge at Wynn.

Karaoke Bars: Although several bars offer karaoke nights once or twice a week, nightly karaoke bars have nearly disappeared from Las Vegas Boulevard and Fremont Street casinos. Amateur crooners can still find a surprisingly fun nightly karaoke scene nearby at Ellis Island. Beginning at 9 p.m. nightly and continuing until the wee hours of the morning, Ellis Island karaoke attracts a huge spectrum of talent levels and welcomes locals and tourists alike.

Clubs: Today's Strip casinos recognize that the young generation of Las

Vegas visitors doesn't care nearly as much about gambling as their parents and grandparents. For them, Las Vegas represents a different experience that centers around hanging by the pool all afternoon and partying at the club all night. A few hands of blackjack or a couple tosses of the dice play secondary roles, at best. As a result, the Strip has seen a club explosion in the past decade. About two dozen nightclubs and poolside dayclubs now occupy the hotels on and near Las Vegas Boulevard. Some Strip resorts now cater to clubbers more than gamblers. At The Cosmopolitan, The Cromwell, and SLS, the casinos seem like an afterthought, with much more attention being focused on the club scene. Poolside dayclubs evolve into nighttime hotspots, keeping the party crowd going almost around the clock.

Most clubs have multiple entry lines.

- **General admission:** Wait in line (possibly for hours) and pay the cover charge ($20-$40).
- **VIP guest list:** Wait in a shorter line, skip the cover charge (if you're a woman), and possibly get a free drink or two (again, limited to humans with XX chromosomes).
- **Table reservations:** Get ushered in almost immediately with no cover charge because you're about to spend a bundle for bottle service.

In all cases, dressing fashionably and not acting like a wanker can help your cause. Guests can get on the VIP list with a little planning. Contact the club a few days in advance, let them know how many men and women are in your group, and ask if it's possible to be added to the list. If your plans aren't firm before you arrive in Vegas, talking to your hotel concierge or a host at the club's entrance a few hours before it opens may also get you on the list. Clubs never want more guys than gals, so women get preferential treatment. Groups of guys should plan to either make friends with a group of women wanting to go to the same club, or plan to make table reservations and lay down some cash for bottle service. While paying $400 or more for a bottle of booze and mixers may seem ridiculous, it's not that bad when split up between several people. Individual cocktails at clubs frequently cost $15-$20, and admission for guys is usually around $30-$40, so you're going to drop some substantial change regardless. Again, table reservations are available by contacting the club in advance or at the club entrance.

During your Vegas visit, you will likely encounter nightclub pass hustlers on the Strip. These passes are typically legitimate, waiving the cover charge (at least for women) and perhaps getting you in a shorter line. If you accept the passes, the hustlers will pressure you for a tip.

For individual club reviews, tips, and contacts for most Las Vegas dayclubs and nightclubs, visit _www.jackcolton.com_. This site provides the most comprehensive guide to Las Vegas nightlife, and makes the admittance process much less intimidating than it may appear for rookies suffering from nightclub jitters.

FREMONT EAST

In Downtown Las Vegas, many tourists never venture beyond the comfort of the Fremont Street Experience canopy. Unfortunately, they're missing out on Fremont East, unofficially the Las Vegas drinking district. Although Fremont East technically stretches three

blocks, from Las Vegas Boulevard to North 8ᵗʰ Street, the majority of action occurs in the one-block area just beyond the huge Slotzilla zip line platform. Visitors will find a few restaurants, shops, and cafés, but the real attractions are the dozen or so bars lining both sides of the street. Each has a different atmosphere and concept, so just about everyone can find a suitable watering hole or two. Favorites include:

Downtown Cocktail Room: Located just around the corner from Fremont at 111 S. Las Vegas Blvd. (look for the neon "downtown" sign), Downtown Cocktail Room is one of the swankier, cozier bars of Downtown Las Vegas. Depending on when you visit, the dimly lit room typically features either piped in or DJ-supplied ambient music. The room can get loud, but most of the din is supplied by customers' voices rather than the music. What sets Downtown Cocktail Room apart from the other bars in the Fremont East District is the variety and quality of its cocktails. One of the best mixology bars in Las Vegas, Downtown Cocktail Room specializes in custom-made cocktails using fresh ingredients and homemade bitters. You've probably never seen a bar menu like Downtown Cocktail Room's. Featured cocktails include a ranking of one to four indicating the complexity of each drink, and a symbol reflecting the type of glass in which each drink is served. Cocktails with lower numbers are likely to provide a consistent, tasty flavor from start to finish. Those with higher complexity will change as your palate gets used to the flavors. A drink ranked as a four may start out smoky and end sweet. If you love cocktails, make this your first stop when visiting Fremont East.

The Griffin: With cheap Hamms or Pabst Blue Ribbon on tap, a jukebox stocked with classic rock, punk, and indie bands, and no cover charge, The Griffin can be a magnet for hipsters, but don't let that stop you from giving it a shot. Its great ambiance, low lighting, and indoor fire pits give this place an old Vegas feel without trying too hard. The Griffin may not have an obvious concept like some neighboring bars, but it doesn't really need one. Cold cocktails, a respectable beer lineup, plenty of lounge seating, a rockin' jukebox, and hopefully some good conversation are enough to make The Griffin worth checking out. Load up the jukebox with The Replacements, Foghat, and The Clash, order a Jameson and ginger, and have a good time.

The Laundry Room: The Laundry Room is the semi-secret backroom speakeasy at Commonwealth—a bar within a bar. Accessible via a hidden door only by those with reservations, The Laundry Room is a small room featuring a few strict rules (no photos, two-hour maximum stay, don't talk about fight club). This place is a cocktail lover's wet dream. Don't bother trying to order beer or wine. They don't have any. The menu features a fantastic variety, but if you want to have real fun, tell the bartender what you enjoy and let him come up with just the right thing. Cocktails run $15 a pop. For access, send a text message to (702) 701-1466 with the day, time and number of people. Someone will respond with a confirmation. Reservations can be made up to one week in advance.

Park on Fremont: Park on Fremont features an indoor bar and restaurant, and two patios. The menu includes more than 100 beers, a creative selection of bloody marys and so-so gastropub fare. The space is designed with a vintage vibe, including an antique jukebox. Make sure to check out all of the artwork and trinkets decorating the back patio. Explore a bit to find the teeter totter. Park is casual, friendly, and fun.

Wayfarer Bar: Tucked away behind a nondescript doorway on Inspire Theater's ground level is Wayfarer Bar, a cozy classic cocktail bar with an appreciation for bourbon and scotch. The people behind Downtown Cocktail Room founded Wayfarer, and it shows. Although the room is smaller and a bit more subdued, Wayfarer's bartenders provide the same great service and attention to detail that brings me back to DCR so often. If you appreciate a great old fashioned, blood and sand or moscow mule, Wayfarer is worth a visit.

Atomic Liquors: Located a couple blocks beyond Fremont East at 917 Fremont, Atomic Liquors is worth the slightly sketchy walk. Opened in the mid-1940s, the oldest bar in Las Vegas took on its current name in the 1950s, when the government began testing atomic bombs not far from the city. The bar is somewhat themed, but not in an obnoxious Hard Rock Café way. A small monitor above the urinal in the men's room shows videos of atomic bomb tests, and some of the artwork harkens back to Nevada's mushroom-cloud-rich past. However, the walls are mostly adorned with artifacts from Atomic Liquors's past. At its heart, Atomic Liquors feels like any small-town or neighborhood corner bar in America. It's a welcoming spot to belly up to the bar, carry on a conversation and have a cold beer or cocktail. It's not overly kitschy and is about as unpretentious as they come. The bartenders are friendly, the music isn't too loud, the always-changing beer menu is vast, and the patrons aren't there to impress anyone.

Shameless Plug: When Fremont East began transforming a few years ago from a collection of mostly empty storefronts to the entertainment district it has become, finding information about the bars in a single location was impossible. To fill this void, I whipped together a website, _FremontStreetBars.com_, which continues to provide information on the bars on and around Fremont Street. Check it out before your visit for the latest information.

FOOD AND BEVERAGE TRENDS

Being one of the nation's culinary hot spots has advantages and disadvantages. Every Tom (Colicchio), Rick (Moonen), and Kerry (Simon) goes to Las Vegas to unveil his latest restaurant concept or

replicate his successes from other cities around the world. As a result, Las Vegas dining options improve year after year. While the Strip features an unmatched variety of top quality restaurants in a relatively small area, this large dining concentration leads to another, less appealing phenomenon. Las Vegas leads the country in running the latest food and beverage trends into the ground.

Remember a few years ago when the world collectively realized bacon makes everything better? This smoked pork renaissance was a wonderful time. Why season food with salt when you could use Bacon Salt? Why just have shrimp when you could have bacon-wrapped shrimp? We've got chocolate. We've got bacon. Why not dip the bacon in chocolate? America's kitchens became delicious bacon fuckfests. Shrewd chefs realized they could wrap otherwise abandoned items from the back of the fridge in bacon, toss it on the appetizer menu, and make a tidy profit. Before the bacon craze, when was the last time anyone ordered dates in a restaurant? Never! But bacon-wrapped dates? Oh yeah. Keep 'em coming.

Bacon is great. Everybody loves it, but enough already. We have enough bacon-related options. Use it to improve otherwise shitty foods like brussels sprouts, but there's no need to sprinkle it on ice cream or wrap it around filet mignon. Those foods are already awesome. They don't need bacon's help.

More recently, restaurants are trying to replicate this success with bacon's Sunday morning fuck buddy—the incredible, edible egg. Few things are as satisfying first thing in the morning as a delicious omelette. It's hard to go wrong with scrambled eggs, fried eggs, and even an occasional hard-boiled egg. Let's leave it at that. We don't need to spruce up other foods by dropping a fried egg on top. The fried egg alone? Delicious. On top of other foods? Still delicious, but unnecessary. A couple years ago, an egg-festooned pie ruined an otherwise perfectly enjoyable evening with friends at Aria's Five50 Pizza. No food needs improvement less than pizza. Dicking it up with an egg is just stupid. And this trend hasn't stopped with pizza. Oh no. Vegas menus are brimming with sandwiches, salads, and burgers unnecessarily adorned with eggs.

While I'm bitching about annoying trends, could restaurants please stop labeling appetizers as "tapas" and "small plates"? We're not in Spain, and a small plate is the dish on which the appetizer is served. We don't order soup from a "bowls" menu. Trying to class up mini-cheeseburgers by classifying them as tapas simply allows restaurants to charge $8.99 instead of $5.99 because it seems more upscale. It's marketing bullshit at its most effective and most annoying.

Restaurants and bars use similar ploys so we feel better about ordering $15 cocktails. I'm a sucker for a delicious boozy drink, so I'm as responsible as anyone for the rise of the specialty cocktail menu at every restaurant and bar in Las Vegas. But these aren't just *any* cocktails. They're "hand-crafted" cocktails. Well, I'm so glad the barkeep is using his hands to make my bourbon berry smash. I'd hate to find out the blackberries were muddled using his toes instead.

Of course, a hand-crafted cocktail isn't delivered in any old high ball, collins, or rocks glass. That would be so 2013. Today, every damn mixed drink with more than three ingredients is required by law to come in a fucking mason jar. How did this happen? Did every grandma who used to can tomatoes die at the same time, resulting in a huge mason jar surplus and subsequent rock-bottom prices for barware distributors? For approximately 10 minutes in the fall of 2013, drinking from a mason jar was quaint. Now it's just annoying.

I can't imagine what the next stupid trend in drinkware will be. If I'm ever at Downtown Cocktail Room and my Laphroaig 18 arrives in a crystal sippy cup, I'm hopping in a cab directly to The Betty Ford Center.

CHAPTER 15

Entertainment

One of the many aspects making Las Vegas an ideal vacation destination is its rich variety of entertainment options. On any given night, visitors can attend terrific performances from talented acrobats, musicians, magicians, dancers, actors, and comedians—or they can go to Criss Angel's show. But Las Vegas entertainment isn't limited to shows. The city has a multitude of attractions, shopping malls, strip clubs, and other destinations for fun and amusement.

SELECTING A SHOW

Right after "Did you win?" the most likely question you'll receive from family, friends, and coworkers upon returning home from Las Vegas is, "Did you see a show?" Even people who rarely or never visit Las Vegas recognize the city as an entertainment mecca. Although you may be tempted to tell them about the unwitting guy at the bar you saw hitting on a cross-dressing hooker, that's probably not the type of show they have in mind.

Much like figuring out where to stay, selecting a show can be daunting because of the large variety of choices. New shows come to Vegas frequently—many for only short stints—schedules vary, and performers often move to different theaters, so you'll need to do a little online research. To help you weigh your options and narrow down the choices, following are some thoughts, tips, and observations about the types of shows you will encounter.

CIRQUE DU SOLEIL

The Las Vegas Strip is home to eight Cirque du Soleil shows. Each of them features Cirque's signature what-the-hell-was-that production values. Acrobats fly through the air, contortionists twist themselves into human pretzels, and guys on stilts engage in sexual acts that have been banned in most states. I made up that last part, but Cirque shows include tons of random weirdness and, in some cases, subtle and not-so-subtle eroticism. Expect impressive staging, athleticism, and choreography. You've likely seen video clips or heard about many of the Cirque shows, but remembering which show is which can be challenging. Here's a quick guide.

- *Mystère*: Performed at Treasure Island, *Mystère* includes pole-dancing lizard people and a man-baby in a diaper. Creepy.
- *The Beatles Love*: Performed at The Mirage, *Love* tells the story of The Beatles—at least that's what it says in the show's official program.
- *O*: Performed at Bellagio, *O* takes place above, around, and in a gigantic water tank. Make sure to pee before the show begins.
- *Zarkana*: Performed at Aria, *Zarkana* performers include a sand painter, ladder acrobats, and other artists who have combined their love of DIY home improvement projects with their passion for the stage.
- *Ka*: Performed at MGM Grand, *Ka* takes place on floating stages and features a bunch of kick-ass martial arts scenes.
- *Criss Angel Believe*: Performed at Luxor, the show should be called *Magique du Douche*.
- *Zumanity*: Performed at New York-New York, *Zumanity* is best known for a scene with two hot chicks in a large fishbowl.
- *Michael Jackson One*: Performed at Mandalay Bay, *Michael Jackson One* focuses on MJ's music rather than his alleged fondness for ruining the lives of pre-teen boys.
- *Le Reve*: Although not actually a Cirque du Soleil show, *Le Reve* may as well be. Performed at Wynn, this tale documents a young girl's strange, erotic journey from Milan to Minsk.

MAGIC

I'm not a fan of magicians. Granted, performing illusions takes great skill, practice, and showmanship. I'm just not impressed by something simply because I don't understand how it occurs. Wow, The Great Jimmy Fuckelstein waved his arms, some smoke billowed out on stage, and his 1979 Ford Granada vanished from sight. Most likely, part of the stage descended or some fancy curtain work was involved. I guess it'll always be a mystery. Whoop-dee-fucking-doo. I'm more puzzled by how Hootie and the Blowfish sold 16 million copies of *Cracked Rear View* and yet nobody I know owns one. Today's magicians must realize that performing slight variations on the same tricks Doug Henning did in 1975 is wearing thin. Many of them now promote their acts as "comedy magic" or "music and magic." If you're going to sit through yet another audience member disappearing from a magic box, at least you can have a laugh or enjoy a shredding guitar solo, I suppose.

With all that said, Penn & Teller put on a funny and irreverent magic show worthy of more than a decade of glowing reviews at Rio. You won't get overdramatic music and a bunch of pseudo-dark-arts bullshit to build suspense, but you may be subjected to Penn's atheist, libertarian commentary mixed in with the jokes and tricks. After each show, the duo signs autographs and poses for photos with audience members—a nice, all-too-rare, personal touch. If you're seeking a more traditional big-time magic show with smoke and flashpots, David Copperfield frequently performs at MGM Grand.

Unfortunately, in the years since Montecore attacked Roy Horn, ending Siegfried and Roy's long-running show, tiger-based magic in Las Vegas has vanished like a volunteer from the audience. Perhaps showroom operators caved to pressure from animal rights activists. Or maybe rumors about tigers getting loose and wandering into the old O'Sheas employee breakroom made executives leery of having wild animals around. Either way, the glory days of white tigers and majestic lions disappearing and reappearing when a creepy dude with a bad dye job waves his arm are now just another fading piece of Las Vegas entertainment history.

MUSICAL HEADLINER

In the 1970s and '80s, Las Vegas earned a stigma as a place where washed up musicians performed at the end of their careers. In recent years, however, fresh-faced hit makers including Rod Stewart, Carlos Santana,

Bette Midler, Cher, and Olivia Newton-John changed that perception. Plus, Def Leppard, KISS, and Guns n' Roses all performed month-long residencies at the Hard Rock, and they all topped the charts as recently as... How about Boyz II Men at The Mirage? They were singing about all the Philly steaks you can eat just yesterday (and by "yesterday," I mean 25 years ago). So, perhaps Las Vegas still is the city where once big-time rock and pop stars go to die. The good news is that we're all getting closer to death too, and many of us are in denial about the music of our youth now being considered classic rock or, worse yet, golden oldies. Las Vegas gives us a chance to see and hear some of the bands we grew up with before they throw in the towel or, god forbid, open theaters in Branson, Mo. Choosing a musical headliner is relatively easy. If you're a fan of their music, consider seeing them. If not, don't. They probably won't look or sound as good as they did in their heyday, but seeing them in a relatively intimate environment in a show customized for Las Vegas helps make up for missed high notes.

BROADWAY

Attempts at turning Las Vegas Boulevard into a second Broadway mirror attempts at making the Strip a family-friendly destination. A few options succeeded, and many died a quick death. With a large, entertainment-hungry audience, Las Vegas seems like a logical fit for shows that have already proven successful in New York. However, access to touring versions of many Broadway shows combined with a Cheesecake-Factory-sized menu of other entertainment options dilutes the novelty of seeing a Broadway-style show in Las Vegas. Consider the typical Las Vegas show options and it's easy to see why Broadway transplants sputter out.

- *The Beatles Love*, a Cirque show unique to Las Vegas.
- Celine Dion, a Vegas-specific show in a much smaller venue than she plays when touring.
- *Jubilee*, a classic Las Vegas variety show with nude breasts.
- *Say Anything: The Musical*, a Broadway show that will likely roll through every major city in the country within the next two years.

The Broadway show is the least Vegasy option. On Monday, when responding to Margie in Accounting's predictable question, "Did you see a show?" with, "Yes, I did—*Pretty in Pink, Live!*" she'll probably tell you she's seeing it in Pittsburgh next month. What fun is that? By the way, neither *Say Anything: The Musical* nor *Pretty in Pink, Live!* exist yet, but they will. Coming up with another *Cats* or *Rent* is too much work when you can just shit out an adaptation of an existing hit movie or television show script and call it a day. That's why we have stage versions of *Dirty Dancing, Ghost*, and *The Wedding Singer*. It's just a matter of time before Lloyd Dobler stands at the front of the stage, hoisting a boombox above his head, while a dozen Julliard-trained actors dance behind him, singing "In Your Eyes." You'll probably have to catch the touring version because it's going to close after a four-month stint at Tropicana.

For visitors who don't live near a major city on the touring circuit or who prefer Broadway shows to other entertainment options, Vegas offers a handful of choices. Because of the high turnover, listing specific options here would be futile. Most Broadway shows that take up residencies in Las Vegas have been successful in New York and are solid choices. Although ticket sales may not keep them around for more than a couple years at most, they rarely close due to poor reviews.

PSEUDO-EROTICA

Adult shows in Las Vegas fall into one of two categories.

- **Burlesque/topless revues:** These shows cater to couples. Because it's Las Vegas and time to get a little crazy, wives grant their husbands permission to gaze at some naked boobies. However, this permission comes with a few conditions.

    1. No strip clubs—getting a lap dance from 19-year-old Destinee is gross. She's somebody's daughter and was probably molested as a child. Otherwise why would she be doing this?
    2. She is going along.
    3. After the show, you're allowed to talk only about the girls' dancing prowess, the quality of the stage production, and the funny comedian who told jokes

between acts. Unless a dancer had a freakish nip deformity, do not vocally evaluate their knockers. You have been warned.

Long-running topless shows include *Fantasy* at Luxor, *X Burlesque* at Flamingo, and *Jubilee* at Bally's.

- **Male revues:** These shows cater to bachelorette parties and packs of ladies. Because it's Las Vegas and time to get a little crazy, wives don't bother consulting with their husbands on whether it's OK to watch a bunch of greased up dudes in banana hammocks shaking their Johnsonville brats. In the event the subject is discussed, seeing the show includes a few conditions.

  1. If you get pulled up on stage and Cody grinds his junk on you, no big deal. You know all those dudes are gay, right?
  2. There's no way in hell he is going along.
  3. After the show, you're only allowed to talk about the show with your girlfriends. If he is within earshot, you have to change the subject. It's not that he cares, but pretending he does makes you feel like you did something naughty.

  Long-running male revues include *Chippendales* at Rio and *Thunder from Down Under* at Excalibur.

TRIBUTE

Long the home to countless Elvis impersonators, Las Vegas now has branched out to become a haven for musical tribute acts of all kinds. These shows either feature a variety of performers impersonating big-time pop stars or pay tribute to a single musical act. Long-running shows include:

- *Big Elvis* **(Harrah's):** For years, 400+ pound Elvis impersonator Pete Valle's tribute to the king has packed Strip lounges. Audiences quickly get over the novelty of Valle's size and realize his voice is the reason this is one of the best free shows in the city.
- *Divas* **(The Linq):** Impersonating Joan Rivers in Las Vegas

for decades, Frank Marino hosts this drag show, which includes dudes performing as Madonna, Lady Gaga, Beyonce, Cher, and Britney Spears, among others.

- *Legends in Concert* (**Flamingo**): The long-running multi-act tribute show stays fresh by periodically changing acts. Although Elvis, the Blues Brothers, and Michael Jackson are staples, acts paying tribute to everyone from Britney Spears to Bobby Darin to Rod Stewart have been part of *Legends* during its 30+ year run.

- *The Rat Pack is Back* (**switches locations often**): The Rat Pack is associated with Las Vegas entertainment history almost as closely as Elvis. *The Rat Pack is Back* pays tribute to the legendary Sands Copa Room shows held by Frank, Dean, Sammy, and Joey in 1960.

- *Purple Reign* (**switches locations often**): Jason Tenner's tribute to Prince nails the Purple Yoda's look, sound, and moves. Backed by a tight band, he covers many familiar hits but also pulls out a few rarities for hardcore fans. The show also includes a Morris Day impersonator for a few songs by The Time.

HYPNOSIS

Plenty of adults are perfectly capable of acting like assholes after downing one too many Jack and Cokes. There's no need to lure them into a hypnotic state to get them to make spectacles of themselves. Tons of opportunities exist to see people dance like fools or howl like dogs. Just visit Fremont Street at 11 p.m. any night of the week. Despite so many free, unofficial shows featuring people acting like fools, hypnotists continue to lure audiences in Las Vegas. They pull a few volunteers from the audience, put them into a relaxed state and then make them do all sorts of humiliating stuff to the delight of strangers just sober/smart enough to have not volunteered. If you find joy in watching some poor jerk act like he's having an orgasm every time a hypnotist claps his hands, check out Anthony Cools at Paris.

VARIETY

Many Las Vegas shows cross genre lines, entertaining audiences with a combination of comedy, dance, acrobatics, magic, and music. Cirque shows sort of fall into the variety show category, but they're a show genre in and of themselves. Some of the topless shows include a comedian or some aerial stunts, but it's the dancing girls exposing their jugs that get patrons in the door. Variety shows appeal to indecisive folks who can't decide between magic, music, and comedy or people who simply want a little taste of everything. One variety show rises above all others. Since 2011, *Absinthe* has received consistently rave reviews. Performed in a tent in front of Caesars Palace, the show features acrobatics, stunts, music, comedy, and burlesque. A little vulgar and a little vaudevillian, *Absinthe* is definitely not for the uptight. Seating is a bit tight and a stage-side seat may result in an unexpected role in the show, so the large and timid should consider sitting near the back.

COMEDY

Since the early days of the Strip, Las Vegas showrooms have featured comics. Redd Foxx, Shecky Greene, Johnny Carson, and Buddy Hackett were among the many legendary comics to play Vegas during the 1950s and '60s. In the 1970s and '80s, David Brenner, George Carlin, and Sam Kinison were regulars on Las Vegas stages. Today, large showrooms feature frequent performances by big-time comics including Jerry Seinfeld, Kathy Griffin, and Jay Leno. With a long-running show at Luxor, Carrot Top performs more standup shows in Las Vegas than anyone and receives surprisingly rave reviews. Several smaller comedy clubs provide the chance to see lesser-known comics, familiar acts who are past their prime (Gallagher) or never made it beyond the club circuit (Jimmie "J.J." Walker), and well-known stars performing one-off club shows or short-term residencies (Brad Garrett). Las Vegas comedy clubs include:

- Brad Garrett's Comedy Club at MGM Grand
- The Improv at Harrah's
- Laugh Factory at Tropicana
- Sin City Comedy & Burlesque at Planet Hollywood

PUPPET SHOWS

More puzzling than the popularity of magicians, ventriloquists continue to attract audiences in Las Vegas. These shows frequently consist of a white male comic who wants to say things that many people would consider homophobic, sexist, or racist if simply uttered by a white guy. Instead, the white guy builds a glorified sock-puppet, sticks his arm up its ass and says the exact same things in character, allowing the audience to laugh as though the otherwise offensive statements are originating from the puppet instead of the white guy. The most distracting part of any ventriloquist's act is watching the awkward facial expressions he makes while focusing on not moving his lips. Less puzzling than how a ventriloquist can talk without moving his lips is how anyone over the age of 11 enjoys this crap.

Performing at The Mirage since 2008, Terry Fator gained fame as the winner of the second season of *America's Got Talent*. Unlike most ventriloquists, Fator not only has zany conversations with his puppets but also sings and does impressions in character. Does performing in this manner take great skill and practices? Absolutely. Is it worthy of a long-running 90-minute show? Well, people keep buying tickets, so apparently it is.

WTF

With dozens of performance spaces to fill, Las Vegas theaters frequently book shows that defy categorization and logic. These shows rarely last long, and discounts are easy to find. If admission is cheap, the novelty of witnessing a horribly misguided concept may be worth the ticket price. Past shows that were destined to fail include:

- *Duck Commander, The Musical:* Hillbilly-based reality television shows and musical theater don't have a huge crossover audience. This was proven when this 2015 show at Rio based on the TV show *Duck Dynasty* lasted only one month.
- *Headlights & Tailpipes:* This 2006 Stardust variety show brought together topless showgirls and classic automobiles into one hot mess.
- *Larry King—Standing Up:* In 2009 at Encore and 2011 at

The Mirage, talk-show host Larry King performed a one-man show, telling stories from his long broadcasting career.

- **Nudes on Ice:** A legendarily weird concept that lasted at Union Plaza for a year and a half in 1988-90, *Nudes on Ice* starred topless, ice-skating showgirls.
- **Panda!:** Throughout 2014 at The Palazzo, this Chinese export featured performers in panda suits dancing and performing kung fu. Surprisingly, the show received many positive reviews.
- **Pawn Shop Live:** Based on the hit television series *Pawn Stars*, this stage show included a puppet version of the Old Man character. The show had "bad idea" written all over it from the start and ended after failing at Golden Nugget and Riviera in 2014.
- **Point Break Live:** A satire of the action movie starring Patrick Swayze and Keanu Reaves, *Point Break Live* lasted just one week at Planet Hollywood in 2008.

AUDIENCE PARTICIPATION IS RUINING THE WORLD

Some people who believe in the concepts of heaven and hell theorize that hell consists of each person's individual worst scenario carried out for all of eternity. If true and if I'm refused entrance through the pearly gates, I'm in for a very long performance of *Tony and Tina's Wedding*. This show combines my low tolerance for wedding receptions with my hatred of shows in which the audience is part of the cast. I can barely tolerate sitting through an actual wedding, so the idea of paying to be part of a fake wedding makes no sense to me. If I have to star as an extra in your community-theater-quality production, you'd better be paying *me* $50—not the other way around.

Slightly less hellish, although not by much, are shows in which I may get randomly selected from the audience to come up on stage to "help out." I'm not interested in selecting a card from your deck, being hypnotized and clucking like a chicken, or playing a tambourine. If you need help doing your job, hire an assistant or get an intern like the rest of us.

Don't get me wrong. I appreciate performers' desire to make the audience feel like they're part of the show and not just seeing the same well-rehearsed, super-choreographed production performed six nights a week. I'll clap my hands at a concert when encouraged. Hell, on a good night I'll even wave my arms in the air like I just don't care if asked nicely. But allow me to carry out my role as an observing member of the audience from the comfort of my seat. Don't bring me up on stage or single me out for "crowd work."

I blame this performer-audience interactivity for spawning another annoying phenomenon—people who insist on injecting themselves into a show even when the performer has not requested audience participation. Insisting that audience members become part of the show creates confusion among stupid people who then assume all shows work this way. Anyone who has been to a rock concert in the past 30 years has been subjected to the asshole who thinks yelling "Freebird" is funny. It wasn't funny in 1985, and it isn't funny today. These are the same fucksticks who believe that by heckling standup comics, they're helping the performance. Any good comic is prepared to verbally crucify these morons, but they certainly don't enjoy having their acts interrupted by some mouth-breather who believes his $15 ticket entitles him to share the spotlight. Although I'm normally not a fan of vigilante justice, in these cases it's completely warranted. Anyone standing near Freebird Steve or Heckler Bob should be legally permitted to administer a beatdown like Joe Pesci after being told to go home and get his shine box.

DISCOUNT TICKETS

With dozens of shows competing for ticket sales daily, paying full price is often an unnecessary waste of cash. Countless resellers offer discounted show tickets online, so a quick Google search can save a few bucks. Two sites that consistently promote a variety of substantial discounts, TravelZoo (*www.travelzoo.com*) and SmarterVegas (*www.smartervegas.com*) compile deals from multiple sources, saving the hassle of having to check dozens of different sites.

If your plans are flexible, consider buying tickets from one of the Tix4Tonight (*www.tix4tonight.com*) booths on the day of the show. Ticket availability and discount percentage are based entirely on demand, so popular shows may be unavailable or have only a 20 percent discount. Less popular shows will likely be available at a 50 percent rate. The service displays the daily discount list on its website, so checking a few times before a trip gives you a reasonable idea of what you're likely to find when ready to buy. For some shows, availability is limited, so lining up before the 9:30 a.m. opening time is common. Tix4Tonight locations include the giant Coke bottle, Showcase Mall, Hawaiian Marketplace (all located between MGM Grand and Planet Hollywood), Planet Hollywood, Bally's, Casino Royale, Fashion Show Mall, Slots-A-Fun, Circus Circus, and Four Queens.

STRIP CLUBS

Las Vegas strippers are nearly as good as casino operators at separating patrons from their cash while making them feel good about it. They may call themselves dancers, but their real talent lies in persuasion and cash extraction. Although none of the resorts on Las Vegas Boulevard or Fremont Street have opened their own strip clubs (yet), topless and fully nude dancers can be found just a short car, cab, or limo ride away. Here's what you need to know about Las Vegas strip clubs.

Nude vs. Topless: Most Las Vegas strip clubs are topless only. If you insist on seeing full beavage, check out Palomino (*www.palominolv.com*) or Little Darlings (*www.littledarlingsvegas.com*). Palomino serves booze, but Little Darlings is alcohol-free. Popular topless clubs include Spearmint Rhino (*www.spearmintrhinolv.com*) and Sapphire (*www.sapphirelasvegas.com*)—the world's largest strip club with more than 200 dancers. Avoid Girls of Glitter Gulch. Although the convenient Fremont Street location may make it tempting, the place is filled with past-their-prime-if-they-even-had-a-prime dancers and high-pressure tactics usually implemented only by timeshare hawkers.

Cover Charge: Many large clubs will gladly send a limo to your hotel, provide a free ride to the club, and waive the cover charge (typically around $30). Arriving with Las Vegas residents or driving yourself may get the cover charge waived as well, but because cabbies get kickbacks from the clubs, taking a taxi guarantees you'll pay the cover.

Dress Code: Many strip clubs have dress codes, so check the club's website before going if you're unsure whether something is appropriate. You can probably get away with jeans, but the club will likely refuse entry if you're wearing a jersey, tank top, sweatpants, or sandals.

Money: Bring plenty of cash. Much like casino ATMs, strip club cash machines frequently carry high fees and low maximum withdrawals. You'll need singles for tipping stage dancers and $20s for lap dances.

VIP Room: When a stripper tries to talk you into a private dance in the VIP room, it's not because she likes you. It's because she makes more money there. Why hustle for $20 lap dances for an hour when she can dance for (and chat with) one guy for $400? Keep a little perspective and show a little restraint. She's only going to fuck you by taking your money quicker, not by giving you any action.

For reliable Las Vegas strip club reviews and additional adult entertainment information, visit _www.toplessvegasonline.com_.

ATTRACTIONS

Las Vegas may be known for gambling, dining, and show options, but like any popular tourist destination, it is also packed with attractions to keep visitors entertained and amused. Discount passes for some paid attractions frequently appear within in-room magazines, free coupon books available in taxis, at hotel concierge desk literature racks, and in purchased _Las Vegas Advisor_ and _American Casino Guide_ coupon books. Many attractions also offer discounted pricing for kids, seniors, locals, and military members.

DOWNTOWN ATTRACTIONS

Fremont Street Experience/Viva Vision (_www.vegasexperience. com_): The most prominent and most popular attraction in Downtown Las

Vegas is the Fremont Street Experience's Viva Vision sound and light show. Featuring a 90-foot-high LED video screen canopy covering four blocks of Fremont Street between Main Street and Fourth Street, Viva Vision runs free six-minute shows hourly beginning at 6 p.m. nightly. Most shows feature classic rock and oldies music with corresponding video. You haven't seen this many gawkers, gazing up with mouths agape, since attending the Blue Angels airshow at the Bumfuck County Fairgrounds. Fremont Street Experience also presents free cover bands and DJs on three stages under the canopy at night. During the summer and periodically throughout the year, familiar bands that normally play the state fair and casino touring circuit (Vince Neil, Everclear, Smashmouth) perform free shows as well.

Slotzilla (_www.slotzilla.com_): The Slotzilla zip line offers Fremont Street's second best adrenaline rush, topped only by the thrill of getting a lap dance from a Girls of Glitter Gulch stripper with visible gunshot scars. Slotzilla's base is a giant model of a slot machine next to Neonopolis, one block beyond the Fremont  Street Experience canopy. The traditional zip line slides riders in seated harnesses from 77 feet above Fremont Street to a platform near Four Queens. The more exhilarating zoom line shoots riders from 114 feet up along the entire length of the Fremont Street Experience canopy, ending outside of Golden Gate. Zoom line riders fly in a horizontal, Superman-style position. Tickets begin at $20 and $40, respectively.

World's Largest Gold Nugget (_www.goldennugget.com/lasvegas_): Located near the registration desk at the Golden Nugget, the World's Largest Gold Nugget weighs more than 61 pounds. Found in Australia in 1980, the Hand of Faith gold nugget was purchased by the Golden Nugget for more than $1 million. It's worth a quick pass-by if you're in the area but isn't impressive enough to justify a special trip.

Neon Museum (_www.neonmuseum.org_): Located a little more than half a mile from Fremont Street on Las Vegas Boulevard, The Neon Museum provides a one-of-a-kind glimpse of Las Vegas's glittery past. The museum's boneyard houses more than 150 historic casino signs. Guided daytime and evening tours are available for $18 and $25, respectfully. Most signs are unrestored and, thus, illuminated only using landscape lighting, so the evening tour may not be worth the extra fee.

The Mob Museum (*www.themobmuseum. org*): The National Museum of Organized Crime & Law Enforcement tells the story of the mafia in America. Located across the street from Downtown Grand, the Mob Museum is open daily. Admission is $19.95. Three stories of exhibits detail the rise and fall of organized crime in Las Vegas and throughout America. Many of the exhibits require substantial reading, so plan to spend about three hours if you wish to thoroughly explore the entire museum.

Gold and Silver Pawn Shop (*www.gspawn.com*): The filming location of the hit TV show *Pawn Stars*, Gold and Silver Pawn is located on Las Vegas Boulevard between the Strip and Fremont Street. The neighborhood is sketchy—fairly typical of neighborhoods with pawn shops—so arrive by car or bus rather than on foot. Most visitors leave disappointed after realizing the store is now a glorified gift shop, peddling novelty items and t-shirts carrying Chumlee's face. Familiar items from the show are on display, but the show's cast rarely appears at the store. Many of the scenes are filmed in areas not open to the public. Despite its popularity, the pawn shop has become one of the most notoriously underwhelming attractions in Las Vegas.

STRIP ATTRACTIONS

Bellagio Fountains (*www.bellagio.com*): The Fountains of Bellagio remain the most dazzling attraction on Las Vegas Boulevard after more than 15 years. The free water and light shows viewable from the sidewalk

in front of the hotel run every 30 minutes each afternoon and every 15 minutes after 8 p.m. Choreographed to songs including "Viva Las Vegas," "My Heart Will Go On," and "Singin' in the Rain," the fountains blast high into the air—and in the case of "Con te Partiro/Time to Say Goodbye," directly into your soul. The fountains should be a must-see for every Las Vegas first-timer. Visitors can pick up a schedule of specific songs at the hotel concierge desk.

Bellagio Conservatory (*www.bellagio.com*): On our way to view the Bellagio Conservatory, I once asked my lovely bride, "What's the current conservatory theme?" Without hesitation, she responded, "Flowers and shit." She wasn't wrong. Although the conservatory, located near the hotel lobby, includes frequently changed seasonal displays, rest assured the true theme is always "flowers and shit." The conservatory is impressive, free, and worth a visit during every trip.

Madame Tussauds (*www.madametussauds.com/lasvegas*): Since you're already a shameless tourist, why not visit one of the most legendary tourist attractions while in Las Vegas? The Venetian is home to one of more than 20 Madame Tussauds locations worldwide. For an adult admission fee of between $24 and $30 (depending on whether you book online in advance), visitors can stand eye-to-eye with life-size wax figures of dozens of celebrities, including Beyoncé, Tiger Woods, and Sandra Bullock. A combination of corny, impressive, and creepy, the wax museum is a fun, once-a-decade attraction.

Caesars Palace Fall of Atlantis (*www.caesarspalace.com*): If the Showbiz Pizza Rock-afire Explosion band, the Disney Hall of Presidents, and Xena: Warrior Princess had an orgy, the resulting lovechild would be the Caesars Palace Fall of Atlantis show. Located near Cheesecake Factory in the Forum Shops, the cheesy animatronic show tells the story of the mythical city of Atlantis. It consists of an awkward exchange between a few robotic statues accented by requisite fire and fountain blasts to keep the kids awake. The free eight-minute show disappoints visitors hourly beginning at 11 a.m. daily.

The Mirage Volcano (*www.mirage.com*): Although not as impressive as the Fountains of Bellagio, The Mirage volcano is still pretty damn cool. The attraction spews water and flames into the air nightly at 8 p.m. and 9 p.m., with an additional 10 p.m. show on Fridays and Saturdays. The volcano accurately reenacts the scene inside my stomach after following up lunch at The Mirage buffet with far too many Fireball shots. Viewable from the sidewalk in front of the hotel and across the street at Casino Royale, The Mirage volcano is another free attraction first-timers should check out.

Gondola Rides (*www.venetian.com*): If you dream of an overpriced canoe ride in the desert, head to The Venetian. For just under $20 per person, you can spend less than 10 minutes drifting around the pond in front of the hotel or along a fancy drainage ditch inside the mall. Your gondolier may sing a lovely song to distract you from the realization that you made an error in judgment when you decided a gondola ride would be fun.

Auto Collections (*www.autocollections.com*): Nestled on the fifth floor of The Linq parking garage, the awkwardly named Auto Collections displays more than 150 classic cars. Because cars on display are available for purchase, automobiles will vary. However, cars owned by President Kennedy, Elvis Presley, and other historical figures frequently appear alongside an interesting collection spanning automotive history. Adult admission is $12, but free passes are often available on the Auto Collections website.

Shark Reef Aquarium (*www.sharkreef.com*): Just about every major tourist city has an aquarium, and Las Vegas is no exception. Located at Mandalay Bay, the Shark Reef Aquarium displays a variety of exotic fish, rays, and sharks, as well as a handful of endangered animals, including green sea turtles and a komodo dragon. Adult admission is $18.

Siegfried and Roy's Secret Garden and Dolphin Habitat (*www.miragehabitat.com*): As close as Las Vegas has to a zoo, Siegfried and Roy's Secret Garden and Dolphin Habitat at The Mirage houses a variety of big cats and bottlenose dolphins. Habitat employees provide interesting facts about the animals but fail to mention that those adorable dolphins everyone loves are known to exhibit rape-like tendencies toward other dolphins. To get the full value from your $20 admission charge, throw out a few questions about that during the dolphin trainer Q&A session. Education is fun!

The Adventuredome (*www.adventuredome.com*): Under the large pink dome at Circus Circus resides the city's largest theme park, The

Adventuredome. Like any decent theme park, this one includes midway games, mini-golf, laser tag, roller coasters, and a variety of thrill rides that spin around and flip riders upside down. Combine your visit with lunch at the Circus Circus buffet for an afternoon you won't soon forget. Admission is free, fees for individual attractions vary, but all-day ride passes are available.

Big Apple Coaster (_www.newyorknewyork.com_): New York-New York's roller coaster begins inside the resort before zooming around the hotel's exterior. A steel-track coaster, the Big Apple Coaster offers a bumpy, two-and-a-half-minute ride beginning with a slow climb and huge drop, and followed by plenty of twists and turns. It's a roller coaster. It's thrilling. It's $14.

CSI: The Experience (_lasvegas.csiexhibit.com_): For $28, MGM Grand visitors can spend an hour pretending they're crime scene investigators. Actors and videos provide clues to help you investigate and solve mysterious murders. If you've always dreamed about examining blood splatter patterns and collecting semen samples, this interactive experience will make you feel like a real Gil Grissom.

The Wildlife Habitat (_www.flamingolv._  _com_): Sometimes you just need to step out of the casino and commune with nature for a few minutes. Located behind Flamingo, swans, pelicans, and flamingos peacefully lounge alongside turtles and koi. The Wildlife Habitat provides a brief sanctuary from the madness of Las Vegas without having to stray from the Strip. It's free and adequately outdoorsy.

Circus Acts (_www.circuscircus.com_): Because Circus Circus is just like a real circus, except with gambling, drinking, and smoking to make it fun, the casino includes circus acts. Acrobats, jugglers, trapeze artists, and creepy-ass clowns perform for free every 30 minutes in the midway above the casino.

P3 Studio (_www.cosmopolitanlasvegas.com_): Located on The Cosmopolitan's third floor, P3 Studio hosts month-long interactive art displays. Although exhibits may include relatively straightforward museum-quality sculptures and paintings, more often than not they're a little weird. This is Cosmo after all, where room service arrives with a Rubik's Cube or Slinky for no reason. Whether the exhibit consists of a body-painted artist immersed in a fluid-filled pod, or a floor-to-ceiling stack of hotel pillows, P3 is worth a glance if only for a what-the-fuck-was-that moment.

Bellagio Gallery of Fine Art (_www.bellagio.com_): A more traditional art gallery, Bellagio's Gallery of Fine Art hosts an ever-changing collection of exhibitions. Past shows have highlighted the work of Claude Monet, Andy Warhol, Roy Lichtenstein, and numerous other masters. Admission is $17.

Bodies... The Exhibition (_www.premierexhibitions.com_): It's pretty easy to learn about the human condition in Las Vegas. Just hang out on Fremont Street around midnight, and you'll see things you wish you could forget. But if that doesn't provide enough educational value, Luxor offers Bodies... The Exhibition. For just $32, you can witness actual human organs and skinned corpses in a variety of posed activities. The exhibit would be much more entertaining if the corpses were posed in Vegas-specific activities—playing craps, visiting the Welcome to Fabulous Las Vegas sign, and loading up plates at the Luxor buffet, for example.

Titanic: The Exhibition (_www.premierexhibitions.com_): More than 100 years ago, a big ship hit a chunk of ice and sunk. Since then, people have been fascinated by the lore surrounding Titanic. Today, Luxor visitors can shell out $32 to see artifacts from the boat. Coincidentally, in 1988 I hit a patch of ice in my 1978 Mercury Cougar, slid into a cement curb and messed up the front axle. It was tragic. For $32, I'll gladly show you the car's hood ornament while recounting the story.

THE LAMEST FREE ATTRACTION IN LAS VEGAS

The Miracle Mile Shops at Planet Hollywood features a free rainstorm show every hour on weekdays and every 30 minutes on weekends. A small pond surrounded by large rocks sits in the middle of the mall floor between the casino and Elara. The show consists of the surrounding lights going dark while flashers along the edge of the ceiling mimic lightning as the sound of thunder fills the mall. Water falls into the pond from several small spigots protruding from the ceiling.

Why would anyone think this was a good idea? It's a fairly safe bet that everyone visiting Las Vegas has seen an actual rainstorm relatively recently. Unless lightning struck their house, causing a fire and ruining their lives, the real-life rainstorm was probably forgettable. And in the former case, it's probably not an experience they wish to relive while sipping an Orange Julius on the way to Foot Locker. So a manufactured version in a shopping mall makes no sense.

To add to the mall's ambiance further, other free Miracle Mile nature-themed attractions are in development. They include mild wind gusts, real-time grass growth, and dirt pile.

OFF-STRIP ATTRACTIONS

Pinball Hall of Fame (_www.pinballhall.org_): With 150 pinball machines and another 50 video games, the Pinball Hall of Fame is a throwback to the days when arcades ruled the land. More game room than museum, the Pinball Hall of Fame charges no admission and encourages visitors not to simply view the classic machines, but also to play them.

Elvis: The Exhibition (_www.graceland.com/vegas_): Celebrating its history as Elvis Presley's Las Vegas concert home throughout the 1970s, Westgate is now home to a collection of memorabilia from his Graceland estate. For $22, visitors can see The King's cars, stage costumes, promotional items, and personal possessions.

Vegas Indoor Skydiving (_www.vegasindoorskydiving.com_): Although the notion of "indoor skydiving" seems contradictory, it is probably the best description of what goes on in the building just a block off Las Vegas Boulevard. For $75, visitors go through a 30-minute class, put on a wind suit, and spend three minutes flying in a vertical wind tunnel powered by a jet engine. If I'm going to spend $75 to get blown in Las Vegas, it better last longer than three minutes.

Machine Gun Shooting Ranges: If you've ever dreamed of being a bad-ass Seal Team 6 member rather than a sackless wuss who works in marketing, Las Vegas has you covered. Several indoor shooting ranges near the Strip offer the chance to fire a variety of automatic weapons. Expect to spend at least $100, but they typically offer free transportation. Google "Vegas machine gun shooting range" to compare options.

Welcome to Fabulous Las Vegas Sign: The iconic welcome to fabulous Las Vegas sign stands on a Las Vegas Boulevard median about half a mile south of Mandalay Bay. One of the city's most popular photo opportunities, visitors typically wait in line for their chance to stand in front of the sign for a quick photo.

You'll probably be recruited to snap a photo of the people lined up in front of you, and the people behind you will gladly do the same for you. If you've lost the family nest egg playing craps, you could just spend the day there, offering to snap photos of everyone for tips.

Driving Experiences: The Richard Petty Driving Experience (_www. drivepetty.com_) offers ride-along and driving experiences in NASCAR and IndyCar race cars. Exotics Racing (_www.exoticscracing.com_) and Dream Racing (_www.dreamracing.com_) offer similar options in Lamborghinis, Ferraris, Porsches, and other high-performance cars. Taking place at Las Vegas Motor Speedway, about 20 minutes from the Strip, these experiences start as low as $90 for ride-alongs up to a couple thousand bucks for a lengthy NASCAR run.

Lion Habitat Ranch (_www.thecathouse.us_): Lions are among the most majestic animals to roam the Earth. In Las Vegas, you can see them up close and personal... in cages... majestic steel cages. Located about 10 miles south of Mandalay Bay, near M Resort, Lion Habitat Ranch admission is $20, with opportunities to hold a lion cub or hand feed a lion for additional fees.

Wet 'n' Wild (_www.wetnwildlasvegas.com_): A few Las Vegas hotels have lazy rivers and wave pools, but if you want a full water park experience, you'll have to head off-Strip to Wet 'n' Wild. The park's water slides and tube rides are guaranteed to make you wet. The park is open daily June through August and weekends in May and September. Adult admission is $40.

National Atomic Testing Museum (*www.nationalatomictesting museum.org*): Learn about a simpler time in American history, when the government detonated atomic weapons in the desert near Las Vegas. The National Atomic Testing Museum features artifacts, videos, and exhibits about the development, testing, and culture surrounding atomic weapons. How quaint. Admission is $22.

Voodoo Zip Line (*www.voodoozipline.com*): Sitting on a small ski-lift bench, Rio visitors can zip from the top of one hotel tower to the next and back again at 35 miles per hour. The ride lasts about 90 seconds, costs $27, and will probably make you shit your pants. Have fun with that.

Hoover Dam (*www.usbr.gov/lc/hooverdam*): Some Las Vegas visitors take a break from the city's buzz in favor of seeing a giant concrete wall. About an hour's drive from the Strip, Hoover Dam provides power for Arizona, California, and Nevada. It is large and impressive. Parking costs $10, 30-minute power plant tours are $15, and hour-long dam tours are $30.

Red Rock Canyon (*www.redrockcanyonlv.com*): Roughly 30 minutes from the Strip, Red Rock Canyon gives nature lovers a chance to explore breathtaking desert terrain. For $7 per car, visitors can access the 13-mile scenic drive and take advantage of nearly 20 hiking trails. Hikes range from easy one-hour strolls to more challenging four-hour climbs. Because the federal government designated it a national conservation area, Red Rock Canyon is one of the few areas in Nevada without slot machines.

BEST VIEWS IN LAS VEGAS

We humans love to look at stuff—especially large stuff. Take something as basic as a wall. Yawn. But a huge wall—nay, a *great* wall—in the middle of China? Get my travel agent on the phone. Rocks? Not so impressive. But big rocks organized in a circle in England thousands of years ago, possibly by aliens? Yes and yes. Let's all go have a good stare. How about a hole in the ground? Supersize it, call it the Grand Canyon, and pack up the wood-paneled station wagon. It's vacation time. With its larger-than-life hotels and shiny lights, the Las Vegas Strip is a gawker's delight. Recognizing what the people want and happy to make a buck from it, hotel owners offer plenty of opportunities to take a gander at the Strip's eye candy from high above ground level.

When paying to take in an impressive view, you surely want to get the most out of your experience. The optimal time for elevated Strip gawking is dusk. Daylight hours provide decent views of the mountains that surround the city. Nighttime views highlight the cool-ass spectacle of the mega-structures lining Las Vegas Boulevard. Seeing the sun fade behind the distant mountains as the hotel lights awaken around you combines the natural and man-made transitions from day to night in one pleasant experience. Besides, people don't make plans for dusk nearly enough. Unless fireworks or the closing time of a public park factor in, when was the last time you suggested doing something at dusk? Nobody has ever uttered the question, "Can I get a dinner reservation for four people at dusk?" So celebrate dusk in Las Vegas by checking out one of the designated observation attractions.

Stratosphere

www.stratospherehotel.com

HEIGHT: 106+ stories

ADMISSION: Free — $20

The most obvious of all Las Vegas observation platforms, Stratosphere towers above the North end of Las Vegas Boulevard like a Viagra-enhanced phallus—tall, proud, and ready for visitors to climb aboard. The observation pod atop the Strat tower includes multiple viewing levels.

- **106:** Top of the World restaurant gives diners a full 360-degree seated view of Las Vegas while enjoying lunch or dinner. The food is decent but expensive. You're paying for the view. No admission fee required.
- **107:** Level 107 Lounge serves cocktails, beer, wine, and appetizers. DJs entertain later at night, but evening hours are more casual and slightly more economical, with happy hour specials nightly. No admission fee required.
- **108/109:** The indoor and outdoor observation decks carry a $20 admission fee plus charges for Strat's four thrill rides.

Thanks to long-dormant Fontainebleau hotel construction, the Strip view includes a giant tombstone-like obstruction, blocking parts of the east side of Las Vegas Boulevard. As with most Las Vegas observation decks, visitors quickly realize that other than the distant mountains—visible only during daylight hours—and the Strip, there's not a ton to see. Compared to the Strip monstrosities, Fremont Street's hotels look relatively small and unimpressive. The rest of the city is visually dull.

High Roller

www.caesars.com/theling

HEIGHT: 55 stories

ADMISSION: $25+

The newest option for views from high above the Strip, the High Roller Ferris wheel at The Linq combines views of the city from mid-Strip with the novelty of riding in a pod. Each High Roller pod can carry as many as 40 passengers, but you're more likely to share the ride with 12-15 others except during unusually busy times (New Year's Eve, perhaps). During the ascent, the first few minutes offer stunning views of multiple Strip hotel parking garages. Once you make it beyond that, you'll see the Center Strip and North Strip hotels, with the South Strip hotels and Bellagio fountains on display during the descent. Don't bother turning around to see the views east of the Strip. They're filled with parking lots, nondescript businesses, and residential areas. Yawn. High Roller rates have been in constant flux since its late 2013 opening.

Eiffel Tower

www.parislv.com

HEIGHT: 46 stories

ADMISSION: $14+

The familiar landmark tower at Paris Las Vegas, the Eiffel Tower gives visitors better aerial views of Bellagio's fountains than any other public observation deck. Although located near the High Roller, Eiffel Tower's closer proximity to the Strip means better views of South Strip and neighboring Center Strip hotels. Because the observation deck and elevator are relatively small, the wait time to get to the actual deck may take longer than the amount of time you'll want to spend there. The entire level is caged in, but openings allow for unobstructed photos.

Foundation Room/Rivea

www.mandalaybay.com

HEIGHT: 43 stories/42 stories

ADMISSION: $30/TBA

At the far south end of the Strip, Mandalay Bay and Delano each feature a restaurant/lounge on the top floor. Guests at the House of Blues Foundation Room and Rivea can view the Strip from indoors or step out onto an outdoor patio for an even better perspective. Although both views are stunning, the edge goes to Rivea for a more complete view of the hotels on the west side of the Strip—Luxor, Excalibur, New York-New York, and Monte Carlo—which are partially obscured from Foundation Room. The restrooms at Rivea even include amazing views, with floor to ceiling windows in the women's room and urinal-crowning windows in the men's room. Plan to dress nicely and pay a cover unless you have dinner reservations. Ask the concierge for details.

Voodoo Lounge/Ghostbar

www.riolv.com/www.palms.com

HEIGHT: 51 stories/55 stories

ADMISSION: $10 (7–9 p.m.), $20-$30 after 9 p.m./$30

For amazing panoramic views of the entire length of the Strip, head to Rio or The Palms and step out onto the patio at Voodoo Lounge or Ghostbar. Because they are located about a mile behind the middle of Las Vegas Boulevard's east side, these clubs provide a better perspective on the entire Strip than any other public observation deck. Expect to pay a cover at both, although diners at Rio's 50th floor Voodoo Steak receive free admission to Voodoo Lounge. Seating at both may be reserved for bottle service, and dress codes are enforced, so nix the t-shirt and sneakers.

Mandarin Bar

www.mandarinoriental.com/lasvegas

HEIGHT: 23 stories

ADMISSION: None

It may be only 23 stories above the Strip, but Mandarin Bar's impressive views, great cocktails, and relaxed atmosphere make it one of the Strip's hidden gems. Floor-to-ceiling windows provide beautiful South and Center Strip views. Located at Mandarin Oriental, the lounge features occasional live music and pricey drinks ($18), so plan to move along after a couple rounds or face a hefty tab. Mandarin Bar enforces a business casual dress code.

Your Hotel Room

If spending more than 30 minutes absorbing the Strip's great views would make your time in Las Vegas more memorable, shell out some extra dough for a Strip-view hotel room. Falling asleep with the LED marquees and remaining flashes of neon in sight is a perfect way to end a day in Las Vegas. And waking up to the sights of the Strip provides a certain feeling that today could be the greatest day ever. Depending on the hotel, you may get a better view than offered by any of the observation decks. When booking, consider the neighboring hotels. A Strip view from Harrah's, for example, may mean views of The Linq, Flamingo, and Bally's, which isn't too exciting. If cost isn't a major factor, book a Wraparound Terrace Suite at The Cosmopolitan and slip the front-desk clerk a $50 while requesting a Bellagio fountain view at check-in. Watching the fountain blasts from your private outdoor patio while enjoying a nightcap and some room-service cookies puts to shame the experience of waiting in line to take a crowded elevator to a public observation deck.

SHOPPING

Some of us gladly spend our allotted Las Vegas entertainment budget on food, drinks, gambling, and shows. Others, however, prefer to receive something more tangible than a full stomach, short-term buzz, or memorable experience in return for their hard-earned money. Fortunately, commerce thrives in Las Vegas. Stores of every variety fill shopping malls and retails spaces on and near the Strip.

The Shops at Crystals

Aria

www.theshopsatcrystals.com

Wedged between Las Vegas Boulevard and Aria, The Shops at Crystals mall isn't the type of mall where you grab an Orange Julius and an Auntie Anne's pretzel between stops at Forever 21 and Spencer Gifts. Instead, it functions like a larger version of Wynn's Esplanade or Bellagio's Via Bellagio shops—expensive designer clothing and accessories for people with a lot of money to blow. The 50+ retailers include Harry Winston, Fendi, Gucci, and Prada. Cha-ching.

The interior design at Crystals is sparse and relatively boring. A three-story, wooden phallus that serves as a restaurant stands out from the mall's otherwise sterile, white design. Much like many Las Vegas casinos, Crystals scents its air in a manner suggesting some sort of vendetta against asthmatics.

Downtown Container Park

Fremont Street

www.downtowncontainerpark.com

Located within the Fremont East entertainment district, just a few blocks from the Fremont Street Experience in Downtown Las Vegas, Downtown Container Park houses more than 30 restaurants and retailers. Stores housed within converted shipping containers consist mainly of independent boutiques selling unique jewelry, clothing, art, and gifts. The container park concept is designed to help small businesses open physical locations with low overhead. As such, the lineup of shops is more interesting than in most malls, but turnover is high.

The converted shipping containers surround a playground and performance stage, which often features bands, movies, and community events. Although the shipping container concept sounds like it would be industrial, ugly, and uninviting, the park is surprisingly welcoming, lively, and fun.

The Forum Shops at Caesars

Caesars Palace

www.forumshops.com

Attached to the casino at Caesars Palace, the sprawling Forum Shops mixes familiar brands found in most suburban shopping malls with high-end, exclusive retailers. Gap, Bath & Body Works, and Sephora live in harmony with Versace, Tadashi, and Gucci.

A visual complement to Caesars Palace, the mall has several interesting design elements. The original space includes faux-sky painted ceilings, complete with clouds—a novel feature in the 1990s—and the equally outdated Fall of Atlantis animatronic robot show. The newer area, opened in 2004, includes a rare spiral escalator and soaring, fresco-covered ceilings, making the Forum Shops feel like a cathedral—a true house of worship for shoppers. Featuring more than 160 stores and restaurants, the mall's biggest downside is its sprawl. Much like the rest of Caesars Palace, the mall is massive, requiring comfortable shoes and plenty of time to get from place to place.

Grand Bazaar Shops

Bally's

www.grandbazaarshops.com

In early 2015, Bally's introduced Grand Bazaar Shops, a mismatched collection of retailers and restaurants housed in open-air rows of small storefronts. The mall is anchored by Swatch and Swarovski, and many shops are either niche boutiques (selling clothing for purse dogs and Disney artwork, for example) or kiosk-quality vendors (selling hot sauce, cell phone covers, and custom t-shirts). It's a larger, less-interesting, low-rent version of Downtown Container Park.

Although intended to mimic the world's great open-air marketplaces, Grand Bazaar Shops lacks such personality. Each row of nondescript storefronts is housed under a pastel canopy used for an underwhelming light show each night. The whole thing changes colors a bunch of times. It's not quite as lame as the rainstorm show at the Miracle Mile Shops, but I don't recommend going out of your way to see it.

Grand Canal Shoppes

The Venetian

www.grandcanalshoppes.com

You can tell that The Venetian's Grand Canal Shoppes mall is fancy by the two extra letters in "shoppes." For each unnecessary letter in a mall's name, add 10 percent over what you would pay elsewhere. Although you'll still find a Victoria's Secret and a Banana Republic amongst the mall's 170 stores and restaurants, Grand Canal Shoppes skews upscale. Anchored by Barney's, the mall's other high-buck retailers include Diane von Furstenberg and Bauman's Rare Books—the bookstore frequently featured on *Pawn Stars*.

The mall's design matches the rest of the resort. Stores surround the mall's namesake canal, where crooning gondoliers offer shoppers short boat rides for $20 per person. Living statues and other street performers entertain shoppers throughout the day in the mall's replica of St. Mark's Square. The winding layout of Grand Canal Shoppes can be a little disconcerting, so consult the mall map often to ensure your safe return home.

Miracle Mile Shops

Planet Hollywood

www.miraclemileshopslv.com

More accessible than its competitors for most visitors, Planet Hollywood's Miracle Mile Shops mall probably doesn't differ a whole lot from the malls in your nearest major city. You'll find Foot Locker, Guess, Kay Jewelers, and multiple Sunglass Huts. I've never understood the point of shopping on vacation at stores available near home, but my resident shopping expert tells me stores in different locations often carry different items.

The 185 stores and restaurants at Miracle Mile Shops surround the casino and Axis Theater. With the exception of one row of shops between the casino and the theater, the layout is a simple U-shape, making it simple to navigate. Much of the mall's design has not been updated since Planet Hollywood's previous incarnation as Aladdin and the mall's original name, Desert Passage. Several years removed from the original concept, the pseudo-Arabian streetscapes seem strange for a mall called Miracle Mile. The mall is also home to the worst free attraction in the city—a fake hourly rainstorm.

Las Vegas Premium Outlet Malls
Off-Strip
www.premiumoutlets.com/vegasnorth
www.premiumoutlets.com/vegassouth
Deal-seekers can venture off-Strip to one of two Las Vegas Premium Outlet Malls. The North location, just a few miles from the Strip and Fremont Street, features upscale shops not typically found at outlet malls, including Armani, Burberry, and Dolce and Gabbana. The South location, two and a half miles south of Mandalay Bay on Las Vegas Boulevard, offers more run-of-the-mill outlet stores, including Ann Taylor, Dress Barn, Calvin Klein, and Nike.

Hotel Shops
Most Strip Hotels
Most Las Vegas Strip resorts include an assortment of shops. Higher end properties, including Bellagio and Wynn, feature upscale shops similar to those at Crystals. Even if you don't have the means or desire to buy anything at these shops, walking by can be extremely entertaining. Never will you witness more hideous fashions at such ridiculous prices than in the windows of the stores at Bellagio and Wynn. Most mid- and lower-tier resorts have a strange mix of stores. Flamingo, for example, has a Pearl

Factory, a generic Las Vegas souvenir shop, a candy store, a Bath & Body Works knockoff, an adult novelty shop, and a clothing store specializing in Cosby sweaters.

CELEBRITY SIGHTINGS

As the world's greatest destination for escaping reality, Las Vegas attracts fun-seekers from all walks of life. As such, seeing actors, athletes, musicians, reality TV stars, and other public figures in Las Vegas is not unusual. Over the years, I've spotted Bono exiting Bally's, Neil Patrick Harris walking with Christina Hendricks through Aria, Kathy Griffin entering Caesars Palace, and Rickey Henderson strolling along the Strip, to namedrop just a few. Residents of Los Angeles may be accustomed to seeing celebrities out in the wild. For us rubes from Middle America, however, getting an in-person glimpse of someone famous is a rare treat. Once every two years, Prince exits his paisley igloo to restock his incense supply, but otherwise we've got no chance of seeing anyone famous near home.

The best way to spot a celebrity is simply scanning faces while you're out and about. Most celebrities won't be surrounded by security or trying to draw attention to themselves, so you have to pay attention. Of course, there are exceptions. I once saw rapper Lil Jon slowly strolling through The Venetian, holding a bejeweled gold pimp cup. Subtle. Most of the time, however, they're just going about their business like any other Las Vegas tourist.

Knowing about special events may tip you off to a high concentration of famous people. Reading Norm Clarke's *Las Vegas Review-Journal* column (*www.normclarke.com*) leading up to and during your trip may tip you off to celebrity charity events and other appearances. Keeping an eye on *Las Vegas Weekly's* event calendar (*www.lasvegasweekly.com/events/*) and even searching Google for "Vegas" and the individual dates you'll be in town may yield some useful event info as well. Reading there was a celebrity poker tournament at the Caesars Palace poker room a few years ago, I wandered by shortly before it began. This effort resulted in sightings of poker pro Daniel Negreanu, *Entourage* star Kevin Connolly, alleged comedienne Rita Rudner, and *The Sopranos* star Steve Schirripa.

As a general rule, I don't approach or attempt to interact with celebrities when they're sightseeing, having dinner, or hanging out with friends. They're trying to have a good time in Las Vegas and don't need some dork from Minnesota pestering them. Just because they're famous doesn't mean they should have to sacrifice their ability to enjoy Vegas in peace. If they're attending a charity event or something similar where their presence is intended to draw attention to a cause and public interaction is expected, I may say hello and tell them I enjoy their work. However, I respect their time and don't have expectations of a budding friendship. It's best to read the situation and keep expectations low. They owe you nothing. That said, anyone who doesn't appreciate being told you enjoy his work, in an appropriate situation, is a dick.

If all else fails, and you want a guaranteed celebrity sighting to impress your friends, you have a couple options. Pay to go to a nightclub event hosted by someone famous. Clubs frequently pay hot celebuchodes with negligible or nonexistent talent to appear on weekends. Clubs usually post signs promoting such appearances near their entrance in the days and weeks before each event. The other option is wandering by the sports memorabilia stores in the Caesars Forum Shops and Mandalay Place Shops (Field of Dreams and Art of Music). Nearly every day, a former athlete or two sits at a table, hawking autographs for $40 a pop. Pete Rose, Jose Canseco, Mike Tyson, Earl Campbell, Jerry Rice, Emmitt Smith, and Roy Jones Jr. are among frequent signers. They usually look bored and lonely. Most people who pony up the cash for a signature seem to be doing so out of pity. Only a folding chair, a sharpie, and a familiar face differentiate them from the people sitting on the Las Vegas Boulevard pedestrian overpasses asking for change. Happy celebrity spotting!

CHAPTER 16

Gambling

Clearly, Las Vegas has become an entertainment mecca with an unmatched lineup of shows, attractions, and activities. Even with this multitude of leisure options, the casino remains the sun around which all other entertainment planets revolve in Las Vegas. Gambling opportunities abound, so you'll probably find yourself spending time in several casinos during your trip. This book isn't a gambling strategy tutorial. However, a Las Vegas guide wouldn't be complete without an overview of the many games of chance and colorful characters you'll likely encounter when visiting the city's dens of sin.

PLAYERS CLUBS

Although you may be eager to demonstrate your phat gaming skills, contain your excitement for a few minutes. Before gambling, swing by the casino's loyalty club booth and sign up for a players card if you don't already have one. Much like the loyalty programs offered  by airlines, grocery stores, and every other retailer, casino players clubs offer incentives aimed at getting you to spend more of your money at one casino, or a group of affiliated casinos, rather than all over town.

Even if you're not planning to play for a significant amount of time at a specific establishment, getting a players card is worthwhile. The simple act of signing up frequently includes $5 in free slot play; a coupon book that may contain free drink coupons, food discounts, and other deals; and discounted hotel room offers for return visits. Asking the players club booth attendants (also known as boothlings) whether any promotions are currently available may yield some additional cool stuff. Frequently, clubs offer free slot tournament entries, promotional slot pulls, or raffle tickets after earning a certain number of players club points.

Every players club is slightly different, and the boothlings can provide a brochure explaining how to earn and redeem. When gambling on table games, give the dealer your card. When playing machines, insert the card in the designated slot and leave it there until you are done playing. Many resorts also accept players club cards at restaurants, gift shops, bars, and anywhere else you spend money in the hotel or casino. Show the cashier your card at checkout. As you play or spend money throughout the casino, you'll earn points. You can later spend points on food, drinks, rooms, and other items throughout the hotel.

Most players clubs have several different tiers with greater benefits for people who play/spend more. At Caesars Entertainment properties, for example, Total Rewards club members start at the gold level. Gold members may receive room offers, restaurant discounts, and other basic benefits. Those who earn 5,000 points in one year become platinum members. Platinums get a couple nominal benefits—a 15 percent discount in hotel gift shops and discounted room offers (although realistically, gold-level members will also receive room offers). Upon earning 15,000 points in one year, players become diamond members. This comes with additional benefits, including admission to VIP lounges with free snacks and booze, waived resort fees when staying at Caesars properties, and an annual $100 restaurant voucher. Achieving 150,000 points in a year earns the player a seven stars card. That tier includes an annual $500 restaurant voucher, a free annual trip to any Total Rewards resort, and the VIP phone number for Gamblers Anonymous. Most casinos offer some variation of this system with different point requirements and incentives.

For those of us who love to visit Las Vegas as often as possible, one of the biggest benefits of using players club cards are hotel room offers. Hardly a day goes by when I don't receive a postcard or e-mail with an offer for free or significantly discounted nights in a Las Vegas hotel. Many of them include dining and gambling credits, show tickets, or similar incentives for returning. Many gamblers mistakenly believe their room offers are tied to their players club tier. This is not the case. The level of offers is generally based on a player's average daily theoretical (ADT) loss—a calculation of the amount of money a gambler is likely to lose to the casino based on his historical level of play. Again using Total Rewards as an example, someone at the platinum level may get better room offers than a higher-tiered diamond member. While the players club level is based on total points earned throughout a year, offers are not. If the platinum member played heavily over just a few days while the diamond member played a much smaller amount but over many days, the platinum's ADT would be higher and room offers will be better than the diamond's. So, if your goal is to maximize room offers, concentrate your play on a specific players club card or in a specific casino rather than spreading it around.

A significant amount of mystery surrounds players clubs. Frequently, even the boothlings don't completely understand how they work. If you ask about average daily theoretical loss and room offers, you'll likely receive a blank stare followed by a suggestion that higher tier levels get better benefits. They'll tell you earning more points is the best way to get better offers. Boothlings are trained for the transactions they complete—signing up new members, giving existing members new cards when they reach a higher level, and writing comp slips when players earn freebies. They rarely understand how the casino marketing department uses the players club data to generate offers.

An even greater mystery is why the hell any customer interaction taking place at a players club booth takes more than two minutes. The number of keystrokes necessary to complete any transaction is matched only by those at airline check-in counters and hotel registration desks. I'm trying to redeem 100 players club points for a free baseball cap, and Mlife Mary is clicking away on the keyboard like she's putting the final touches on the great American novel. I wrote this entire section on players clubs in less time than it takes to get my monthly two-for-one El Cortez restaurant vouchers at the Jackie's Club booth. Meanwhile, three octogenarians behind me in line just keeled over while waiting to get a duplicate card. I completely understand that casinos need to diligently track transactions involving freebies for players, but let's be reasonable.

Fortune 500 mergers have wrapped up with less paperwork and fewer signatures.

GAMES

Once you have your players card in hand, it's time to get your gamble on. Just about everybody understands that all casino games carry a mathematical advantage for the casino. Even if you know the best possible strategies for your games of choice, you're going to eventually lose. If you manage to hit a good run, the casino will win it back as long as you keep gambling. Now, before you start tapping out an e-mail telling me about the bank of full-pay double bonus video poker machines at Main Street Station that carry a .17 percent player advantage, save the effort. It's true that such favorable games do exist, and someone could even eke out a long-term profit. All they have to do is learn perfect strategy for every hand, make no mistakes, play only favorable games, and withstand long losing streaks in pursuit of relatively small long-term profits. Few people are disciplined and dedicated enough to bother. For most of us, gambling is a chance to be entertained and potentially leave the casino with some short-term wins.

Fortunately, casinos offer a variety of games to entertain and delight the masses. Let's take a look at the exciting options awaiting us on the gaming floor.

Big 6: Among the first table games you'll encounter in many casinos is Big 6. Frequently positioned at one end of the casino pit, this game features a large vertical wheel covered with various denominations of currency and a dealer who  looks like she's being held against her will. I wouldn't be surprised to see a Big 6 dealer holding up a newspaper while the pit boss snaps a photo. This poor gal has one of the dullest jobs in the casino. Hours sometimes pass with little or no action. The game itself is simple to learn and nearly as exciting as Rock-Paper-Scissors. Bettors choose which denomination they think will land behind the stationary arrow on top of the wheel following a spin by the dealer. The odds heavily favor the casinos, which is why they can justify making the game available despite relatively few gamblers dumb enough to play it.

Slots: The most plentiful game on any casino floor, slot machines come in countless varieties. Although traditional three-reel mechanical slots still exist, most machines are now video slots. They typically have five or more virtual reels and a nonsensical hodgepodge of paylines, making it nearly impossible to know what the hell is happening once you push the button. Spins that look like they should be big winners result in tiny payouts, and screens with no noteworthy winning combinations suddenly come to life  with random wild symbols, leading to big jackpots. Slot machines are the ultimate game for anyone who wants to gamble without learning any sort of actual strategy. Insert money, push a button, see colorful symbols and hear exciting sounds, repeat. Pavlov would be proud.

Some gamblers play slots because they offer the potential for big jackpots with the perception of minimal risk. But more than that, they can be extremely entertaining. Many video slot machines carry familiar themes based on popular movies, television shows, and bands, including *Grease*, *Dirty Dancing*, *Footloose*, *Mad Men*, *The Sopranos*, *The Godfather*, KISS, Michael Jackson, Elvis, and The Rolling Stones—to name only a few. Lucky players hit bonus rounds that feature video clips, music, and animated mini-games within the main slot game. As slot manufacturers work harder to capture just a moment of our increasingly short attention spans, slot games are taking on more video game characteristics. Some even allow players to unlock additional features and save their progress for later. Isn't technology great?

Baccarat: Despite having a simple set of rules, baccarat is the most confusing game in any casino. The dealer draws two two-card hands, designated as the player and banker hands. Gamblers bet on whether the sum of the player's cards or banker's cards will be higher. They have three choices—player, banker, or tie. There are a few other nuances, but that's the general gist of baccarat. So what's confusing? How can this idiotic game make or break a casino's bottom line? Asian high rollers love baccarat and risk ridiculous amounts of money on what is only slightly more intricate than betting on a coin flip. The game is so boring that casinos allow players to blow on, bend, and rip the cards all in the name of building tension and catering to nonsensical superstitions. If you believe in buffoonery like numerology, voodoo, or magical pixie dust, baccarat is your game.

Video Poker: Called the crack cocaine of gambling by people who have never done crack cocaine, video poker takes the strategy of playing cards and gets rid of the most annoying part—the other players. Based on the drawn cards and the payouts offered, players decide which cards to hold and discard in pursuit of winning hands. The game involves decisions and strategy with no social interaction, making video poker the perfect option for analytical introverts. Much like blackjack, every dealt hand has a correct  strategy for players wishing to decrease the house odds and improve their chances of losing less money over the long term. Most players interested in learning the correct strategy begin with the most basic game, jacks or better. Most other video poker games (bonus poker, double bonus poker, double double bonus poker) have similar strategies with slight variations to account for higher four-of-a-kind payouts. Because jacks or better doesn't have as many high-paying hands as its various bonus poker cousins, the chances of large jackpots are lower. However, the game is less volatile, meaning you have a better chance of playing for longer periods of time on the same amount of money. Games that include wild cards (deuces wild, jokers wild) have substantially different strategies from jacks or better and bonus poker variations, but they can be loads of fun. The joy of hitting four deuces for 1,000 credits on a deuces wild machine is topped only by the ever-elusive royal flush.

Regardless of which games you play, one piece of video poker advice applies: with rare exception (games that have unusual paytables), play the maximum number of credits accepted—usually five per hand. If playing five credits is too rich for your blood at the quarter level, find a nickel or dime machine instead, and play five credits per line there. Because the royal flush for five coins pays more than five times the amount of a royal flush with one credit, failure to play five credits substantially increases the house advantage. Even though royal flushes are elusive, you'll feel like a fool when you eventually hit one on only three credits.

Keno: Have you ever dreamed of playing the lottery but not having to wait hours or even days for the results? Welcome to keno. With some of the worst odds in the casino, keno's lure is the dream of winning a big chunk of change for only a dollar or two. It works just like the lottery. Choose your numbers and hope they are randomly drawn. The more numbers you get correct, the more you win. Today, most keno play takes place on machines similar to or, in many cases, the same terminals as, video poker. However, a few casinos still have live keno pits, where the numbers are drawn bingo-style using numbered ping-pong balls. Casinos that offer live keno usually display winning numbers on video monitors in their cafés and provide keno cards on the tables for convenient mealtime wagering.

Roulette: Offered in most Las Vegas casinos, roulette gives gamblers a chance to see how lucky their lucky numbers really are. Simply place chips on one or more numbers, number combinations, or a corresponding color—red, black, or green—and watch the ball roll around the roulette wheel before dropping onto the winning digit. Most roulette tables include an LED display showing the most recent dozen or so winning numbers. Ignore it. Past results have absolutely no effect on future games. The past six spins have landed on red  numbers, but that doesn't mean the next spin is any more or less likely to do the same. Roulette players wanting the best odds seek out elusive single-zero wheels, which have only one green digit instead of the usual two (zero and double-zero) and, thus, a casino advantage of 2.7 percent rather than 5.26 percent. Unfortunately, such wheels typically carry high table minimums of $25 and up.

Blackjack: The most popular casino table game, blackjack is simple and fun. Players try to get a higher hand than the dealer without exceeding 21. Unfortunately, a dark cloud hovers over Las Vegas casino pits, decreasing  your chances of turning a profit. This cloud is called 6:5 blackjack. Not so long ago, casual gamblers heard many stories about the wonders of blackjack in books, articles, and then only moderately outdated Vegas programming on The Travel Channel. They learned to hunt for advantageous blackjack tables by looking at the number of card decks used. One deck is ideal. Two decks is still pretty good. Six or eight decks dealt from a shoe? The worst! Realizing the fewer-decks advice told only part of the story, casinos began offering more one- and two-deck games. The catch was that hitting blackjack (21 on the first two dealt cards) on these new games paid only 6 to 5, rather than the traditional 3 to 2. This change in payouts added 1.39 percent to the casino's advantage. That may not sound like a huge amount, but considering that the typical six-deck 3:2 Vegas game has a house advantage of less than .3 percent, a 1.39 percent bump is huge. Casinos soon found that many players pay no attention to payouts and rule differences at all and began converting all of their blackjack tables to 6:5. So while finding games with fewer decks is a worthwhile pursuit, first identifying the ever-dwindling 3:2 tables is much more important. Of course, if you have no idea what you're doing, the casino's advantage will be much higher, making blackjack no better of a gamble than keno. Using a blackjack training app or website will do wonders for helping you learn the proper strategy relatively quickly. Much like with video poker, a little practice can do wonders for preserving your gambling funds.

You may encounter gamblers who get irritated over how you play—especially if you deviate from basic strategy (whether on purpose or accident). If you hit when you shouldn't have or stay when you should have hit, it affects the rest of the dealt cards. If other players lose after you make an incorrect move, they may blame you. On the equal chance that your errant move benefits them, they will give you no credit. They're hypocritical assholes that way. If you wish to rid the table of them, split dealt pairs of 10s—always a no-no—until they leave in a huff. Problem solved.

Craps: The energy level in many casinos is dictated by what happens at the craps tables. Because most players are betting on the same outcome, craps players quickly form an us-against-the-house bond. Winning dice rolls elicit cheers matched only by make-or-break plays during sporting events broadcast in sports books. It's an individual game that takes on the excitement of a team sport. As a result, craps tables also spawn many legendary stories. If you find yourself on a table with a roller who hits a lucky streak, controlling the

dice for 45 minutes, you'll tell the story again and again for years—mainly because it resulted in the most profitable night you've ever had, but also because of the experience. You were part of something, and it felt magical.

If you've never played craps, the huge table with a multitude of betting options may intimidate you. Don't let it. Most of the betting options are long shots with a high casino edge. Ignore them until you have the basics down, and then decide whether you're feeling lucky. Most players start with a pass line bet and take the odds once a point is established. The odds bet carries no house advantage, making it the best wager in the casino. Continue this strategy on subsequent roles by betting the come line and taking odds. Or, if you're too impatient to wait until the shooter establishes a point, making place bets on 4, 5, 6, 8, 9, or 10 will give you the action your racing heart and degenerate mind crave.

Poker: Thanks to the meteoric rise in popularity of online and televised poker about a decade ago, Las Vegas poker rooms were flooded with wanna-be Chris "Jesus" Fergusons and Phil "Unabomber" Laaks. Although the hype has since declined, it's still fairly common to see some tool who thinks wearing a hoodie and sunglasses while he plays will intimidate his opponents and hide his tells. Never mind that his costume doesn't disguise the obvious tongue clicking he does every time he's bluffing. Fucking amateurs.

While most casino games pit the player against the casino, poker players battle each other. The luck of the draw maintains the chance element necessary for casinos to legally offer the game, but many serious players rely on skill to outplay and outwit opponents. With this in mind, the key to winning at poker is finding a game with less skilled players than you. If it's your first time playing, for example, avoid the high-limit games in the Bellagio poker room. Playing at the same table as a guy you saw last week on ESPN2's replay of the 2009 World Series of Poker may be thrilling, but the novelty will wear off when he's making you his hold 'em bitch. A low-limit game at Flamingo or Bally's might be a better choice.

Carnival Games: Familiar blackjack, roulette, and craps games share space in most casino pits by a variety of newer gambling options, including Three Card Poker, Crazy 4 Poker, and Blackjack Switch. These and other casino carnival games are typically variations on more popular games but with more complex strategies and horrendous odds. The appeal of a potentially large payout for a tiny bet draws players to some of these games, but they're often rapid money vacuums.

Sports/Horse Betting: When it comes to casino sports betting, the two most important considerations are the odds being offered and the quality of the sports book for viewing live events.

Comparing odds usually means either visiting multiple casinos or checking a website like *www. vegasinsider.com/odds*, which shows current betting lines across several sports books. All sports books managed by a single company (MGM Resorts, Caesars Entertainment, William Hill, CG Technology) will offer the same odds, so don't waste your time checking Flamingo and then wandering next door to The Linq. They'll be identical.

The layout and quality of sports books for viewing events varies widely. Lagasse's Stadium at The Palazzo, for example, seats hundreds of spectators, sells decent food, and functions as much as a bar and restaurant as a sports book. Westgate's SuperBook takes up a huge chunk of the resort's casino floor, with a massive wall of monitors displaying dozens of events simultaneously. New York-New York's sports book, on the other hand, is wedged in the corner of the casino, has few seats, and offers neck-craning viewing angles.

RESOURCES

Players can find an endless supply of gambling strategies, tips, and theories online. If you're thinking about trying a new game, do a little research to understand the basics before your trip. Video tutorials on YouTube are plentiful, and can help you understand table game layouts and betting procedures. Dependable sources for detailed information include:

- *The Wizard of Odds (www.wizardofodds.com):* No other site matches *The Wizard of Odds* for information on virtually every game on the casino floor. It includes mathematically correct strategies, detailed analysis of casino game odds, and overviews of gambling conditions in casinos throughout Las Vegas.
- *The Vegas Parlay (www.thevegasparlay.com):* Blogger Tommy Lorenzo packs this site with dependable sports book reviews, betting tips, and free picks.
- *VPFree2 (www.vpfree2.com):* This site tracks video poker conditions at casinos not only throughout Las Vegas, but also across the country. When trying to find the video poker games with the best odds in any casino, check *VPFree2* for the exact machine location with each casino.

THEORIES AND SYSTEMS

When discussing your Las Vegas plans with friends and colleagues, or speaking with another player in the casino, you're likely to receive unsolicited gambling advice. Many people love to share their secrets about how to beat the casinos. "When someone who has been playing for a long time leaves, move to her machine right away." "Play one credit only for about five minutes until the machine has time to warm up. Then switch to max credits." "Only play at night. The machines never hit jackpots in the morning." Bullshit, bullshit, and bullshit. Because we're all somewhat ego-driven, we look for explanations why we won or lost. Some people develop theories based on something that happened to them a couple times, even though they're not able to duplicate the results on a consistent basis. Most gambling theories are little more than superstition. Just because you won $300 on a machine at the end of an aisle doesn't mean the best machines are always located at the end of an aisle. You may have eaten a donut 45 minutes before hitting your jackpot, but that doesn't mean if you eat another donut you'll hit another jackpot in 45 minutes. However, donuts are delicious, so adopting the donut/jackpot theory is still a victory.

Even lamer than gambling theories are gambling systems. If someone tells you he has a system for beating the casino, tell him you have a system for silencing morons and then knee him in the groin. Typically, gambling systems involve a specific betting sequence based on the game's previous outcome. For example, if you lose a hand in blackjack, double your bet on the next hand. Continue this until you win. This system may work a few times, but you'll eventually experience a run of consecutive losses that will result in huge bets. You'll either deplete your bankroll or run up against the table maximum to simply get back the money you previously lost. Nice system.

If you'd like to test someone's gambling theory or system without risking any money, simply ask him how many millions of dollars he's worth as a result of casino wins. If he has such a great system for winning, surely he's exploited it to its fullest and is living the life of a king. You'll probably learn that he drives a PT Cruiser and works at a bowling alley.

CASINO CUSTOMERS

Whenever a large number of people with nothing in common except the dream of winning money get together, there's bound to be more than a few wackos in the bunch. Some of the colorful characters you're likely to encounter in the casino include:

- **Slot Sorceress:** The ultimate in superstitious slot players, the Slot Sorceress waves her hand in front of the machine before each spin. Adapted from the methods spelled out in ancient texts, her efforts have never resulted in a major jackpot, but she once inadvertently conjured up a fertile goat, making for an awkward flight home.

- **Poker Nutjob:** The Poker Nutjob attempts to hide his tells and intimidate his opponents by covering as much of his face as possible. Unfortunately, the sunglasses and tightly pulled sweatshirt hood do little more than caution people to closely watch their prepubescent children when he's around.

- **Codependent Couple:** Some married couples are so incapable of functioning individually that they turn video poker—a solo game—into a fun together-time activity. They discuss each hand and come to a mutual decision about which cards to hold and discard. When they aren't at the casino, they enjoy riding their tandem bicycle and wiping each other's asses after shitting.

- **Machine Abuser:** The Machine Abuser takes out pent-up rage by hammering the slot machine spin button or video poker machine hold and draw buttons with unnecessary force. Inevitably, his aggression results in a jammed button, leading him to respond with self-righteous dismay and anger toward responding casino employees. Avoid conversation and eye contact with this guy. He's an asshole.

- **Your New Best Friend:** When playing blackjack or craps, players frequently strike up an us-against-them camaraderie, pulling for each other to beat the casino. Some people mistake this mutual support as the basis for an actual relationship. They're frequently playing alone and take every open opportunity to interject themselves in conversations between you and your actual friends, laughing at references they couldn't possibly get and acting like one of the gang. Even though you want to be kind, encouraging their behavior is like feeding a stray dog. They'll follow you around looking for love and acceptance the rest of the day. Smile and nod, but don't engage.

- **The Lurker:** Gambling is super fun. Watching other people gamble is super dull. People who hang out in casinos and watch other people gamble but never actually play are just plain weird. When noticing a lurker standing behind you and watching you play, the best strategy is to stop playing, turn around, and stare at them until they go away.

- **Victim:** Some gamblers can't handle losing streaks at all. Seeking sympathy, they like to make sure everybody at the blackjack table knows they're having a bad day. "You've got to be kidding me" and "You're killing me" follow just about every hand, but rather than cutting their losses and leaving the table, they just keep playing—and bitching about how badly they're doing.

- **One-Upper:** When hitting a large jackpot or winning a big bet, being congratulated by other gamblers always feels nice. However, there's inevitably someone in the mix who lets you know he won a bigger jackpot or had a more impressive win earlier in the day. Fuck that guy.

- **Unsolicited Advisor:** When playing a game, you occasionally may be unsure about the best strategy for a given situation. Asking other players what they recommend provides welcomed assistance or reassurance that you're making a reasonable move. Some players don't wait until they are asked before offering advice. These know-it-all asshats love to assist those not blessed with their superior gambling skills. The only ways to deal with these wildly narcissistic clowns are moving or telling them you don't want their advice. This response will be met with self-righteous indignation and a proclamation that they were just trying to help. Sorry to offend you, Mother Teresa, but I can split a pair of 8s without your assistance.

You can't always dodge these people in the casino, but being able to identify them may help you respond to them or, even more importantly, avoid being one of them.

GO-GO DANCERS

Over the past several years, an increasing number of Las Vegas casinos have added party pits, featuring scantily clad female dealers who double as go-go dancers. This is an obvious ploy to get male gamblers to hang out longer and part with more money. Big surprise—many men like spending time near jiggly boobs. Most casinos have figured out that the key to a successful go-go pit is stocking them with young, attractive dancers. Unfortunately, a few miss the mark. Following are signs that you've chosen to gamble in a bad party pit.

- The pit boss welcomes you to Las Vegas Club.
- Your dealer won't quit talking about her affair with Jack Klugman.
- You can't look at the dancers' thighs without thinking about 1970s Major League Baseball outfielder Oscar Gamble's afro.
- Employees keep chatting about how much better the new uniforms mask lactation stains.
- That rash wasn't there when you started playing.
- The player sitting at third base whispers, "I love it here. I have a thing for scabs."
- Each song begins with an introduction by Dr. Demento.
- Something smells like cat food.

Returning to Reality

For many of us, Las Vegas represents our escape from reality. It's our happy place, where we throw routines out the window and pretend to have no responsibilities. Unless you spend most of your time lounging by the hotel pool and getting hot stone massages at the spa, you probably won't return home feeling relaxed, recharged, and ready to resume your normal life immediately.

Be prepared for a post-Vegas crash. It's inevitable and unavoidable. However, proper planning can ease your post-Vegas reality whiplash and minimize emotional trauma.

CHAPTER 17

The Post-Vegas Aftermath

Upon returning home, you'll be greeted with all of the responsibilities you've conveniently shunned during your trip. That big work deadline you left behind? You're one week closer to it. That house-painting project you need to complete before the in-laws visit? It's still waiting for you. Welcome back to reality.

You can't fully avoid the post-Vegas crash, but you can decrease its harshness. Do not return to work on the first day following a Las Vegas trip. When planning your trip, factor in at least one full cushion day between returning home and working. You may be sleep-deprived or hungover, and still functioning with a Vegas mindset when your trip ends. Rushing back to work without proper acclimation increases your chances of doing something problematic, like ordering a Jack and Coke when Jessica from Accounting walks by your desk.

Allow yourself adequate time to catch up on sleep and adjust to your regular life before subjecting yourself to coworkers and customers. Conversations with friends and acquaintances who truly get what Las Vegas is all about give you a chance to relive your trip. Prolonged discussions with people who don't appreciate Las Vegas, however, will compound the effects of post-Vegas depression. You'll inevitably get stuck in a conversation with Judgy McJudgerson, who disapproves of most of your life choices, especially vacationing in "Sin City." Use your cushion day to prepare standard responses to the most likely questions you'll receive from everyone who knows you were just in Vegas.

- **Did you win?** If you boast about winning, your dimwitted colleague will likely suggest you should have sprung for donuts for the whole department. If you say you lost, you'll cement your reputation as a degenerate. It's best to be vague. "I did okay" is an acceptable nonresponse. If pressed for more details, try, "Well, I'm back at work, so I obviously didn't win millions."

- **Did you see any shows?** Unless you want a thorough recounting of the time three years ago when Judgy saw Terry Fator at a local casino, respond with something like, "I saw a drunk club girl throw up on her boyfriend. Best free show in Las Vegas."

- **Where did you stay?** Unless you stayed at a well-known, iconic hotel like Bellagio or Caesars Palace, lie and say you did. Saying you stayed at Vdara or The Cosmopolitan will result in an avalanche of annoying follow-up questions, like "Is that the one with the waterfall?"

Because of that whole "what happens here stays here" campaign, people at home will expect to hear a good story. You'll likely tell the same story multiple times, so keep it concise. Or, if your coworkers are exceptionally annoying, simply say, "Some crazy stuff happened, but HR would frown on me talking about it in the workplace." Shake your head, smirk, and walk away.

Many of the best Las Vegas memories are completely meaningless to anyone except your vacation companions. Recounting "you had to be there" moments with those who were there can help extend the Vegas euphoria for a few days after arriving home. Swap photos, remind your friends, travel companions, or spouse of their unintentionally hilarious antics, and try to patch together any missing details from your experience.

There exists only one surefire way to minimize post-Vegas depression. Begin planning another trip immediately. Even if it's a year away, knowing you'll return to Las Vegas in the foreseeable future can squash the feelings of sadness, annoyance, and frustration that follow a trip. Begin making a list of things you didn't get a chance to try along with the things you loved and want to repeat. Booking flights and a room will make the next trip even more real. If that's not practical, figuring out tentative dates and scoping out potential room choices are great options. The sooner you begin planning, the quicker your post-Vegas crash will subside.

For many of us, Las Vegas gets under our skin. It becomes more than just a place to vacation. When we're not there, we're plotting ways to return. We read Las Vegas blogs, listen to Las Vegas podcasts, and participate on Las Vegas forums. Keeping up with openings, closings, and future development plans helps us bridge the time between trips. We think about it. We talk about it. We dream about it.

Our experiences in Las Vegas occupy many of our favorite memories. We take comfort knowing Las Vegas Boulevard and Fremont Street always stand ready to serve as our home away from home—our escape from reality.

Whether you are already an obsessive Las Vegas visitor, are on the way to becoming one, or are preparing for your first visit, may your next trip be filled with great food, delicious drinks, successful gambling, entertaining experiences, and unimaginable fun. Viva Las Vegas!

Las Vegas Music

Crafting the perfect Las Vegas playlist is an unending pursuit. To help expand yours, following is a list of songs that include gambling and/or general Las Vegas themes.

AC/DC: "Sin City"

All Time Low: "Vegas"

Tori Amos: "Don't Make Me Come to Vegas"

The B-52s: "Queen of Las Vegas"

Backyard Babies: "I Got Spades"

Gerald Bair: "Hanging out with Elvis"

Clint Black: "A Good Run of Bad Luck"

The Bleeding Hickeys: "Roadkill"

Blink 182: "The Rock Show"

Blobots: "Vegas Bars"

Bobby and Jeannie Bare: "Vegas"

Sara Bareilles: "Vegas"

Bianca: "Vegas"

Bon Jovi: "Roulette"

The Bouncing Souls: "Punks in Vegas"

Kevin Bowe: "Las Vegas is Waiting"

Kim Carnes: "Draw of the Cards"

Ray Charles: "Blackjack"

Cheap Trick: "High Roller"

Richard Cheese: "Christmas in Las Vegas"

Tony Christie: "Las Vegas"

Chumbawamba: "Jesus in Vegas"

Petula Clark: "Downtown"

Charlie Clouser: "Let it Ride"

Clowns for Progress: "Leave Me in Las Vegas"
Clubstrophobia: "Vegas"
Cocteau Twins: "Heaven or Las Vegas"
The Cougars: "Vegas Makes Her Fuck"
Jonathan Coulton: "Gambler's Prayer"
Cowboy Junkies: "Ooh Las Vegas"
Sheryl Crow: "Leaving Las Vegas"
Dead Kennedys: "Viva Las Vegas"
Death Cab for Cutie: "Little Bribes"
Adam Derry: "Vegas"
Dessa: "Dutch"
Mike Doughty: "The Gambler"
Mike Doughty: "Strange Powers"
Drive-by Truckers: "Checkout Time in Vegas"
Duran Duran: "Hallucinating Elvis"
Matt Dusk: "Two Shots of Happy, One Shot of Sad"
Electric Lights Orchestra: "Poker"
Everclear: "Blackjack"
Everclear: "Learning How to Smile"
Firewater: "The Vegas Strip"
Brandon Flowers: "Welcome to Fabulous Las Vegas"
The Four Aces: "Meet Me in Las Vegas"
The Free Design: "McCarran Airport"
Gomez: "Las Vegas Dealer"
Hall & Oates: "Las Vegas Turnaround"
Calvin Harris: "Vegas"
Faith Hill: "Let's Go to Vegas"
Hootie and the Blowfish: "Las Vegas Nights"
Walt Hudson: "Adios Las Vegas"
INXS: "Pretty Vegas"
Jimmy Eat World: "Big Casino"
Julius Airwave: "Lost Vegas"
Stephen Kellogg & the Sixers: "Vegas"
Lady Gaga: "Poker Face"
Limbeck: "Sin City"

LMFAO: "I'm in Las Vegas Bitch"

Kirsty MacColl: "There's a Guy Works Down the Chip Shop Swears He's Elvis"

Marlee MacLeod: "Las Vegas"

Madonna: "Gambler"

Barry Manilow: "Here's to Las Vegas"

Dean Martin: "Ain't That a Kick in the Head"

Dean Martin: "I Love Las Vegas" (aka "Drink to Me Medley")

Midi Mafia: "PHamous"

Conor Maynard: "Vegas Girl"

Tom Meny: "When I Win"

Jeff Mix: "Fremont Street"

Motorhead: "Ace of Spades"

Bob Neuwirth: "Lucky Too"

New Found Glory: "Vegas"

Wayne Newton: "Danke Schoen"

Nico: "Vegas"

O.A.R.: "Crazy Game of Poker"

OK Go: "The House Wins"

Evan Olson: "Vegas Bound"

Buck Owens: "Big in Vegas"

Papa Kreak: Gambling Blues"

Gram Parsons: "Ooh Las Vegas"

Katy Perry: "Waking Up in Vegas"

Kevroy Potter: "Elvis Chapel of Love"

Elvis Presley: "A Little Less Conversation"

Elvis Presley: "Night Life"

Elvis Presley: "Viva Las Vegas"

The Quiet Few: "Hungover for Vegas"

Jimmy Ray: "Goin' to Vegas"

Dean Rockwood: "Fool on a Slot Machine"

Kenny Rogers: "The Gambler"

The Rolling Stones: "Casino Boogie"

The Rolling Stones: "Tumbling Dice"

The Seriouslys: "24 Hour Vegas Buffet"

Frank Sinatra: "Luck be a Lady"
Size 14: "People Get Really Drunk in Las Vegas"
Sonia Dada: "Las Vegas Virgin"
Southern Culture on the Skids: "40 Miles to Vegas"
Spazboy: "Vegas"
Bruce Springsteen: "Roulette"
Bruce Springsteen: "Viva Las Vegas"
Steely Dan: "Do It Again"
Stereophonics: "Vegas Two Times"
Suitcase Pimps: "Vegas"
Geggy Tah: "Las Vegas with the Lights Out"
The Thrills: "Your Love is Like Las Vegas"
Vegas in Flames: "Vegas"
Tom Waits: "Mr. Siegal"
Dale Watson: "Christmas in Vegas"
The Weepies: "Vegas Baby"
Who Da Funk: "Shiny Disco Balls"
Wilco: "Casino Queen"
Robbie Williams: "Me and My Monkey"

Sites, Podcasts, and Apps

Following are recommended websites, podcasts, and apps to help you plan your trips and fan the flames of a growing Las Vegas obsession.

WEBSITES

- *FremontStreetBars.com:* A guide to Downtown Las Vegas bars from this book's author.
- *JackColton.com:* The most thorough source for Las Vegas nightclub reviews and host contact information.
- *Little Vegas Wedding (www.littlevegaswedding.com):* A helpful guide for planning and executing Las Vegas weddings.
- *Topless Vegas (www.toplessvegasonline.com):* A comprehensive guide to Las Vegas strip clubs.
- *The Vegas Parlay (www.thevegasparlay.com):* A thorough, well-written blog focusing on Las Vegas sports books and sports betting.
- *The Vegas Solo (www.vegassolo.com):* A dependable blog dedicated to helping solo travelers improve their Las Vegas trips.
- *VegasTripping (www.vegastripping.com):* A no-holds-barred site featuring news, in-depth reviews, and insightful commentaries about all things Las Vegas.
- *VPFree2 (www.vpfree2.com):* A directory of the best video poker paytables in Las Vegas and other locations.
- *Wizard of Odds (www.wizardofodds.com):* The most comprehensive source for gambling odds, strategies, and information.

PODCASTS

- *Five Hundy by Midnight (www.fivehundybymidnight.com)*: The weekly Las Vegas podcast hosted by this book's author and his wife.
- *Vegas Gang (www.vegasgangpodcast.com)*: A roundtable discussion examining the business side of Las Vegas and the gaming industry.
- *VegasTripping (www.vegastripping.com/podcast)*: A roundtable discussion focusing on a different Las Vegas topic each episode.

APPS

- **Blackjack Card Counting Trainer Pro (iTunes app store)**: An iOS app for learning to count cards.
- **Blackjack Strategy Practice (iTunes app store)**: A simple but helpful blackjack strategy training app for iOS.
- **Blackjack Trainer Pro (Google Play store)**: A useful Android blackjack training app.
- **Bravo Poker Live (iTunes and Google Play stores)**: An iOS and Android app for tracking live poker room tournaments, current games, and promotions.
- **Poker Atlas (iTunes and Google Play stores)**: Another iOS and Android app for tracking live poker room tournaments, current games, and promotions.
- **VegasLists (www.vegaslists.com)**: An iOS app for creating Las Vegas to-do lists.
- **VegasMate (www.vegasmate.com)**: The definitive iOS app for Las Vegas trip planning and on-location information.
- **WinPoker (iTunes app store)**: The best iOS video poker training app available.

APPENDIX C

Casino Maps

Downtown Casinos

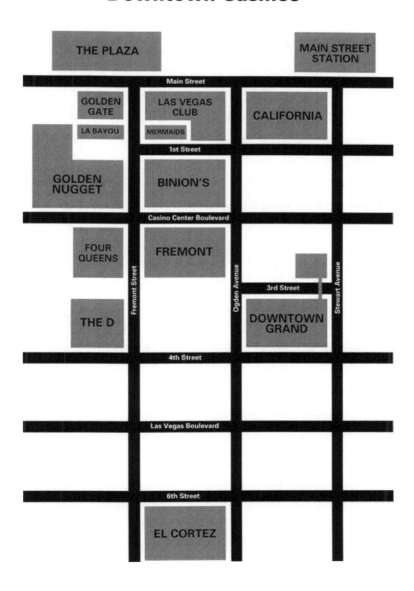

Strip Casinos

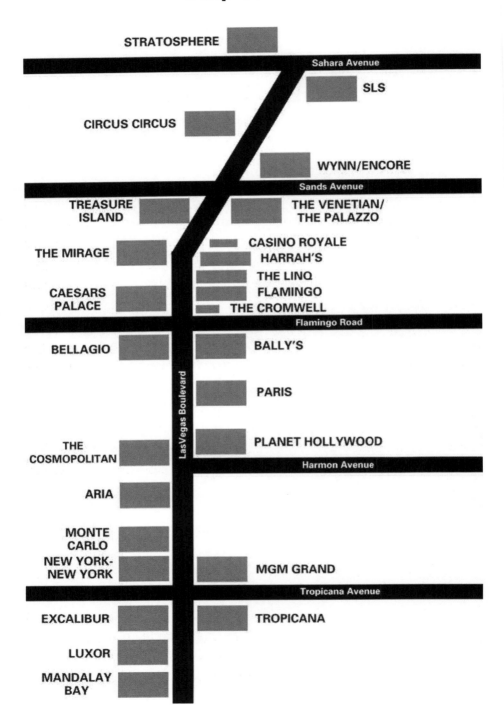

Acknowledgments

T*he Outsiders' Guide to Las Vegas* would not exist without encouragement, support, friendship, and inspiration from many people.

Among the first people to offer words of encouragement when I began podcasting in 2005 were Hunter Hillegas and Chuckmonster. They were also waging war online against the growing mountain of PR-generated Las Vegas fluff, Hunter with *RateVegas.com* and *TwoWayHardThree.com*—and more recently the VegasMate iOS app—and Chuckmonster with *VegasTripping.com*. Joining Hunter and Chuckmonster as the third panelist on the *Vegas Gang* podcast, Dr. David Schwartz knows more about the history of gambling and Las Vegas than anyone. His articles for *Vegas Seven* and his books—*Suburban Xanadu, Roll the Bones,* and *Grandissimo*—are required reading for anyone interested in how Las Vegas became the city it is today. Joining Chuckmonster at *VegasTripping* are Mike E, John H, and Misnomer, who continually offer thoughtful and funny reviews and opinions on all things Vegas. These guys have inspired me through their creative, intelligent, and entertaining approach to Las Vegas commentary. I'm honored to call them my friends.

Five Hundy has changed my life in countless ways. Thanks to the thousands of listeners who have contributed to the success of the show over the years. You generously share information, offer insight into different ways to experience Las Vegas, and provide endless motivation to keep the show going. Every week, I learn new things about Las Vegas from your e-mails, calls, comments, and Facebook group discussions. Much of that knowledge helped me write this book. I am continually amazed by the positive feedback and support you provide. I'm honored to play a small part in your lives and thank you for collectively playing a huge part in mine.

After leaving my job of 20 years in July 2014, I soon began considering whether to write this book, an idea I had tossed around a few times over the years but never had time to pursue. I launched a crowdfunding project on Kickstarter to gage interest among *Five Hundy* listeners. In 30 days, the project closed with contributions totaling more than 500 percent of my original goal. Thank you to all of the Kickstarter project backers, many of whom are listed here: Eric A., The Admiral, Chuck "bitcoin" Ahrens, Chris Anderson, Richard Andrade & Aimee Poirier, Todd Arnold, Jordan Ault, Bruce Bacher, bcmike, David Berryman, Kelly Blair, Brian & Lauren from St. Louis, Steven R. Brown, Shaun Barnes, Phillip Bennett, Brian Bounds, Doug Bowers, Jody Brooks, Sue Bunce, Jim Busfield, Scott Byron, Jeff C., Jim & Jan C., Tommy Canale & Melissa McBride, Dominick Cancilla, Captain Jack, Captain X Dave, Carl & Laura from Austin, Robert and Keri Carlson, Jon Carter, Steve Carter, Nick and Michelle Castle, Brian "BC" Chevrier, H. Y. Choi, Chris from Portland, Chris in Missouri, Randy & Melanie Chumchal, Gordon Clark, Coach & Ayo, Jeff Cohen (Vitaphone Varieties), Rick Collins, Jared Cook, Jim Cook (@MnEsdad), Craig Cornwall, Linda Craig, Grant Crawford, James Cummings, Dan & Kate from New Jersey, Dave in Calgary, Dave from New Hampshire, David in Carson City, Bobby D., Casey Davis, Craig T. Davis, Denton Dallas and Beyond, Maria DePaolo, Giulio DiCicco, Lee Dioso, @dm49323, Richard Downs, duckflambe, Ian Dunk from Leicester, England, Jen & Ted Dunleavy, Mike E., Harvey T. Enokida, Peter Erickson, JJ & Amy Evans, Glen Farrell, Steve Feitl, Frank Fernholz, Jeremy Fleming, Tony Fry, David Fulton, Brian G., Mark & Kirsten Garka, Gary from the Southwest metro, Steve Gedville from Lindenhurst, Ill., James Gillette, Bill Gillingham, Glen & D'Andra, João Ramos Graça, Steve Grantz, Brian Grapes, Richard Greenberg, Greg from Birmingham, Mich., Gregg & Michelle from Buffalo, Brandon Griffiths, Erik H., Chris Hall, John Hall, Mike Halston, Geoffrey Harm, Seth Harper, James Haste, Karl Herbert from Wales, U.K., Damon Herft, Ryan Hess, Hetz, Andy Hoffman, Joe Hortsch, Nick Houlding, Scott Howard, Michael Howie, Andrew D. Huber, Michael Hummer, Andrew Huntley, Mark Ickert, imforiu, J-Dub & Danielle from Maine, Jeff and Connie from Ohio, Jim and Mary, Jim from Liberty Skis, jkhoch, John the Electrician, Sean Johnson, David

Jones, Jeff Jones, Joanne Jones, Dr. T. Taylor Joo, Michael Joy, John K., Karen & Chris, Pete & Heather Kennedy, Keno is Bad Guy, Seth Kerney, Joe & Tiffany Koltunowicz, Sammy Kowall, Rodney Kraisinger, Joe Kro from Motown, Randy Kuper, Don Kurklis, Kyle & Andrea, Stacy & Al Laufer, Bryon Leach, Robert Scott Leavesley, Malcolm Leeder, Didcot, England, Rodger LeFlore, Dave Lifton, Lin from New Jersey, Carmen & Edwin Lipscomb, Listeners Bob & Beth, Oliver Lovat, John & Ute Lowery, Chris Lynn, Evan M., Donny Mac, Holly Mac, Peter A. Machon, John Mangrich, Gregg Matsumoto, Tony McKay, Allen Magee, Danielle Mallek, Rick "Manny" Manifold, Mark, Jaime Martinez, Marty & RJ from San Francisco, Pinata Massengil, Matt & Crishna, Don McGill, Bill & Kate McGuinness, Pat McNeely, James McVay, John & Melanie Melius, Tom Meny, Michael from Raleigh, Scott Mineart, Misnomer, Jeff Mix, Kevin & Doreen Monsebroten, Nicole, Nick Moore, Mark & Diane Moormann, Scott Nash, Thomas E. Nelson, Val Nelson, Kevin Nielson, @NoDeuces, Brian Noe, Reed Nolen, Ed O'C in New Jersey, Dorian Oldham, Olonzo, Matt Olsen, Amy Olson, oupiglet aka Mara, Graeme Overton, Paul from St. Augustine, Fla., Jon P. in Pa., Bogan Painter, Gina Palmacci, Chris Peacock, Al & Erin Perry, Original FHBM Fan Club Members Pete and Ellen, Philip from Palm Springs, Stephen and Heather Pingry, Jersey Bill Pittock, Stuart Poyner, Mike Prescott, Kenny Preston, Steve & Mandy Price, Johnny Puke, Mark & Anne Quigley, Eddie & Claudia Ramos, Ranelle, Alan Reed, Tim Reich, Kurt Rickhoff, Robert Riddle, John & Natalie Riegelman, Ricardo Rodriguez, Scott Roeben, Matt Ross, Matthew Ross, Kathryn Rushe, Russ & Pat from Indy, Roland Ruth, Eric Rzeszut, Tina Sahli, Russ Sauve, Mike Schechter, Dr. Dave Schwartz, Chris Scott, Team Shimbaleen, Jeff Short, Michael Simonds, Mark Skaggs, George Skrypek, Christopher W. Smith, Dan Smith, David I. Smith, Money Well Spent, Matthew Stanford (@matthewinuk1), Bob Stepp, Michael Storino, Su father and son, Darrell and Murray Sully, @SweepstakesGuru, Diane Taylor, Rob Taylor, Kristopher Tenney, Chris Thompson from the U.K., Michael Ticich, Tim from Boston, Richard Timperley, Roland and Cathy Tomsons, Guillermo Trabado, William Trost, Tricia Truscott & Michael Williams, Tom Uglean, Brian & Sarah Ulrich, Dale Uselton, Jason Vasquez, Brendon Wagner, Marcie Walcott, Dave Wang, Katherine

Webster, Trace Webster, Will Weider, Greg Weight, Eric Weinstein, Eric C. Whitaker, Justin M. Wilson, WRXDreamer, Danny Z., and Kelly Z.

Several people offered invaluable assistance and advice while I produced this book. Thank you to Dave Lifton for Kickstarter campaign help, Hunter Hillegas and Chuckmonster for editing assistance, Dr. David Schwartz and Todd Arnold for production advice, George Geddes for legal tips, Nicole Parthum for pep talks and moral support, and Cathy Zielske for design, layout, photography, and assorted other consulting services.

My love of Las Vegas is so deeply ingrained that I assume it's genetic. Thanks to my parents, Bill and Pat Dressen, for passing along the Vegas gene and for raising me to be a semi-productive member of society. Thanks to my brothers, David, Mike, and Dan, and my nephew Phillip, for helping me appreciate Las Vegas in new ways during our guy trips. Thanks to my younger nephew, Chris, for his patience whenever he's subjected to stories about our Las Vegas antics. Twenty-one is approaching. You'll understand then.

Thanks to the former coworkers who helped shape my communications, management, and workplace-coping skills during 20 years of employment at ACA International, especially Kira Marsyla, Cathy Zielske, Shalla Kierzek, Jill Schaefer, Anne Rosso, Ted Smith, Toni Nuernberg, and Gary Rippentrop.

Several artists have influenced me with their approach to work and the manner in which they treat their audiences. Although they will likely never read this, I want to publicly thank them for their inspiration: Chris Hardwick, Dave Grohl, Brian Fallon, Frank Turner, Dan Wilson, The Dollyrots, and Dave Hause.

Most importantly, thanks to Michele. In 1996, when wedding plans began to get out of control, she said six words that would forever change our lives: "Screw this. We're going to Vegas!" In 2004, when I told her I had been listening to a bunch of cool, independent Internet radio shows called podcasts and that I was thinking about starting one about Las Vegas, she said, "You should definitely do that." In 2014, when my job left me feeling demoralized and beaten down, she said, "Don't go back." A few weeks later, when I told her I was thinking about launching a crowdfunding campaign to see if anyone would be interested in a *Five Hundy* guide to Las

Vegas, she said, "You should give it a shot." In other words, she's to blame for all of this, and I couldn't be more grateful. Thanks for believing in me, pushing me to take chances, and making me laugh every day. I love you more than chili cheese fries after a night of drunken gambling on Fremont Street.

Index

About the Author

Tim Dressen is producer and cohost (along with his bride, Michele) of *Five Hundy by Midnight*, the first podcast devoted to Las Vegas news, reviews, and commentary. Debuting on Jan. 9, 2005, the show has attracted thousands of devoted listeners in all 50 states and more than three dozen countries. *Five Hundy* has also garnered media attention from publications including *The New York Times*, *The Boston Globe*, and *Las Vegas Review-Journal*. The readers of *VegasTripping* voted *Five Hundy by Midnight* the Best Las Vegas Podcast eight times—every year it has been eligible— and voted Dressen the Las Vegas Person of the Year in 2015. He is also the editor of *FremontStreetBars.com*, a guide to the Downtown Las Vegas bar scene.

A professional writer and editor by trade, Dressen earned a bachelor's degree in print journalism from the University of St. Thomas in St. Paul, Minn. He has visited Las Vegas more than 60 times since 1997 but has no desire to live there. He remains an unapologetic Las Vegas outsider.

Printed in Great Britain
by Amazon.co.uk, Ltd.,
Marston Gate.